DISPATCH FROM BERLIN, 1943

ANTHONY COOPER is a retired schoolteacher with a PhD in German civil aviation in the Weimar Republic, and is the author of *HMAS* Bataan *1952* (NewSouth, 2010); *Darwin Spitfires* (NewSouth, 2011 and 2022); *Kokoda Air Strikes* (NewSouth, 2014); *RAAF Bombers over Germany*; *Paddy Finucane and the Legend of the Kenley Wing*; and *Sub Hunters*.

THORSTEN PERL is an investigator of historical and scientific topics. He has been involved with official agencies in the search for and clarification of missing crew members of the Second World War for twenty-seven years. Thorsten works in research and development of regenerative agriculture and lives with his family in Eberswalde near Berlin in Germany.

'An extraordinary tale of five brave reporters and their eyewitness accounts of the horrors of aerial warfare during and after a raid on Berlin. A compelling tribute to the 57 205 young men killed while serving with bomber command during the Second World War.' **IAN McPHEDRAN**

'This book captures the life and death drama that saw five war correspondents, two of them Australian, assigned to RAF Bomber Command to report on the most dangerous campaign of the Second World War – bombing Berlin. Neither they nor the crew knew if they would survive the night. A compelling story of a single raid that has remained untold for too long.' **PETER REES**

'A deep, intimate and remarkable story – indeed, a rare personal window into the huge and devastating machinery of the air war over Europe during World War Two. The trials and tribulations of five intrepid journalists is an exciting tale in its own right, but it simultaneously gives a unique keyhole with which to view the tenure and drama of the era. Well-written and equally well-researched, this book is a gem for those with even a passing interest in military history of the Second World War, and scholars of the field alike.' **CRAIG STOCKINGS**

'*Dispatch from Berlin, 1943* takes you on a heart-stopping bombing raid over enemy territory as brave allied air crew battle flak, fighters and fate. Told through the eyes of five brave journalists who went with them, this is a remarkable book about the horror and humanity of war.' **MARK WILLACY**

DISPATCH FROM BERLIN, 1943

THE STORY OF FIVE JOURNALISTS WHO RISKED EVERYTHING

**ANTHONY COOPER,
WITH THORSTEN PERL**

NEWSOUTH

A NewSouth book

Published by
NewSouth Publishing
University of New South Wales Press Ltd
University of New South Wales
Sydney NSW 2052
AUSTRALIA
https://unsw.press/

© Anthony Cooper, with Thorsten Perl 2023
First published 2023

10 9 8 7 6 5 4 3 2 1

This book is copyright. Apart from any fair dealing for the purpose of private study, research, criticism or review, as permitted under the *Copyright Act*, no part of this book may be reproduced by any process without written permission. Inquiries should be addressed to the publisher.

 A catalogue record for this book is available from the National Library of Australia

ISBN: 9781742237923 (paperback)
        9781742238661 (ebook)
        9781742239590 (ePDF)

Design Josephine Pajor-Markus
Cover design Peter Long
Cover images LiliGraphie, iStock
Printer Griffin Press

All reasonable efforts were taken to obtain permission to use copyright material reproduced in this book, but in some cases copyright could not be traced. The author welcomes information in this regard.

DISPATCH FROM BERLIN, 1943

THE STORY OF FIVE JOURNALISTS WHO RISKED EVERYTHING

ANTHONY COOPER,
WITH THORSTEN PERL

NEWSOUTH

A NewSouth book

Published by
NewSouth Publishing
University of New South Wales Press Ltd
University of New South Wales
Sydney NSW 2052
AUSTRALIA
https://unsw.press/

© Anthony Cooper, with Thorsten Perl 2023
First published 2023

10 9 8 7 6 5 4 3 2 1

This book is copyright. Apart from any fair dealing for the purpose of private study, research, criticism or review, as permitted under the *Copyright Act*, no part of this book may be reproduced by any process without written permission. Inquiries should be addressed to the publisher.

 A catalogue record for this book is available from the National Library of Australia

ISBN: 9781742237923 (paperback)
        9781742238661 (ebook)
        9781742239590 (ePDF)

Design Josephine Pajor-Markus
Cover design Peter Long
Cover images LiliGraphie, iStock
Printer Griffin Press

All reasonable efforts were taken to obtain permission to use copyright material reproduced in this book, but in some cases copyright could not be traced. The author welcomes information in this regard.

CONTENTS

1	A big opportunity	1
2	The lucky five	15
3	Forerunners	50
4	Bomber boys	57
5	A gathering storm	82
6	The raid	104
7	'Orchestrated hell'	132
8	Survivors	162
9	The dead	201
10	Reporting the raid	216
11	Prisoners of war	240
12	A grand tour	254
13	Personal impacts	295
14	Aftermaths	314

Author's note	323
Select bibliography	325
Notes	327
Index	340

CHAPTER 1

A BIG OPPORTUNITY

Lowell Bennett was bored. It was the autumn of 1943, now into the fifth year of the European war, and this young and ambitious American reporter was working long hours in the drab London office of the International News Service (INS). His job was to collate the news copy teletyped in from the INS reporters at the battlefronts, to type up the resultant news articles about the progress of the war, and to wire these to the US for distribution to the newspapers. It was an important job, editing war correspondents' raw copy into ready-for-publication stories for the people back home. But for an adventurous soul like Bennett, it was dreary, anonymous office work. He did it loyally enough but thought it a second-rate occupation to be writing up other people's stories with other people's by-lines. He was able to stifle his impatience and frustration on the assumption that the Allies must soon launch the much-anticipated 'Second Front', an event which would surely give him his next opportunity to escape the office by going ashore with the troops on D-Day. But it was too late for this to happen that year, as the winter weather would preclude any cross-channel operation. The invasion, and Bennett's own hoped-for role in it, would have to wait until 1944.

It was on 26 November 1943 that the phone rang in Bennett's busy INS office. Many, many phone calls came through to the news desk each day – the damned phone never stopped ringing. But this call was different. This time there was an official from the British Air Ministry on the other end of the line, advising that there were seats available on RAF bombers going on a raid, and that one of these seats had been allocated to INS. The voice of the air force official directed that the news bureau send 'their man' for a meeting at the ministry premises in Adastral House, on Kingsway. This was only a couple of hundred metres past the end of Fleet Street, where all the press agencies had their offices. It would be a short trip, but full of portent. The phone call electrified the office, particularly the bureau's two most ambitious young journalists. The only question was, which one would get to go?

> Two reporters were in line for the job, William Wade and Lowell Bennett. Both wanted to go. Bennett took a shilling out of his pocket, they flipped, and Bennett won. 'Two out of three', Wade protested. 'Nothing doing', said Bennett. 'I go.'

And so, Lowell Bennett had made his date with destiny. He had booked a flight to Germany. The next question was: which raid? To what target? But Bennett already had his suspicions: he had recently worked the news copy about the big RAF raids to Berlin on the nights of 18 and 22 November. And there would be another one that very night. After all the media trumpeting of the RAF's achievement in opening a powerful bombing offensive against Hitler's capital, surely another such raid was on the cards? For Bennett, the prospect was intriguing and disturbing in equal measure.

The phone also rang in other Fleet Street newspaper offices, triggering the same excitement about who would go. Unusually, two of the chosen media organisations were Australian. At the office of the *Sun*, a popular Sydney tabloid, 39-year-old veteran war correspondent Norm Stockton was itching to go, having transferred from Sydney to London earlier in the year with precisely this sort of expectation. The phone also rang in the offices of the respectable broadsheet, the *Sydney Morning Herald*. In this case the paper's senior correspondent, 46-year-old Alf King, pulled rank on the junior reporters and put his own name on the list.

The Berlin raids were certainly a big story, justifying the reporters' avid interest. By November 1943, British bombers had already been pounding the cities of the German Reich for three years. Or at least they had tried to: Britain's strategic bombing campaign against German cities had commenced during the critical period of the Battle of Britain, symbolised by the RAF's first-ever raid upon Berlin on the night of 25 August 1940, but these early operations had been quite ineffective, more or less scattering their bombs randomly across the German countryside in the general region of the targeted cities. As someone said, the night sky over blacked-out Germany sure was *dark*. It was only in 1943 that the RAF got into its stride, just as its heavy bomber squadrons were newly equipped with powerful four-engine machines, of which the Avro Lancaster was the best example, as well as the most numerous. By 1943, Bomber Command had been trying to win the war for two years by smashing German cities but results always fell far short of ambition. A few successes had punctuated the 1942 campaign, such as the well-publicised 'thousand-bomber raid' upon Cologne on the night of 30 May, as well as the destructive conflagrations visited upon Lübeck and Rostock over March and April of the same year. By contrast, numerous and repeated raids upon the industrial cities of the Ruhr district in western Germany failed to produce comparable results despite the large effort expended. A big success finally came with the notorious firestorm raid upon Hamburg on the night of 25 July 1943, in which about 40 000 people died and another 1.2 million fled the city. Air Marshal Arthur 'Bomber' Harris, at the helm of RAF Bomber Command, intended to do the same thing to Berlin later that year.

Certainly, the resumption of raids on Berlin in 1943 was symbolic of Bomber Command's growing power and ambition. As a target, Berlin was not only the political power centre of the Nazi regime and the administrative centre of its government and military authorities, but it was also one of Germany's most important industrial centres, producing about 8 per cent of Germany's total output: the Berlin conurbation hosted twelve aircraft factories, twenty-five armaments facilities, and 40 per cent of Germany's electronics industry (for example, Berlin-based firms developed and produced the very radio and radar equipment that the Luftwaffe was using to combat the raids).

However, viewed from England, the German capital was such a faraway and difficult target that it had been kept off the RAF's target list for more than a year. Now that new and better bombing aircraft and bombing technologies were available, what better way for the RAF to flex its newly developed muscles and proclaim its growing retributive power to the world than to send repeated large raids deep into Germany to batter Hitler's capital? By the late autumn of 1943, Air Marshal Harris was certain that his air assault upon the cities of central Germany would cause the Third Reich to collapse. Harris was thinking big: as the RAF's most fundamentalist believer in the holy RAF doctrine of strategic bombing, he believed that his bomber force could defeat Nazi Germany all by itself, so ruining the 'morale' of the German people as to render redundant the need for the much-prefigured Anglo-American invasion of occupied Europe and the consequent ground fighting to invade Germany. The RAF, so he believed, would in effect do the army's job for it, and it would do it alone (although possibly with a bit of help from the Americans). According to this script, Germany would surrender before the Allied invasion needed to be launched, because it would be bombed by the RAF into chaos, collapse, sedition and mutiny. Hitler would be deposed by the Germans themselves and peace terms made. It was quite an ambitious aspiration.

Berlin was by far the largest city in Germany, indeed the third largest city in the world, 40 kilometres wide north to south, and 50 kilometres wide east to west, measuring 624 square kilometres. To the RAF, such a huge target must have seemed deceptively difficult to miss, but on the other hand, it was too big for Harris's bombers to do a 'Hamburg' in one night – rather, an extended sequence of raids would be needed to achieve a similar measure of apocalyptic devastation. Harris was convinced his bombers could do it. He sold his Berlin Blitz to Prime Minister Winston Churchill on the basis that, 'It will cost between us 400–500 aircraft. It will cost Germany the war.' As events would prove, he was optimistic on one count, and hopelessly deluded on the other: the raids ended up costing Harris 625 aircraft, and it would take bloody ground offensives by both the Soviets and the Western Allies for Hitler to lose his war.

Buoyed by his dazzling expectations, Harris dispatched the first raid of his Berlin winter offensive on the night of 18 November 1943. Three further raids followed before the end of that month, each involving powerful raiding forces of about 400 Lancasters. But the Nazi capital was formidably well defended by night-fighters, flak guns and searchlights, so that by the end of November, this assault on Berlin had already cost Harris a total of eighty-three RAF bombers and their crews. So far, the resultant average loss rate was 4 per cent of bombers dispatched; this was less than might have been feared, but as the raids continued the loss rate was expected to climb.

Harris's bombers might not have knocked Germany out of the war, but they certainly knocked Berlin about badly. The second raid in the series, on the night of 22 November, became 'the most effective raid on Berlin of the war', with at least '3000 houses and 23 industrial premises' completely destroyed, an estimated 2000 people killed, and 175 000 people rendered homeless. Several firestorms burned a 'vast area of destruction', producing a smoke cloud which by the next day had risen to an altitude of nearly 19 000 feet. On that night the bombs fell thickly in the central city area, and then a rising wind fanned the flames set by the incendiary bombs, so that the resultant firestorms consumed not only whole blocks but whole districts. This raid was not dissimilar in its effects to the Hamburg firestorm raid earlier in the year, although the death toll was far lower. Nor was this highly destructive raid a one-off: the three-raid sequence on the nights of 22, 23 and

26 November saw a total of 1450 bomber sorties to Berlin. On the night of 23 November, Berlin's flak command tallied about 200 bombers penetrating right into the heart of the city to bomb, with heavy damage to central Berlin, causing further firestorms. Three nights later, on 26 November, the raiders again succeeded in flying another 200 bombers across Berlin itself. Because of wayward target marking by the pathfinder crews, the bombs fell five miles north of the central district, but they fortuitously fell in unusually concentrated fashion upon 'the most important industrial area of Berlin', namely districts such as Siemensstadt, Reinickendorf and Borsigwalde. The defending Luftwaffe was so impressed by this seemingly surgical strike upon the industrial plants in the northern suburbs that it summarised the purpose of the raid as: 'Besides the terrorisation they had the objective of destroying the armaments firms in the north and northwest of the Reich capital.' In fact, the bombing of these specific facilities was a fluke, the designated aiming point having been central Berlin. Despite the imprecision, together these three raids dropped a total of 5500 tons of bombs, cumulatively inflicting 'severe damage' to Hitler's capital.

Harris was encouraged enough by the early results to take this as a promising start to the Berlin offensive and a sign of things to come. Hence the invitation for the journalists to fly to Berlin. As journalist Lowell Bennett recalled it, for the next raid 'four correspondents would fly with the bombers to witness the execution and effect of one such attack'. The RAF's expectation in making this invitation was that the next raid would be as spectacularly devastating as the earlier ones, and hence would provide great news copy. Such positive media coverage would almost guarantee ongoing political and public support on both sides of the Atlantic for the American and British bomber barons' costly and brutal combined bombing campaign.

For his part, Adolf Hitler bloodthirstily accepted the challenge offered by the stepped-up Allied bombing raids of 1943. On 8 November, only days before the onset of the main sequence of Berlin raids, the Führer performed the last public speech of his notorious career, an address which was broadcast over the radio at 8.15 pm. He brushed off the property losses the Allied bombers had inflicted so far upon the German people; indeed, he declared, 'let them destroy as much as they want'. Although expressing himself as pained by the 'anguish' thereby inflicted upon German women and children, he also thrilled to the thought of Germany's 'hundreds of thousands' of bombed-out citizens spurring the nation on to revenge. The growing trend of large-scale devastation, destruction and death in Germany's cities was mere grist to his rhetorical mill. Hitler emphasised that the bombing was secondary to the bigger issue of defeating the Soviet Army on the Eastern Front and keeping the Russian hordes far beyond the borders of Germany, and to that end he promised that unlike in 1918, this time there would be no seeking of peace terms to end the war at 'fifteen minutes to midnight'. This time, he declared, Germany would fight on, despite the bombing, and according to him, this time Germany would win: 'You can count on that. The last one to lay down his weapons, that shall be Germany, and it will be five minutes *after* midnight.' Other than a vague promise that 'the hour of reprisal shall come', he laid the emphasis not upon what the Third Reich would specifically do to turn the tables upon its tormenters, but rather upon how much of a pounding the German people could in fact take. The industrial damages he declared to be 'inconsequential', while the three million ruined residences 'could be rebuilt in no time'. The Führer virtually revelled in the vastly increased sufferings imposed upon the German people in the present war, compared to back in the First World War: 'Could you imagine, my party comrades, that in the World War we could have suffered and withstood for even a month what we have now been enduring for years?' It is hard to see how this speech could have given any rational person grounds for confidence in Germany's self-proclaimed 'greatest-warlord-of-all-time', but it was within the terms of this mutually agreed apocalyptic contract that Britain's Air Ministry invited five journalists to go on a flight to see Hitler's capital burn.

Lowell Bennett had nabbed the sole place on a Berlin-bound bomber allocated to the American print media in London. Three approved US news agencies had been eligible: Associated Press, International News Service, and United Press. From the perspective of the Air Ministry's media managers, these three formed the 'American Pool', and whichever agency got to send a reporter on the trip would share its news copy with the others. To decide which agency would get the seat, representatives from the three news organisations had agreed to draw lots. Three small slips of paper were thus placed into a service cap provided by a US Army officer who had agreed to act as a 'neutral referee' of the ballot. That officer drew out of his cap the paper marked 'INS', and then the phone call had gone through to the Air Ministry, advising them of which agency to ring to make the offer. And hence came the subsequent Air Ministry phone call to the INS office in London. After this serendipitous opening had come a second recourse to pure chance, when Bennett and Wade flipped a coin to determine which of them would go – with the coin falling Bennett's way.

It was in this manner that the RAF extended its invitation for the five journalists to witness the next Berlin raid from the cockpit of a Lancaster. Lowell Bennett attended the portentous meeting in Adastral House, and recalled the terms of the invitation:

> ... we four reporters were summoned to the British Air Ministry in London and offered, in the words of a Wing Commander, 'an opportunity to see a big raid against Berlin in fairly clear weather'. 'If you accept', he cautioned in tones overlaid with solemnity, 'you'll have to accept the risk which, at the moment, is the highest for any target in Germany. You'll have to take the chance of being shot down and having no story at all. On the other hand, in a Berlin blitz, you'll have a good big story if you do come back.
>
> 'The Germans know we are out to destroy their capital', he added with a furtive, confidential air. 'And we know they know it. But the old man [Air Marshal Harris] is determined to finish the job. So there you are – do you want to go?'

The journalists had been presented with a stark take-it-or-leave-it proposition, but after all the anticipation and build-up, it was an offer they could hardly refuse: they had been summoned to the Air Ministry to hear just this offer; they stood there now as lucky representatives of a press corps that had been collectively hankering for just such an opportunity; and they were further impelled by the force of implicit peer group pressure. Trapped in this coercive logic, all four journalists accepted. All were ambitious, talented correspondents for whom the trip represented the chance to get their by-lines on the front page and their names in the public eye.

Nonetheless, the participating journalists' assent did not come without internal misgivings, as Lowell Bennett afterwards related:

> The Wing Commander noted our names and next of kin, then announced that we would take a train the next day to the various air bases from which we would fly. We walked out of the closely guarded Air Ministry to return briefly to the routine of London reporting. With me went that irresistible premonition: it was going to be a one-way ride.

Bennett was so sure of it that he wrote a letter to his wife, to be posted off to her address in New Jersey when he failed to return. He wrote her, 'When you receive this, I shall be walking home through Germany ... Please do not be perturbed by the report, "missing in action".' The lucky war correspondents presented with this unmissable opportunity were a diverse group which ultimately numbered five: two Americans, two Australians, and the late addition of one Norwegian. The latter had not been privy to the initial round of invitations but had got himself on to the program through his own insistence and the string-pulling of the London-based Norwegian government-in-exile. The omission of any Britons amongst the invitees suggests the Air Ministry's concern to get the message of its Berlin raids out to an international audience – the US, the British Commonwealth, and the peoples of the occupied and neutral countries in Europe. Alf King and Norm Stockton comprised the contingent of 'veteran Australian war correspondents', both professional newspapermen of long standing. Their reach was far broader than the Australian newspapers they represented, however, as their reports would be carried by British papers as well. Most prominent among the chosen five was the world-renowned American radio broadcaster Ed Murrow, who had been heading up the London office of the CBS radio network since 1938. By contrast Lowell Bennett was the least experienced reporter of the group, only 23 years old, and new to journalism; he had cut his teeth as a correspondent during the Tunisian campaign, only one year previously. In broad terms, therefore, Murrow represented the US broadcast media, Bennett represented the US print media, while the two Australians represented the syndicated print media of both Britain and the Commonwealth. The last man in the contingent was the odd one out: Nordahl Grieg, one of Norway's greatest living intellectuals, a poet, novelist, playwright, war correspondent, inspirer of the Norwegian and Danish resistance movements, and radio broadcaster for the Norwegian government-in-exile in London.

On 27 November, the selected reporters travelled the North-Eastern Railway from London King's Cross to

Lincoln. Lincolnshire was the heart of 'bomber country', and Lincoln was the connection point to the air bases clustered across that county. During the rail journey, Lowell Bennett mused quietly by himself, by turns fatalistic and melancholic, staring disconsolately at the unprepossessing sights presented by the winter journey: inside the train compartment he critiqued the 'faded, peacetime advertisements still on the carriage walls', while his morbid gaze out the window was sullenly returned by the 'dirty November fog'. But at the end of a dreary rail journey, he arrived at Lincoln Station to find it a hive of activity, with a '... seemingly aimless rush of uniformed travellers along its bleak platforms':

> But it was a brief picture, for the RAF awaited us, and all the reporters were mysteriously bundled off in a car to the base where we would await the launching of the attack we would accompany.
>
> And thus began a six-day wait, a delay until Bomber Command ordered another mammoth night raid against Berlin.

The journalists arrived on their allocated bomber bases just in time to see the aftermath of the latest Berlin raid on the night of 26 November. That night the bombers returned home just in the nick of time, to get their wheels back on their runways right in the face of rapidly deteriorating weather. Some didn't make it. The days following that raid saw such persistent poor visibility over England's 'bomber counties' that there could be no repeat operation for several days – it remained foggy, misty, rainy and hazy. This left the journalists at a loose end, detained on their air bases, and presenting the various commanding officers with yet another administrative detail to attend to in looking after the guests. Their RAF hosts were obliged to be solicitous of the reporters' welfare, as they bore the imprimatur of none less than Air Marshal Harris himself, who had condescended to extend his 'permission' for each of these five journalists to fly on the raid.

CHAPTER 2

THE LUCKY FIVE

Alf King: The professional newsman

At 46 years old, veteran Australian journalist Alfred King was the most senior reporter to fly on the raid. He found himself allocated to No. 467 Squadron, an Australian Lancaster unit at RAF Waddington, about 7 kilometres south of Lincoln. By then Waddington had become an Australian colony, with two Australian bomber squadrons in residence, No.s 463 and 467. The former was an inexperienced outfit, having only been established on 25 November, just days before King's arrival, so he was allocated to the more senior unit, and like Murrow and Bennett was assigned to the most experienced crew available, that of Squadron Leader William Forbes, the Acting Commanding Officer (CO).

Bill Forbes was only 23, but he and his crew had flown twenty-six missions since completing their training and joining the squadron less than six months previously. They were acknowledged as the squadron's 'gen' (expert) crew, and on the verge of completing their tour; this next raid would be their last before being 'screened' from operations. It was unusual for a crew to be withdrawn from operations before completing the requisite thirty 'ops', and the fact that this was about to happen to Forbes and his crew points to the fact that Bomber Command's losses had

Alf King, senior correspondent in the London office of the *Sydney Morning Herald*, who pulled rank on his junior reporters to take the risk of personally writing an eyewitness report of a raid to Berlin.

Courtesy Valda Curcuruto

been so high that there was an urgent need for instructors at the bomber training units to increase the flowthrough of replacement crews. It is probable that Forbes's crew was also being screened prematurely for morale purposes, to demonstrate statistically to the squadron's other crews the mere possibility that they could survive a tour. This message was apposite, for like all the other heavy bomber squadrons in Bomber Command, No. 467 had had a hard war, losing twenty-seven aircraft and 189 men on operations during the five-and-a-half month period of Bill Forbes's tour of operations. And so when Alf King arrived at Waddington to fly his trip to Berlin with Bill Forbes and his crew, these men had just this one last mission to fly before they could be rested from ops. But first they would need to survive the ride. And with a journalist on board! The pressure, tension and anxieties of getting through their tour seems to have told on the airmen, for having met his crew, Alf King found Forbes to be 'an old man of 23'.

By the youthful standards of the aircrew, Alf King himself was also an 'old man'. As befitted his age he was a senior journalist, the London editor for the *Sydney Morning Herald*, and so had pulled rank to get himself on to this flight, rather than allocating the opportunity to one of his more junior reporters. King had been the *Sydney Morning Herald*'s 'special reporter' in London as far back as 1929. Before that he had enlisted in the Australian Imperial Force in 1915, and by the end of the First World War was an artillery lieutenant with the 1st Australian Division. Through the 1930s, however, his career had not taken off as he might have hoped, for after his spell in London he was back in Sydney, reduced to reporting on the horse-racing scene for lifestyle magazines. But his career had taken an upward turn by March 1941, when he left Australia and the racing round for London, having regained a position with the *Sydney Morning Herald* as the paper's 'staff correspondent' in Britain. Like Lowell Bennett, King was then confined to the news desk in the London office, composing print-ready reports of war news, the raw copy of which had been generated by other, more junior journalists.

King's status is shown by the editorial freedom he enjoyed to write not only human-interest stories from the front, but also issues-based articles framed within a broader geopolitical canvas. With privileged access to a range of sources, such as interviews, press briefings, press conferences, press releases, and cables from journalists in the field, King wrote wide-ranging articles about such topics as the campaigns in North Africa and the Pacific Theatre, Middle Eastern politics, Britain's wartime science and industry sectors, Allied war leaders, the Allied war conferences, US forces in Britain, and the Allied bombing campaign over Germany. As a result he had by 1943 become a very well informed commentator with a shrewd understanding of the big picture of Allied strategy, familiar with Allied generals and politicians and with the politics of the war. He enjoyed the benefits of his insider status and found his work 'absorbingly interesting', as it allowed him to keep a 'watch' on 'history in the making'. King was just too busy in his job and too stimulated by his ringside view of big events to get restless or homesick, writing to his family in Sydney, 'I suppose I do so much, hear so much, and see so much that I have little time left to ponder on exiledom'.

Although a loyal spokesperson for the Allied cause, King could also be parochial, criticising what he saw as the discrimination shown by British officialdom against representatives from the 'Empire press' (namely from Australia and the other self-governing dominions). He alleged that preferential treatment was accorded to reporters for British and American media outlets in gaining access to good stories, declaring indignantly that, 'The Empire press ranks as a Cinderella in London, where it is invariably omitted when any discrimination is shown between the home, American and Empire press.' In relation to one of the biggest ongoing stories, the bomber offensive against Germany, King cited specific incidents in which British and American press representatives had been given special access to interview aircrew after raids, whereas 'Empire press representatives were not invited'. It may be that the officials in the Air Ministry had taken note of the complaint and of his press campaign for greater antipodean access to stories, for the phone rang in the *Sydney Morning Herald*'s London office just as it did in Bennett's INS office, requesting that the *Herald*'s man present himself for the same portentous meeting. Indeed, the fact that two Australian press representatives were included amongst the invitees may show that the Air Ministry was consciously seeking to smooth over ruffled Australian feathers.

And so now King was not only permitted to interview aircrew participants of a big raid, but he would be going on one himself. And not only would he be exercising the muscles of the 'Empire press' by gaining privileged access to the inside story of the Berlin Blitz, but he would also be able to home in from war politics in London to a more fine-grained story about the men at the 'pointy end' of the war. More than a year previously he had visited one of the factories turning out the then-new Lancaster bombers and had marvelled at the new machines' power: 'I saw six bombers fresh from the production lines capable of carrying about 50 tons of death and destruction in one journey over Germany.' Now he would get to fly in one and to see for himself those tons of high explosives dropped on Berlin. He knew it would be risky, but after agitating for the Australian press to be accorded unmediated access to the bomber boys, he was in no position to refuse the invitation, and like the other invitees was morally and professionally obliged to take the chance and go.

Ed Murrow: Voice of the 'Free World'

At RAF Woodhall Spa in Lincolnshire, No. 619 Squadron was obliged to host perhaps the most famous broadcast journalist in the world, Ed Murrow of CBS. From his first live broadcasts in 1938, Murrow had reinvented radio news by providing serious coverage on the threatening rise of Hitler's Germany, thereby developing an intense, direct, and ethically engaged form of first-hand reportage. Through his broadcasts he became so identified with the cause of the free world in the struggle against Nazi Germany that he became a 'major international celebrity'. After the outbreak of the European war in September 1939, he popularised Britain's cause in the war for his American audience, notably through live trans-Atlantic broadcasts during the Battle of Britain in

Ed Murrow, distinguished American war correspondent and pioneering radio broadcaster, in trademark chain-smoking pose at his typewriter in the London office of CBS. Like the other journalists who volunteered to fly on a raid, Murrow set great store in authentic, first-hand, morally engaged reporting.
Alamy EG6MRW

1940 and the subsequent German 'Blitz' upon London. He memorably started his broadcasts with an impeccably timed, 'This ... is London', and signed off with his trademark, 'Good night and good luck'. Murrow's on-air reportage during this crisis period of the war made him 'the most sought-after American in London', attaining trusted insider status among the British military, governmental, social and media elites. Through creatively redefining the rules of broadcast journalism, Murrow and his team of radio reporters became 'the first electronic news stars who attained their stardom as bona fide, on-the-air reporters who had seen and lived the stories they covered'. By 1943, 35-year-old Murrow's on-air persona was invested with unsurpassed credibility and moral prestige.

When a public figure of this stature presented himself at RAF Woodhall Spa to fly on a very 'dicey' operation to Berlin, it was unsurprising that the squadron CO, Wing Commander W 'Jock' Abercromby DFC, himself took on the role of being Murrow's pilot. Abercromby, a 33-year-old veteran of more than forty bombing operations, was understandably anxious not to get his VIP visitor killed. Bomber squadron COs did not need to fly more than the occasional raid, as their role was predominantly administrative; moreover, Abercromby was to be transferred out of the squadron within days, and so under normal circumstances he would hardly be expected to take the risk of flying another mission now. Nonetheless he put himself back on the operations roster, for Murrow's sake. The CO's readiness to personally fly Murrow on the mission was a generous act, suggesting that he was not willing to take the risk of assigning the great man to one of his less experienced junior pilots. This was typical of the solicitude extended to the other journalists when they reached their assigned squadrons.

Murrow was perhaps too senior a figure to have been allocated such a risky assignment in the first place, but he had volunteered himself for his own reasons. Like Alf King, the boss had pulled rank on his subordinates to get himself on the flight. This was because Murrow chafed under the notion that since witnessing and reporting so memorably on the Battle of Britain back in 1940, his role since then had been less that of a first-hand war reporter, and more that of media manager and editor. Serving as the London chief for CBS, he had been directing his team of broadcast journalists as they reported on the various war fronts in the European theatre; his task was to organise, co-ordinate and compere the resultant broadcasts, rather than going to the front himself. But by November 1943 Murrow was intent upon recapturing the immediacy of his earlier role by again reporting the sharp end of the war as an eyewitness.

One of Murrow's CBS correspondents, Dick Hottelet, admitted that he himself was prepared to fly in a bomber to get a story only 'because it was, unhappily, part of my job'; but he thought that Murrow did so because he was 'driven' to prove himself all over again. Another of Murrow's colleagues, Eric Sevareid, reported that while reporting on the London 'Blitz', Murrow had repeatedly placed himself in harm's way under the bombing to get the first-hand stories he wanted. Sevareid recalled Murrow's remarkable coolness and personal poise even in the face of bombs falling so close that the detonations caused water to gush from broken hotel plumbing and the ceiling plaster to fall 'like snow' onto the carpet. After watching him up close under the duress of personal peril, he considered that Murrow was not afraid of dying so much as he was 'afraid of being afraid'. It seemed as if Murrow maintained his personal style of affected nonchalance in the face of danger not just to stay close to the events he reported on, but also to live up to the standards of his own self-created persona. Clearly, the Air Ministry's offer of a seat on a Lancaster coincided with Murrow's professional and personal yearnings, and so he jumped at the chance to go himself, rather than extending the offer to one of his reporters, as might have been more appropriate.

Murrow's whole life seemed to have led up to his participation in the struggle against Hitler's Germany. After graduating from Washington State University in 1930, his early career was framed by the rise of Hitler and the Nazi seizure of power in Germany in 1933. Appointed as the assistant director of the Institute of International Education, he found himself dealing directly with the impact of the Nazis' persecution of Germany's Jewish population. The institute was an 'unofficial educational embassy' funded by the Carnegie and Rockefeller foundations, committed to the work of peace activism through the instrumentality of arranging student and academic exchanges. As it turned out, Hitlerism was *the* peace issue of the time, so Murrow's office had to respond to the spiralling humanitarian catastrophe of Nazi atrocities inside Germany. He bent his efforts towards raising funds to bring German academics to the United States to escape Nazi persecution. Of course, a large proportion of these refugees were Jewish, so Murrow collaborated closely with Jewish organisations like the American Jewish Joint Distribution Committee, a humanitarian group supported by luminaries such as Albert Einstein, working to fund placements for persecuted and displaced scholars in US institutions. Murrow's four-year tenure with the institute also gave him superb networking opportunities with members of the diplomatic, academic and financial elites on both sides of the Atlantic, contacts which he would build upon further when he moved to London to build a new career in broadcasting.

In 1937, Murrow negotiated what would prove to be a breakthrough, self-defining career change, joining the CBS broadcasting network. Having been engaged for five years as a facilitator, organiser and advocate on behalf of the victims of Hitler's fascism, from 1938 Murrow shifted to a more public role. Initially appointed as director of talks, from 1938 he was posted to the network's London office, responsible for providing live broadcasts of European stories for the audience back home, and specifically charged with improving CBS's coverage of European news. This appointment was tailor-made for Murrow, for starting with the Sudeten crisis of 1938, he was able to exploit international concerns about the bellicose trajectory of Hitler's foreign policy by upgrading CBS's coverage to a daily news feature, the 'CBS World News Roundup'. Both Murrow in London and his Berlin-based CBS colleague, William Shirer, were sure that Hitler was trying to start a war, and both were determined to make this *the* story in their on-air reportage back to the States.

Once the war broke out, and particularly from the crisis point of the Battle of Britain in 1940, Murrow's self-appointed task became one of popularising Britain's war for his American audience. He had in effect become a propagandist for the Allied cause, influencing Americans to side with Britain in the struggle against Nazi Germany. As Walter Cronkite, one of Murrow's peers, admitted, accredited war correspondents 'abandoned any thought of impartiality'. It followed that accompanying the RAF on a return visit to Hitler's capital, and reporting on it by radio, was a logical next step in the trajectory of his life's work so far as an activist for the Allied cause against the Nazi regime.

Lowell Bennett: Cub reporter

Lowell Bennett had the shortest car trip of any of them from Lincoln railway station, bound for RAF Skellingthorpe, only five kilometres out of town. He was assigned to No. 50 Squadron, one of the senior heavy bomber outfits in Bomber Command. Compared to his more illustrious colleague from CBS, Bennett arrived on his assigned bomber base as a relative unknown. Despite his ambition, he was at the time only a fresh-faced 'cub reporter', and so had no public profile comparable to Murrow's. However, upon arrival at Skellingthorpe he was assigned to the squadron's most experienced crew, captained by Flight Lieutenant Ian Bolton. Bennett found that Bolton's crew was coincidentally composed entirely of Scotsmen: Bolton and five others 'hailed from Scotland', while the seventh man was Scots-Canadian! The men's nationality must have been congenial to Bennett, as his wife Elizabeth was Scottish-born. Although Bolton was only 20 years old, he was as safe a pair of hands as you could find in a frontline Lancaster squadron

Young American war correspondent, Lowell Bennett, after repatriation from his POW camp in Germany, reunited with wife, Elisabeth, and sons, Alan and David. This is the type of uniform he wore when he was shot down, and in which he undertook his remarkable guided tours of bombed-out German cities.
Courtesy Alan and David Bennett

in 1943: he was about to fly the final trip of his 30-operation tour, and by surviving so long he and his men had become the acknowledged 'gen crew' of No. 50 Squadron. The squadron executive officers thought their best crew 'ought to take the American', rather than assigning Bennett to the tender mercies of a less experienced team. From the squadron's perspective, it was self-evidently imperative to keep 'the American' alive, and they considered the best chance of that happening was if Bennett flew with their best pilot, Bolton. Like Jock Abercromby at Woodhall Spa,

Bolton was generous in agreeing to take the journalist on this one last trip. For him and his boys, there was at least the consolation of knowing that this op would certainly be their last before getting rested from combat flying.

With his assignment to these frontline warriors at No. 50 Squadron, Bennett's war-reporting career was now back on track. His first big journalistic opportunity had come one year earlier, in November 1942, when he was sent out to Algeria to report on *Operation Torch*, the Anglo-American invasion of Vichy French North Africa. There he showed himself to be venturesome to a fault, going forward to the sharp end of the war to report from the battlefront in Tunisia. If Ed Murrow's artform lay in well-crafted and delivered radio broadcasts, Bennett's would prove to be longer format – the book. Indeed, his first book, *Assignment to Nowhere*, a personal narrative of reporting the war in Tunisia, was released in mid-1943 to favourable reviews. He almost certainly intended that his next book would flow from the adventure upon which he was now embarking.

If Murrow was a culture warrior in opposition to fascism, Bennett was a free spirit and a restless questor after new experiences. He was the product of the Franco-American alliance in the Great War: Lowell Bennett senior, his father, had married a Frenchwoman named Marguerite, one of the translators at General John Pershing's American Expeditionary Force headquarters in France. His siblings' names – Micheline, Charline and Georgette – suggest the French cultural tone set for the resultant family. His culturally blended and bilingual family was sufficiently well-off that even during the straitened times of the Great Depression, his parents retained the means to finish off his school education with a year at a boarding school in France to perfect his French. He duly returned home with a 'flawless Parisian accent', but also with a growing impatience for the conventional routines of workaday life in America. Although of a literary bent and with a talent for language, Bennett remained too full of wanderlust to toe the academic line at college, so dropped out of his studies at 19. He escaped his 'nice, suburban upbringing' in America by going abroad, living cheaply and travelling as a 'hobo' as he journeyed to South Africa and Australia, in a similar manner to that of contemporary upper middle-class 21st-century backpackers going abroad on a 'gap year'.

He was back in France by the time the war started in September 1939, joining the American Volunteer Ambulance Corps in time for the German assault on France in May 1940. After the French defeat he was captured by the German Army and interned, but in July that year was released from confinement alongside other American volunteers for repatriation to the US. Bennett never lacked enterprise and initiative, as we shall see, and instead of returning to the US, he stayed in England, serving as an ambulance driver for the Free French forces during the London Blitz. During this time he married a British woman, 'Liz' Walker, who worked at the American Eagle Club, a soldiers' canteen in London. She delivered their first son, Alan, towards the end of 1941, but despite his new commitments, Bennett was not for settling down: ever resourceful and persuasive, he succeeded in launching himself on a new career as a journalist, getting himself appointed as a war correspondent with the International News Service. The INS was an American wire service owned by media tycoon, William Randolph Hearst, sending syndicated news copy to print media outlets in the US.

After achieving this career upgrade, he got his next big break when he was assigned to report on the war in Tunisia. Bennett's colleagues were quickly impressed by the inexperienced correspondent's reporting from the combat zone: INS's seasoned columnist, Bob Considine, declared Bennett to be the 'fastest developing newspaperman I've seen in my twenty-odd years around copy-desks'. However, having proven himself by cabling stories from the frontline, Bennett was disappointed to be recalled to London before the campaign ended, after only two months in the field. Although reunited with his wife and son in Hampstead, he was not pleased to be confined again to INS's London office: 'Suddenly and emphatically, the North African episode was ended. I was back in the routine that is London – the "desk", the blackout, the sandwiches, the race to catch the last bus home, the anonymity of news-agency work.' As it had been prior to his North African interlude, Bennett's job in the office was as a news editor, not reporter. In this role he got no by-line by which to get his name out to the public. As a self-described 'romanticist', Bennett found it deflating to edit other journalists' stories, rather than collecting those stories himself. He itched to get the chance to go back into the field, as he related:

> Reporters can go dashing off to the fronts, get themselves shot at, come back feeling very colourful and maybe a little brave, but the office routine goes on as always. For two months, Charlie Smith and others had been receiving our stories of the fighting,

had been relaying them to newspapers in America.
And now it would be our job to help do that, for other correspondents in Moscow, Algiers, Cairo, New Delhi and elsewhere.

Bennett was prepared to perform this prosaic duty in the expectation that his turn would come again. When he resumed work in London after returning from Tunisia, the press corps expected that the next big story would be the Anglo-American invasion of occupied Europe – the event which would become known to us as 'D-Day'. Perhaps this would present the ambitious young reporter with his next opportunity to report from the front? Bennett waited in tightly strung expectation of his next big break:

> Our job was to report news to America, and a spell of excitement and adventure in North Africa was, after all, only an interlude. But there would probably be another interlude just around the corner.
>
> It would probably be much the same as last time: a telephone call, a mysterious order to get ready for some 'camping out', then another trip.
>
> And perhaps the next time it would be the Second Front.

With Liz pregnant again, he took the precaution of sending his family home, away from the war and the German bombing of London, to live safely with his family in New Jersey; there his second son, David, would be born in 1944. This move was ostensibly to keep the family safe, but it seems likely that an additional reason was that with his appetite for combat reporting whetted by Tunisia, he sought to spare his wife the worry of knowing what he was actually doing when he went off on his next field assignment. Indeed, once she was gone, he reportedly presented his boss, Leo V Dolan, the head of INS's London bureau, 'with a request to be dropped somewhere behind Hitler's defences for a "more adequate" news coverage'. This fanciful request was of course denied, leaving Bennett impatiently seeking and questing after the next big thing. One of his drinking buddies from the press corps remembered Bennett in this period:

> Among his newspaper friends both at the office and at Ye Olde Bell, the pub around the corner, he was known as a fellow who found it rather difficult to take himself seriously, who had a laugh for everything and everybody, who was full of wisecracks and could argue anyone under the table, and whose restless mind was constantly making jabs for new horizons.

As it turned out, Bennett did not need to wait for D-Day for his next injection of action. There were so many media agencies in Britain that opportunities to be embedded with a combat unit had to be rotated among the rival claimants in the interests of organisational equity. And so it happened that when the Air Ministry decided to send journalists on its next Berlin raid, INS's turn had randomly come up. And the phone had rung in the London bureau office, and rival reporters Lowell and Wade had randomly flipped their coin. Bennett's resolve not to defer to Wade must have hardened with the thought that Wade had already flown a bombing mission with the US 8th Air Force, whereas Bennett had never been on a raid. And thus a few days later Bennett found himself at RAF Skellingthorpe with Bolton's boys, waiting for flying weather to return.

Norm Stockton: Man in a hurry

Meanwhile, veteran Australian war correspondent Norm Stockton was one of three journalists awaiting a flight at RAF Binbrook, billeted together in the officers' mess. As we have seen, the two American reporters were stowed away respectively at Woodhall Spa and Skellingthorpe, while Stockton's fellow Australian, Alf King, was at Waddington. Besides Stockton, those at Binbrook were the Norwegian Nordahl Grieg, plus yet another Australian reporter, Colin Bednall. The latter was not one of the original invitees, but like Grieg was a late addition to the program. But whereas Grieg and Stockton had 'Bomber' Harris's permission to fly on the *next* raid to Berlin, Bednall only had permission to go on the following raid after that – and when that took place it would not be to Berlin. With Bednall left to nervously wait on the ground in the meantime for his turn to fly, Stockton and Grieg were the lucky ones.

All three of these reporters were allocated to Binbrook's resident Lancaster outfit, No. 460 Squadron, which was the senior Australian unit within Bomber Command, having been flying operations over Germany since early 1942. It was commanded at the time by Wing Commander Frank Arthur, who was a navigator, not a pilot, so was in no

Australian war correspondent Norman Stockton, at right, interviews General Scanlon (centre) of the USAAF, in front of a B-17 bomber at an RAAF base in Australia, during the Allied air forces' 1942 bombing campaign against Japanese bases on New Guinea and New Britain. Stockton wanted to experience air combat, not just write about it, so the next year he took up a post in Britain to get himself closer to the fighting. He got closer to it than he would have wished.

AWM Negative 012356

position to fly one of the journalists himself, as No. 619's CO, Jock Abercromby, would do for Ed Murrow. Instead, Arthur assigned Stockton to one of the unit's most experienced pilots, Pilot Officer James English, a 27-year-old teacher only two trips away from completing his tour, along with his equally experienced crew.

Stockton's host outfit was a hard fighting unit and had an eye-watering loss record to prove it. One of No. 460's aircrew, Flight Sergeant Norman Ginn, who would fly on the same mission as squadron guests Stockton and Grieg, had by now – midway through his tour – become 'numb' in his fatalistic expectation of his own inevitable demise. He had been on the squadron long enough to see a lot of crews come and go; he now realised that 'few people got through their tour' and so had just come to accept that as a brute fact. All he could do was fulfil his 'part of the bargain' by doing his job as the wireless operator in his crew, right up until the moment when they were inevitably shot down. It helped psychologically that crews flew, lived and died together, and Ginn indeed identified strongly with his crew: he thought his captain, Flight Lieutenant Tom Alford, to be 'marvellous'; he found the navigator, Flight Sergeant Eric Daley, to be 'very clever'; and thought the rest of them were all 'good' at their jobs. It was small-group identity like this that enabled bomber crews to ignore the odds and accept their chances; they were resigned to die together if that's what it came to. This was the straitened cultural world into which Stockton and the others had been inserted.

It is noteworthy that each of the journalists so far slated to fly on the 2 December raid had been assigned to fly with a crew of considerable operational experience. This shows that although the air force was prepared to accept the risk of having journalists killed while embedded in a bomber crew, it wanted to create the best chance of getting the reporters safely back on the ground. This was not only a humanitarian consideration, but pragmatic as well: the reporters needed to get back alive if they were going to write their stories and put Bomber Command's Berlin offensive on the front page of the newspapers – which was of course the object of the exercise.

Like Alf King, Norm Stockton was a middle-aged and mid-career professional journalist, for whom the war had presented a career opportunity to report on serious news for reputable Australian newspapers. He was 39 years old in 1943, with a wife and child back home. In 1937 he had married Marie Bishop, a journalist from Melbourne with whom he had shared the adventure of reporting on Japan's war against China while based in Hong Kong. Earlier in the 1930s he had worked as a freelance journalist in Sydney but had in effect dropped out of society after his divorce from his first wife in 1935. After that disruptive event in his personal life he had resorted to employment far from the madding crowd as a wireless operator: first he marooned himself at the remote meteorological station on Willis Island, 450 kilometres off the North Queensland coast, and then worked a passage aboard a ship plying the route between Sydney and Hong Kong. Clearly a very resourceful man with considerable initiative and know-how, Stockton then left the ship in Hong Kong after talking himself into a job with the *South China Morning Post*. After this breakthrough, his career progressed well, as he had no doubt hoped: he became an editor for the *South China Daily Telegraph*; the overseas correspondent for several newspapers, including the Melbourne *Argus*; and the chief correspondent for the London *Daily Express*, reporting on Japan's war in China. His secure work in Hong Kong also provided the opportunity for his wife to work professionally, and she too reported the war news, for London's *Daily Express* and *Daily Telegraph*. However, the war in China was escalating, and after the devastating Japanese bombing 'blitz' upon Canton over May–July 1939, Marie Stockton and their baby daughter, Anne, evacuated to Manila. They arrived back in Australia on 20 September, where Marie found herself newsworthy – not on account of her status as an informed observer of the Japanese war upon China, but rather for the patronisingly trivial novelty of being an 'Australian girl' doing war reporting.

After the evacuation of his family, Stockton himself remained at risk as a reporter covering the China war, and two months later he had a brush with death, when the aircraft he was travelling in came close to getting shot down by the Japanese. Flown by Australian pilot JN Wilson, Imperial Airways airliner DH 86 *Dardanus* was heading for a refuelling stop at Hanoi, en route from Hong Kong to Bangkok, when it allegedly entered prohibited airspace near the Japanese-held island of Weizhou in the Gulf of Tonkin. The airliner was intercepted and forced down by five Japanese fighters, which fired at it throughout a 20-minute-long engagement, only ceasing fire when the airliner's wheels touched the ground at Weizhou's military airbase. The five occupants were lucky to escape unscathed, although the aircraft was temporarily impounded, and both Stockton and the pilot arrested. This became known as the

'Weichow Incident', causing a flurry of diplomatic protests, so that the two Australians were safely released, but the incident was one more step in the process of the geopolitical estrangement between Japan and the Western powers that would soon lead to the outbreak of the Pacific War. Given the excellent gunnery standards demonstrated by Japanese fighter pilots in the opening phase of the ensuing war, there can be little doubt that they had aimed to miss Stockton's aircraft, firing streams of tracers across the airliner's bows to intimidate the pilot and give the signal to land. Certainly, no German fighter pilot over Berlin would be giving any British bomber similar leeway.

After this scare, it was perhaps unsurprising that Stockton put some distance between himself and Japanese forces by moving to Manila, where his China experience opened doors for his next career move: he was appointed as a correspondent on the staff of General Douglas MacArthur, the US Generalissimo in the Philippines. But Stockton was fated to live dangerously, for the war then followed him to Manila, with the eruption of hostilities between Japan and the Anglo-American colonial powers. Japan invaded the Philippines in December 1941, but Stockton got out before the Japanese conquest, following MacArthur and his entourage when they evacuated to Australia. There he was accredited as a war correspondent with MacArthur's general headquarters in Melbourne.

Professionally, the move back to Australia provided an opportunity for Stockton to report on the operations of the US Army Air Forces striking back against the Japanese outposts on New Guinea and New Britain. In the early months of 1942 his reportage focussed on the only Allied units in Australia doing any hard fighting – the air force. Accordingly, he visited air bases in Queensland to interview the crews of American B-17 and B-26 bombers after their return from raids on the Japanese outposts of Rabaul and Lae. But the closest he himself got to the war was by vicariously experiencing the thrills and spills of bombing, flak and fighter attack while safely behind his typewriter in Townsville, writing up the stories of the American airmen for publication in the newspapers 'down south'. He also reported avidly on the achievement of his British colleague, Harold Guard of the United Press, in accruing 22 flying hours on operations in B-26 bombers based out of Queensland.

Judging by what he did soon after, Stockton must have felt envy and frustration with regard to Harold Guard's exploits, for writing up the stories at second hand was as close as an Australian journalist could get to the air action over New Guinea. This was because Guard was accredited to the US press, so was given access reserved for US reporters only. As for Lowell Bennett, reporting other people's stories was not enough for Stockton, who harboured the professional ambition of writing up the action from first-hand observation. At the time (and since), Australian servicemen and reporters tended to regard the Australian battlefront as a sideshow, remote from what many perceived to be the main struggles of the war – in Europe. Despite his access to good combat stories from the American airmen, and his by-now deep expertise in reporting on Japan's war, Stockton seems to have shared this preference for the higher-status European theatre, for by November 1942 he had got himself transferred to the London office of the

Sydney Sun. From there he undertook field trips to North Africa to report on the Tunisian campaign (as Bennett did), and then on the invasion of Sicily in July 1943. By late 1943 he was back in London, looking for another active assignment. While there, he submitted a 106 000-word manuscript for a personal memoir entitled *My Typewriter and Me*, or *From China to Charing Cross*. But before he could get it published, that phone call came through, requesting that the *Sun*'s man present himself at the Air Ministry. Stockton had certainly spoken to enough bomber crewmen in Australia and written enough about their experiences of air combat. He had read Harold Guard's accounts of his participation in bomber missions with professional envy in his heart. And now he finally had permission to go and see for himself. He was hardly likely to turn down such an opportunity, for his own reasons impelled and obliged to go forward and take the risk alongside the others.

Nordahl Grieg: Norwegian patriotic icon

The most enigmatic of the five journalists, and also the man most invested in the struggle against Hitler's Germany, was Nordahl Grieg. The other four were redoubtable journalists, but Grieg was a renaissance man by comparison, his written output spanning not only journalism, but poetry, novels, and successful drama scripts. Although he would come to win renown in Norway as an inspiring patriot, Grieg had a restlessly cosmopolitan, international outlook. After graduating from Royal Frederick University, he spent much of his life abroad, travelling the world as a sailor aboard Norwegian merchant vessels, studying in England, travelling in Greece, working as a newspaper correspondent in China during the Chinese Civil War, living in the Soviet Union to study Soviet film and theatre, and serving as a war correspondent during the Spanish Civil War. And of course, once Norway was invaded and occupied by Hitler's forces in 1940, he lived in Britain once again, working once more as a war correspondent. Like his four colleagues invited to participate in the raid, Grieg certainly had no lack of initiative, curiosity and drive.

But to a greater extent than any of the others, Grieg applied an ideological perspective to his life's work. He was chair of the Norwegian Friends of the Soviet Union from 1935 to 1940, so was rightly regarded as a communist 'fellow traveller'. Although he never joined the Norwegian Communist Party, he acted as if he had, gaining notoriety by defending Stalin's show trials in 1937, and for making tendentiously ideological attacks upon Stalin's purged rival, Leon Trotsky. As a cheerleader for the communists, Grieg gave staunch support for Norway's initial policy of neutrality in the Second World War, taking his lead from the fact that the Soviet Union had contracted the Soviet–Nazi non-aggression pact of 1939.

It was Germany's invasion of Norway in April 1940 that brutally altered Grieg's perception of the world situation. Throughout the 1930s he had warned that the rise of the Hitler regime in Germany meant war, and now that war had come – and to his own country. On 8 April 1940, the day before the invasion, Grieg was in Oslo, on leave from national service to enjoy some time with his soon-to-be wife, the famous Norwegian film and theatre actress,

Gerd Egede-Nissen. That evening they were both deep in conversation with their friend and artistic collaborator, Hans Jacob Nilsen, the former artistic director of *Det Norske Teatret*. They were discussing their respective film and theatre projects for the 1941 season when the air-raid sirens started wailing and the lights went out.

The friends broke off the meeting and the couple headed back to their hotel through darkened streets. With the morning came the sad, sobering clarification that Norway had indeed been invaded by Hitler's Germany: first German bombers droned overhead, and then while he was at breakfast in the hotel dining room, Grieg saw an officer in German uniform rush up to the reception desk and ask to see 'Herr Quisling', the notorious pro-Nazi leader of the *Nasjonal Samling*. This was Norway's Fascist party, which although electorally unsuccessful previously, collaborated with the Nazi invasion and occupation once the war began. Unbeknown to Grieg, German troops had already landed in multiple harbours to secure Norway's cities, ports and airfields.

Fired up with vengeful indignation, that morning Grieg reported to the War Ministry looking for an assignment to active service, but the ministry was evidently administratively overwhelmed by the situation, so he was told to go home. Remembering that his reason for visiting Oslo from his home city of Bergen was that he had an appointment with his dentist, he presented himself at the appointed time as he now had nothing better to do. After getting his dose of drilling, filling and filing, Grieg was still lying in the dentist chair, his sore mouth still full of cotton buds, when the dentist blurted out, 'Damn, the Germans are here!' Grieg sat up and looked out the window to see a party of German infantrymen disembarking from a truck in the street outside. He watched them set up a machine gun outside the entrance to the National Theatre, where they were peacefully greeted by a troop of Norwegian mounted police. Grieg raged at his fate in thus 'becoming an eyewitness to the surrender of Oslo'. That night Grieg heard repeated radio announcements from the new Quisling government threatening punishment against any who resisted the German occupation.

He escaped occupied Oslo for the countryside, heading for the Gudbrand Valley, which had become a rallying point for Norwegian forces continuing armed resistance. There Grieg was able to join a thirty-man unit which was dispatched to the Lillehammer train station, where a massive transshipment was underway, with more than 1500 boxes and barrels being unloaded on to a special train from a convoy of lorries. It was Norway's gold reserve, all 240 million kroners' worth, being shipped out from under the Germans' noses. Norway's finance minister, Oscar Torp, had organised the move on the first night of the war, and now he was in Lillehammer supervising the transshipment. Starting on 19 April, Grieg was now committed to a seven-week expedition to take the gold to safety, becoming an assistant leader within a party of thirty soldiers and forty civil servants. The party stayed just ahead of German pursuit in an arduous odyssey which culminated in a British warship evacuating the gold from the northern port of Tromsø for safekeeping in England.

Grieg accompanied the gold shipment as it departed Norwegian waters aboard British warship HMS *Enterprise* on 25 May, leaving his unhappy country in the ship's wake.

Finding himself suddenly exiled, Grieg was both disturbed by the loss of homeland and resolved to return: 'I knew that I would one day return to a free Norway. But that would cost many more battles, and our homesick yearning would become greater than any other Norwegians before us had felt.' Grieg felt Norway's defeat as a humiliation and a betrayal, and was consumed by an extravagant sense of self-sacrificial devotion to his country. To him, Norway's long 'night of shame' could only be brought to an end by a flaming 'dawn', with the 'light' of that bonfire kindled by Norwegian patriots such as himself: he boldly declared, 'We must burn' in the act of resistance, and even dwindle 'to ashes' in the heroic attempt.

With the national gold reserve safely deposited in the Bank of England, Norway's government-in-exile set up shop in its embassy at Princes Gate in Knightsbridge, London. Grieg was proud of the success of the gold shipment and of his own role in it, and had now abandoned his erstwhile role as a political dissident, instead unreservedly identifying himself with the Norwegian state: '... on board our ship lay the preconditions for a free Norway, the possibility of buying weapons and rebuilding an army, so that one day we could free the country from the slime with which it had been covered ...' Norway's government-in-exile in London represented not only its constituency of Norwegian exiles in Britain, but also the population back home under German occupation. To reach this audience, the government created 'The Royal Norwegian Information Service' to broadcast Norwegian radio news, talks, performances and readings. However, it seems that the conservative Norwegian authorities in London continued to regard the former left-wing firebrand Grieg with suspicion, for despite his pre-eminent qualifications as a patriotic wordsmith it was only after an interval that he was appointed as a press officer for this wartime propaganda organisation: a year would elapse before he regained a Norwegian army uniform and the officer status that went with accreditation as an official war correspondent. Grieg was of course superbly qualified for the role of press officer, being one of Norway's greatest living writers, a master of propaganda, a man with a matchless record of anti-fascist activism, and with fluent English.

Having been given access to the powerful, popular medium of radio, Grieg anchored the Norwegian information service's syndicated radio program in an equivalent manner to that of Ed Murrow. The program was entitled 'Norway fights on', and he soon became well known for his patriotic broadcasts and inspirational poetry readings. Grieg's task was to boost morale amongst Norwegian fighters, both those serving alongside British forces as well as those seeking to resist the German occupation within Norway. His broadcast poetry readings expressed his countrymen's yearning to create 'a Norway/Whence the tyrant has been hurled'. As a spokesperson for his fellow exiles, he also used his radio broadcasts to give poignant expression to Norwegian homesickness. In one of his poems, he speaks for all exiled Norwegians by writing from the perspective of one of the thousands of Norwegian seamen who crewed Allied merchant ships; to this Norwegian Everyman, home was 'present' only 'in his dreams', nostalgic dreams in which he 'fondles' the remembered trees and stones of his lost homeland with the 'tender touch of a lover'. Grieg declares that only to exiles is 'the Meaning of Norway' truly known.

Grieg's poetic broadcasts into occupied Norway revolutionised his public image, turning the controversial pre-war radical into an iconic symbol of 'good' Norway. Dr Andreas Winsnes, the director of the British Norwegian Institute from 1942 to 1945, described the impact of Grieg's broadcasts during the occupation:

> There is hardly a Norwegian who has not been affected by Grieg's lovely poems. We sat listening to them all over our far-flung country during the first year of the war. When our wireless sets were seized we read them in underground newspapers.
>
> His words sent out a ray of light when the prospect looked darkest. It was our land itself that spoke to us through his verse.

Besides his patriotic radio broadcasts, Grieg operated as war correspondent based in England. Like Bennett, it was not Grieg's style to write stories in his London office by collating other people's copy, so instead he sought to write about the war by embedding himself with the most forward-deployed units of the Free Norwegian armed forces. Thus he wrote about the Battle of the Atlantic not only by visiting hospitals full of ship-wrecked survivors to obtain first-hand survival stories, but also by taking ship aboard a Norwegian warship on convoy escort duty in the Atlantic, and by flying an anti-submarine patrol over the Atlantic in a Catalina flying boat of No. 330 (Norwegian) Squadron. As with the four colleagues who would also go on the flight to Berlin, it was a logical next step to go on a bombing raid in order to write authentically about the bomber crews who did the bombing.

Once Grieg's flight was lined up, his friend Olav Rytter visited him in his hotel room in London, to find that 'Grieg was a little worried but seemed excited' about going on the raid. However, despite his nervousness, Grieg remained good company, regaling Rytter with 'intriguing, fun' anecdotes about the RAF flyers he had interviewed after their return from bombing raids. Grieg described for Rytter his profound admiration for the *sang-froid* of the aircrew living in the suspended sentence between missions:

> The most striking thing is that it's so unreal. [After] the show, these poor devils are strolling around and joking with chess and bridge and reading a book or writing. But you would need to have seen it yourself to understand what they'd been through just the night before. I never stop wondering about human nature.

Indeed, his vicarious identification with the bomber crews in their 'closet of death' had given Grieg cause to ponder deeply on the nature of courage. In his July 1943 poem, 'The Best', he reflected upon the fate of Danish resistance fighters in terms that he could equally apply to his RAF flyers, declaring that 'They are the best who die'. In his view, it was the 'strong and single-hearted' individuals in occupied Denmark who 'willed and dared the most' by opposing German tyranny. He hailed the courage they showed when facing death – 'calmly' taking 'their parting' – in terms that applied equally to the stoical endurance of the airmen.

Grieg told Rytter that he had discussed with an RAF bomber pilot friend his intention to fly on a mission (the pilot was probably Tor Anundskås, a Norwegian Halifax bomber pilot). His pilot friend had told him, 'I admire war correspondents for one thing: You are doing the same as we are, but of your own free will,' whereas by contrast, he and his comrades did it out of duty: '... it is a destiny we are subject to and to which we bow'. The pilot considered that if a war correspondent found himself 'in trouble' flying on operations, it was his own fault for choosing to go on the flight, whereas if an airman found himself 'in trouble, it is by order of others, an outsider's higher power'. This grand fatalism made it 'easier' for the flyers to bear the risk, or so this pilot thought. For his part, Grieg was amazed that a man who was obliged by his superiors to fly thirty missions to Germany before being rested from operations should consider this 'easier' than a war correspondent flying only a single mission to get a story. Grieg had no pretence to fearlessness, summing it up with the Old Norse saying that 'It's a scared man who does not dare to tremble'. Grieg explained it thus for his friend, Olav Rytter:

> The difference between courage and cowardice is whether you react uncontrollably to the fear or not, because obvious fear is contagious. It would hurt the whole, the collective. If you look around in the plane, everyone sticks with their [job]. Everybody is pale, tense, but does their job.

Grieg's words were consistent with his ideals, for he persisted with going on the Berlin trip despite, like Lowell Bennett, having a premonition that he would not return from it: he told his wife upon his departure for Binbrook that, 'They will never take me alive!' In anticipation of being shot down, and evidently intent on depriving the Germans of the satisfaction of identifying his body as that of the famed Norwegian patriotic propagandist, he left his identity tag behind in his flat, taking with him only a pendant inscribed 'Nordahl'.

Grieg went ahead with the flight because only by doing so could he live and write with the authenticity his soul craved. It was this basic motivation that he shared with the other journalists who flew. Amongst the five journalists slated to fly on the big raid to Berlin, Grieg was the exception to the pattern of being hosted by the most experienced crew available on the squadron: he was assigned to Flying Officer Alan Mitchell's crew, a less experienced team who were only halfway through their tour. But whether this made any difference to the outcome is questionable, given the randomness of fate in the skies over Germany, as we shall see.

CHAPTER 3

FORERUNNERS

Despite the apparent novelty of five journalists flying on the one raid to Berlin, our five reporters were not the first to blaze a pathway into the skies over Germany. As early as March 1942, the Air Ministry had permitted war artist David Thornton-Smith to fly on a raid to Essen in a Stirling bomber, 'to gain a first-hand impression of Bomber Command at work', and to represent those impressions in oil paintings. More recently, one of the BBC's 'most distinguished war correspondents', Wynford Vaughan-Thomas, had succeeded in getting a trip in a Lancaster to Berlin on the night of 3 September 1943. His sound engineer, Reg Pidsley, accompanied him to make a live recording of the flight, cutting the sound directly on to an acetate disc, using a portable turntable placed on the floor of the cockpit. Once their Lancaster was safely home to the RAF base at Langar in Nottinghamshire, the two men rushed their freshly cut discs to the BBC studios in London, where an edited version of the recordings was transmitted over the BBC Home Service the very next evening. Vaughan-Thomas, Pidsley and the seven-man crew of Squadron Leader Ken Letford's Stirling bomber 'F for Freddie' had needed some luck to regain *terra firma* alive on that evening of 3–4 September 1943. On that night twenty-two Lancasters out of 316 were shot down, a loss rate of almost 7 per cent.

Despite the well-known risks, journalists were more than willing to hazard their lives to get their stories. Indeed, our risk-taking five were following a trail blazed by others. Before Vaughan-Thomas scooped his rivals by broadcasting a sound recording of his participation in a raid, in January 1943 eight journalists had been allocated places for the RAF's first raid on Berlin since 7 November 1941. This raid occurred on 16 January, symbolically raising the curtain on Bomber Command's ongoing and costly 1943 offensive against the German capital. The *New York Times*' Jamie MacDonald was among those who went, with his story appearing in that paper two days later. The other journalists who accompanied the raid that night were Colin Bednall of the *Daily Mail*, and Reuters correspondent Stewart Gale. Their stories were syndicated to media outlets throughout the world.

It is telling that in all three cases during 1943 when RAF authorities allowed journalists to go on a raid to Germany – the 16 January raid, the 3 September raid, and the raid flown by our five reporters – the target was Berlin. This was deliberate, as Berlin was the jewel in the crown of the RAF's bombing campaign, the nerve centre of the Nazi state apparatus, the most difficult target on Bomber Command's hit list, and the one that most clearly symbolised the Allied aspiration of using the long reach of airpower to strike back at the monster in his lair.

Careful management of public relations was essential to sustaining the costly Anglo-American bomber offensive into Germany, and so by the end of 1942 the Allied air forces were realising that first-hand news stories about raids to Berlin offered a means of controlling the story for global media consumption. Prior to 1943, both RAF Bomber Command and the US 8th Air Force had stalled persistent requests from media organisations to allow journalists to accompany bomber crews on raids. But eventually, both air force bureaucracies conceded that the public relations gains of first-hand news coverage outweighed the risks of adverse publicity if a journalist were lost. As far as Britain's Air Ministry and Ministry of Information were concerned, the successful completion of a flight carrying a journalist offered a threefold benefit: firstly, it would boost the British public's support for Bomber Command's controversial strategic bombing campaign against Germany's cities; secondly, it would improve national morale by offering credible assurance that Britain was striking back against Hitler's capital; and lastly, it would show the Americans that Britain was 'punching her weight' in the Allied war effort, and would therefore help shore up this vital alliance.

For journalists, therefore, getting a 'seat' on a bomber was not a tribute to their personal powers of persuasion, but rather the outcome of a carefully and deliberately strategised *invitation* on the part of the air force authorities. For example, in Vaughan-Thomas's case, the RAF had suddenly contacted the BBC 'with a dramatic offer' to take a two-man recording crew to Berlin. As far as the BBC was concerned, this offer came as a sudden breakthrough, following a four-year campaign to get permission for a journalist to fly on a raid aboard a bomber. Jamie MacDonald's flight too had been the culmination of his employer's four-year struggle to get a journalist aboard: only a single 'seat' was offered to the American press, and that to the *New York Times* alone. In time-honoured fashion the two eligible journalists had vied for the spot by flipping a coin, and MacDonald had won. Jamie MacDonald's feat in January 1943 of getting aboard an RAF bomber, flying to Berlin and getting home alive to file his story aroused great excitement among other American journalists in Britain, which only added steam to the pressure of pent-up demand for seats aboard bombers.

Of course, it was not only British bombers that proved to be magnets for ambitious journalists. Throughout 1942 the Americans had been building up the 8th Air Force, their own bombing force in England, and after a series of heavy losses and modest results this force too needed all the good public relations it could get. Of course, Americans did not need any tuition from the British about marketing, and so the 8th Air Force appointed four public relations officers 'to promote the daylight bombing strategy', and 'to sell the American public on its requirement for more men and equipment'. And so a team of cameramen led by film director William Wyler were taken aboard American bombers during early 1943 on raids over France and Germany to take footage for what became the 'morale-building' feature film, *The Memphis Belle*. The risks of such journalistic commitment to their craft were underscored when one of Wyler's sound engineers, Harold J Tannenbaum, was killed as the B-17 he was travelling in was shot down over France. In addition, the 8th Air Force's Public Relations Office submitted the names of thirteen carefully vetted journalists from approved news organisations to begin training on 1 February 1943 to fly on a raid.

The journalists who went on this raid have provided illuminating accounts of how civilian reporters responded to the life-threatening hazard of flying in a bomber on an operation. One of the thirteen embedded journalists who trained for participation in this bombing mission was Walter Cronkite of United Press, who went on to become the 'personification' of American television journalism in the post-war years, the 'most trusted man in America'. Cronkite recounted that in a discussion among themselves before their flight, one of his colleagues, Bob Post of the *New York Times*, had remarked with gallows humour that given the 8th Air Force's loss rate on bombing raids, out of the ten journalists in the room still intending to fly on the raid, one would not return. In the event, only six journalists actually went on the raid when it finally occurred, as an attack upon the German naval port of Wilhelmshaven on 26 February 1943. It was no coincidence that the raid the journalists were permitted to fly on was another symbolic occasion – the first time that 8th Air Force bombers ventured into Germany, previous raids having confined themselves to targets in occupied France and the low countries. The prophetic Bob Post did not return from Wilhelmshaven, killed in a B-24 bomber shot down by a German fighter. With seven bombers lost out of the sixty-four that went over the target, his acerbic assessment both of the loss rate, and of the proportional mortality rate amongst the participating journalists, had been confirmed in tragic fashion. He had had a premonition of his death while waiting to go, telling his friends, including 'actress Leonora Corbett and war correspondent Helen Millbank of the *Chicago Daily News*', that 'he thought he was going to die'. As a tribute to his dead colleague, Cronkite filed a story for the *New York Times* in Post's stead which was run on the front page.

Given such a risky proposition, it is telling that out of the thirteen correspondents appointed to go on the American raid, only eight made it to the point of actually getting ready to fly on the day of the take-off, and of these, two pulled out at the last moment as 'they were not well enough to go'. One of the resolute final six, Andy Rooney from *Stars and Stripes*, had also considered pulling out, and for similar reasons, as he related later: 'The thought crossed my mind that I didn't feel too well myself.' Indeed, as he sat anxiously through the pre-flight briefing and nervously waited to go, his resolve almost failed:

> A thousand things went through my mind. I wondered what I was doing there. Was it really necessary for me to volunteer for a mission that could easily cost me my life simply to get a story for the newspaper or to appear legitimate in the eyes of the crewmen I was covering on a daily basis?

Besides simple professional ambition, Rooney's self-reflection shows that one reason why journalists accepted such risks to get their stories was something akin to survivor's guilt. The unlucky Bob Post was an example of this: although in his more cogent moments he had considered his role as a war correspondent to be a 'more important' service to his country than serving in the armed forces, he nonetheless remained uneasy about having dodged the draft on the basis of his reserved occupation, knowing that other men had enlisted and were now shouldering the risk of flying operations on almost a daily basis. Somehow, the resultant troubled conscience had prompted him to volunteer to fly on his fateful mission. Similarly, Andy Rooney recalled that his decision to take the risk of flying on a raid 'probably grew out of that uneasy feeling we all had that we were watching too many young men our age die while we were writing stories about them and then going back to London for dinner'. For men like Post, Cronkite and Rooney, their ongoing moral credibility as war correspondents required them to go.

So too would it be for Murrow, Bennett, King, Stockton and Grieg, when their turn came later in the year.

CHAPTER 4

BOMBER BOYS

Despite their acceptance of a very hazardous assignment, the five flying journalists were only too keenly aware of their privileged status as 'one-trip tourists', trespassers in the deadly game of chance played by the full-time airmen. As we have seen, one of these five was Lowell Bennett, who at the end of November 1943 found himself at RAF Skellingthorpe waiting to fly on the raid. But Lincolnshire's weather remained 'appalling', with persistent fog and low-hanging cloud that meant they had to take a six-day hiatus before the weather allowed operations to resume. While waiting for the weather to improve, like his four colleagues Bennett was left ensconced at his assigned base, getting to know the flyers. The young American reporter was described as 'lanky, boyish, and exceedingly good-natured', and he had the engaging personal style to get the men to talk, perhaps with their tongues loosened by a pint or two in 'Beer Alley' – the bar in the officers' mess. To take advantage of the waiting time, he made a start on the human-interest angle by socialising with the aircrew he would fly with; he made a point of being winningly self-deprecating, disparaging himself as an 'operationally useless load' who needed to be 'ferried' to Berlin.

In particular he got to know his pilot, Ian Bolton, whom he found to be an intelligent, reflective and mature man for his 20 years, and from whom he gleaned insights into the

'Beer Alley' in the Officers' Mess at RAF Waddington. While waiting for the weather to improve enough to permit the big raid to be launched, our five correspondents had several days in this sort of convivial environment to get to know their hosts; this is the mess where Australian war correspondent, Alf King, got to know the officer aircrew of the Australian 467 Squadron.

AWM Negative UK2210

culture of the 'bomber boys'. Bolton led what was regarded as the best crew in the squadron, he was a flight commander responsible for one of the squadron's three flights of bombers, and was himself on the verge of completing his operational tour, so Bennett might have thought his pilot could offer some pearls of wisdom about how to survive and thrive in the bombing business. But he did not; indeed, it was hardly reassuring for Bennett to hear Bolton ascribe his survival so far to luck. Bolton explained how it all worked:

> You have to calculate that the Germans are going to shoot down from five to ten percent of every bomber force we send against Berlin ... If they get you – well, you're unlucky; you're one of the five to ten percent.

Then he casually pointed out, unreassuringly, 'so far we have been lucky'. And that was that.

Bennett had previously gotten to know plenty of frontline American and British soldiers in Tunisia, so thought he knew something about warriors, but he found the 'bomber boys' to be 'unique' in their attitude towards an extreme form of war service in which their 'life expectancy' was 'reckoned not in years but in weeks':

> The constant turnover of new crews to replace battle casualties, the ever present uncertainty, the youthful fatalism – these brought on a cordiality and a comradeship one might ascribe to condemned men living together, and accepting a close intimacy before their ultimate and collective end.

Especially in the RAF, the time had long since passed when much conversation was devoted to discussions of death which clutched, in its myriad and awful forms, at these fresh-faced fliers of Britain. To the outsider, their attitude seemed at first one of adolescent indifference to a subject which they could not fully understand. But it was not that. Death had become a routine corollary to their business; and they ignored it as they ignored the deadliness of their bomber cargoes.

The squadron as a whole had been lucky in the preceding month despite its participation in all of the Berlin raids so far, for during November it launched a total of ninety-eight Lancaster sorties on bombing operations but lost 'only' three out of the twenty-six crews which had flown on operations that month. That gave a relatively encouraging loss rate of just over 3 per cent of sorties – more or less a best-case scenario for an RAF heavy bomber crew operating over Germany at the end of 1943.

At Skellingthorpe, six days of taut anticipation and anticlimax went by for Bolton and Bennett – and for all the others – during which time operations were first declared to be 'on', then 'scrubbed' because of adverse weather forecasts. However, the pre-operational 'flap' on 2 December turned out to be for real. Squadron bomb aimer Les Bartlett had adopted the habit of walking from the sergeants' mess to the airfield at about 10 am to see if 'there were "ops" cooking'. Upon arrival that day he found the signs plain to see: 'Men were dashing in and out of flight offices; crews in flying kit were piling into transports, and everyone was generally busy.' This flurry of activity was because each crew had to test-fly their aircraft before returning it to the ground staff for fuelling up each bomber in time for their take-off around nightfall. Bartlett and his crew also undertook this pre-operational test flight, sure they would be on '"ops" tonight', as the weather was 'bang on' for operations. Somewhere nearby, Lowell Bennett too was reading the signs plainly enough, and did not need to be told what was going on: he watched the armourers swarming over the bomb dump and loading the bomb trolleys, and the fleet of heavy fuel bowsers making their way around the perimeter track, calling in turn at the parking bay of each of the Lancasters slated to fly on the operation. Bennett was amazed how quickly the ground crew divined the identity of the target, in advance of the official notice of the operation which would be given at the aircrew briefing in the early afternoon: the prescribed loads of 10 000 pounds of bombs and 1800 gallons of fuel suggested that it was to be another trip to Berlin. Once the briefing went ahead at 1.30 pm, the ground crew's educated prediction was confirmed – the bombers were off on another visit to the Big City that night.

Bennett's privileged status as an embedded reporter permitted him access into the inner sanctum of the base operations building, where he observed the special advance briefing given to those ten aircraft captains whose names had been chalked on to 50 Squadron's ops board. The scene reminded him of his geography classes back at school: with a large map on the front wall, beside a blackboard covered with 'sharply' chalked-on operational data, each pilot sat behind a school desk, which he covered with charts and an open notebook. The pedagogical theme was further accentuated by the short lecture delivered schoolmaster-style by the civilian meteorological (met) officer, who stood gesturing at his weather charts, talking disinterestedly about isobars and pressure gradients with 'a stingy, rasping voice'. Bennett found the meteorologist 'a lean, thin-jowled Northcountryman who seemed, if anything, slightly bored with the whole business and more than a little dubious of the value of his information'. Of course, his off-hand tone reflected the fact that he himself did not have to go to Berlin. But the pilots in front of him did. And they knew that the odds were good that one of them would not return. It was best not to think too much about that, and they took their minds off it as best they could by busying themselves with copying down the operational data of the mission.

Meanwhile at RAF Binbrook, where Norm Stockton and Nordahl Grieg similarly sat in on the 460 Squadron briefing, Flight Sergeant Norm Ginn, the wireless operator in Flight Lieutenant Tom Alford's experienced crew, heard a chorus of gasps from the assembled aircrew when the curtain was pulled aside to reveal the map, with its taped-on route pointing all the way to Berlin and back. Ginn and his crew had been on each of the previous four trips to Berlin and had found them very 'nerve wracking'. Ginn was discouraged by his realisation that the Germans were always 'ready for us', and he found it 'terrifying' seeing other aircraft shot down around them 'all the time'. And now Bomber Command HQ had thoughtfully laid on another such trip to the Big City! While experienced crews were aghast, for new crews the ignorance could be bliss. That afternoon at RAF Bardney, Sergeant Norman Wells was the rear gunner in Sergeant Phil Plowright's crew from No. 9 Squadron, going on their first op. Wells remembered

Aircrew from 460 Squadron undergoing the pre-mission briefing in the Ops Room at RAF Binbrook, November 1943. The target was Berlin, but one of the briefing officers has evidently lightened the atmosphere by cracking a joke. On average, about one in twenty of these men would not return from the night's raid, and they knew it.

AWM Negative 069822

the reaction of his freshman crew upon the awesome revelation of the target for tonight:

> When we went into the briefing room and saw we'd got Berlin for our first, we thought Christ Almighty and yet, the same time, it was something good. We were going to Berlin. That was the heart of the war.

The self-belief of this 'sprog' crew might have been bucked up by the identity of the aircraft to which they had been assigned: she was a thirty-two-trip veteran formerly assigned the radio callsign J-Jig, but recently rechristened by her ground staff as J-Johnnie Walker, with reference to that whisky's advertising slogan, 'still going strong'. The aircraft's longevity and auspicious new callsign were taken as a good omen by her green crew, but at the briefing the freshers noted the other crews' expressions of concern that the 'bombers had been given a direct route ... straight to the target, and there were no diversionary raids'. With that, any interior mental calculus the other airmen might have been making of their survival chances had to be adjusted downwards, an unspoken cogitation which must have occurred too amongst the assembled crewmen at Binbrook, Waddington, Woodhall Spa and Skellingthorpe.

At the 460 Squadron briefing, the twenty-five operating crews similarly confronted the enormity of another dicey trip to the Big City. Journalist Norm Stockton must have been at least a little reassured that his assigned crew was highly experienced, had done it all before, and had come back alive the previous twenty-eight times. Moreover, he had found a compatriot in the crew's navigator, Pilot Officer Neville Anderson from Brisbane in Queensland. As a fellow 'Brisbane boy', and because he wrote for Queensland newspapers, Stockton had identified Anderson as good talent for the story he wanted to write about Brisbane's own 'bomber boy', to create a local connection with his readers back home. Anderson was a 24-year-old former law clerk who had spent more than a year in the Australian Army before joining the RAAF in January 1941. After training in Canada, he had qualified as a navigator in August 1942, joining No. 460 in June 1943. By the standards of Bomber Command aircrew longevity, by December of that year he was a veteran. Stockton had found a human-interest story in him, but despite the parochial angle he was planning for his feature about the boys from the Aussie bomber squadron, Stockton's 460 Squadron crew was in reality a British Commonwealth crew, just like Alf King's crew from the Australian 467 Squadron: in Stockton's case, only three of the seven crewmen were Australians, alongside three British flyers and one Canadian; whereas in King's case, only two of the seven were Australian, with the others comprising two Scots, two Englishmen, and a Canadian. This mixture of nationalities was typical of all squadrons in Bomber Command, whatever their official national designation.

Over at RAF Woodhall Spa, Ed Murrow similarly sat through the briefing for the 619 Squadron captains, similarly sizing up the flyers around him as 'talent' to be included and quoted in his story. When the curtain was dramatically opened to reveal Berlin as the target, he noticed a 'big Canadian' pilot's self-contained response: he simply 'printed "Berlin" at the top of his pad and then embellished it with a scroll'. Back at the Skellingthorpe briefing, Bennett heard the met officer explain that they would have to fly through two weather fronts to reach this faraway target, with one front lying across the English coast and one over Germany. Beyond this prediction, the met officer had to resort to quite imprecise prognostications: at the Lancaster's cruising altitude of 20000 feet, the air temperature would be something between −36 and −50 degrees Celsius; and while there might be plenty of cloud cover over Germany – and hence more safety from night-fighters, searchlights and flak guns – on the other hand 'it might be completely clear'. The met officer finished on an even vaguer note by telling the pilots that they would simply have to take 'potluck' with the weather. On that unreassuring thought he scooped up his charts and left the room.

The meteorologist's place on the Skellingthorpe ops-room stage was taken by No. 50's commanding officer (CO), Wing Commander Robert McFarlane DFC, whom Bennett found to be an impressive 'twenty-nine-year-old Scot and veteran of more than sixty raids against Germany'. McFarlane outlined the raid's tactical details 'with the clarity and precision of a good business executive', detailing the raiding force, the route, target, aiming point, target-marker flares, and bomb-load; as well as the expected defensive measures from searchlights, night-fighters and flak. He explained that No. 50's ten operating crews were part of the third wave, out of five waves of bombers scheduled to bomb, with all five waves crammed within a twelve-minute bombing window. McFarlane emphasised that the squadron crews were to bomb within a stated four-minute time window, and so pilots and navigators were to manage their navigation to ensure that they went over the target strictly within this timeslot. McFarlane wrapped up his presentation with an exhortation:

> This is the most important target of the war, chaps. Go in there and bomb hell out of them. Make everything count – then bring yourselves and your planes home again safely. Keep your eyes open for fighters. Watch

for those flares they drop to light up your route. Good luck to you all.

The CO's peroration was long on aspiration and affirmation, but it was short on actionable tactics for survival: what were the pilots to do about those flares, once they saw them, given that they were simultaneously enjoined to stay tightly on track, to flock together within the bomber stream, and to keep rigorously to the time schedule at each waypoint? Bolton's fatalistic acceptance of the whims of 'luck' was probably as practical a focus as anything for men about to 'dice' the odds over Germany.

Over at Woodhall Spa, Ed Murrow found a similar content and tone in the 619 Squadron briefing to that which Bennett found at Skellingthorpe, observing that 'The atmosphere was that of a church and a school':

> The weatherman gave us the weather. The pilots were reminded that Berlin is Germany's greatest center of war production. The intelligence officer told us how many heavy and light ack-ack guns, how many searchlights we might expect to encounter. Then Jock, the wing commander, explained the system of [target] markings, the kinds of flares that would be used by the pathfinders. He said that concentration was the secret of success in these raids; that as long as the aircraft stayed well-bunched, they would protect each other.

Like Wing Commander McFarlane's closing words to 50 Squadron, this last point too was well-meaning 'eyewash' from a CO somehow trying to provide a note of reassurance for his men. As everyone knew, it would be too dark for the aircraft to consciously stick together; everyone knew that each crew would be on its own, navigating autonomously from waypoint to waypoint, and adjusting its aircraft's speed to stay on schedule and to bomb within the assigned time window. The only co-ordination that would be possible in relation to other bombers would be last-second manoeuvring to avoid mid-air collisions. Alongside No. 50, No. 619 was assigned to the third wave, so Bennett and Murrow would be travelling through the same skies not far apart, timed to pass over Berlin within a minute or two of each other.

With the captains briefed, the other crew members were now allowed into the ops room for the 'mass briefing', whereby each captain met with his crew to go over each member's specialist concerns: for the navigator, the route, waypoints, timings and the radar fixes to look out for on the H2S ground-mapping radar; for the bomb aimer, the bomb load, aiming point and target markers; for the flight engineer, the fuel load, power settings, fuel consumption and airborne endurance; for the air gunners, the night-fighter defences; for the wireless operator, the wireless frequencies, codes and transmission schedule. With information imparted, notes taken, and maps and logs stowed in flight bags, at 3 pm Skellingthorpe's operating crews met to take their 'special pre-mission meal'. Bennett found that this included 'wartime rarities' rarely seen by lesser mortals in rationed wartime Britain: 'a real egg, ... real bacon, and fresh milk'. He partook of this repast, appreciating the egg as 'a real treat', but along with his gustatory appreciation came the nauseating return of his previous 'hunch' that this was going to be a 'one-way trip'.

Suppressing the thought, and managing to keep the food down, Bennett went with the others to the operations office to get kitted up for the flight. No. 50 Squadron navigator Les Bartlett described this pre-flight ritual as 'the great bind of getting dressed' to fly at high altitude in an unpressurised, poorly heated aircraft: after undressing, he would pull on two pairs of underpants (one of silk, one of wool), a white polo-neck sweater, and heated electric waistcoat and slippers; over this ensemble he would put back on his normal RAF battledress – woollen trousers, battledress jacket and socks. Then came insulated flying overalls, the yellow 'Mae West' inflatable life preserver vest, parachute harness, and flying helmet. Into his bomb aimer's leather 'gen bag' he would stuff six maps, torch, RAF-issue escape kit, silk gloves, leather gauntlets, two spare pairs of gloves, handkerchiefs and goggles, as well as his personal 'evasion kit' crammed into a 'Craven A' cigarette tin. This latter contained razor, shaving cream, toothbrush, toothpaste, soap, comb and sticking plaster. For Bartlett, once he was trussed up in all these layers and carrying both his tightly stuffed gen bag and his heavy, rock-hard parachute pack, he could barely walk. As he recalled, 'what a bind it is moving about getting into the aircraft in that outfit'.

For non-flyer Bennett, over the top of his war correspondent's uniform he drew on a shoulder holster with a .45-inch pistol. Over that he donned his army-issue greatcoat, then a Mae West life preserver, and finally a US Army musette bag loaded with what amounted to Bennett's own idea of a survival kit for shot-down reporters on the

Aircrew from 467 Squadron getting kitted up in the ready room at RAF Waddington, before undertaking a raid in August 1943. Personal lockers are visible at right. The pedantic process of putting the kit on in the correct order was a calming ritual in itself, but pre-flight nerves could be further eased by smoking, joke-telling, singing and whistling. Clearly visible on the man at left are the 'Mae West' life preserver, the parachute harness, and one of two spring-loaded hooks for attachment of the chest parachute pack. A parachute pack lays on the floor in the centre. On the floor at right are the navigator's and/or bomb aimer's 'gen bags', which they use to convey their maps and equipment to their respective compartments in the aircraft.

AWM Negative UK0544

run inside Nazi Germany: a carton of cigarettes, a notebook, pencils, heavy winter underwear, toilet articles, and 100 rounds of .45 ammunition. The pistol and ammunition contravened the rules for civilian war correspondents, but as Bennett's conviction was that he would be shot down, he justified it with the consideration that it would help him to evade capture and get home to file his story. The other articles were similarly chosen to support his anticipated heroic feat of filing a story while on the run, deep within enemy territory. Over the top of this already-bulky ensemble went the tightly done-up constriction of the parachute harness, with its two snap hooks on the chest straps by which to attach the parachute pack. Given his premonition, he must have carefully noted those hooks on the front of the harness, and their corresponding fittings on the back of the parachute pack, as well as the location of the parachute ripcord on its side.

Bennett had to hurry, for from 3.30 pm lorries started pulling up at the crew room to pick up the crews. Once embarked, each crew would be driven along the taxiway and dropped off in front of the parking bay where their bombed-up and fuelled-up Lancaster sat waiting for them. As the overburdened and trussed-up Bennett struggled out towards his crew's lorry, carrying his parachute pack, an RAF officer noticed the 'Yank' war correspondent and his civilian shoes, and stopped him: 'You'll probably be cold wearing those light shoes. Why not borrow my flying boots?' Having already noticed the snug-looking sheepskin flying boots of the RAF flyers, Bennett readily accepted, but the thoughtful officer added, 'Just one thing, though. Of course you'll come back all right. But, if you don't mind, would you sign for the boots in case anything happens to them – then I can draw another pair.' The premonition hit Bennett again. He signed.

After the briefing, Bennett was so sure of his premonition that he had gone aside to compose a report of the raid, and of his participation in it, for release upon his non-return. It seems that as a result he missed out on the 50 Squadron pre-operational ritual of collectively listening to a gramophone recording of the Andrews Sisters' rendition of the sentimental song, 'The shrine of Saint Cecilia'. This was an obligatory requirement for squadron crews departing on a raid, as Bartlett explained:

> If you were a superstitious type it was a must, if not then you still listened to it because it was considered extremely unlucky not to have done so, and you did not want to push your luck – not to mention the wrath of your crew if they found out.

The plea in the song's lyrics for heaven to protect them was indeed apposite, invoking the hope of a sacred place of refuge, and their yearning to survive and return to their loved ones. Many of the airmen must have found the song lyrics comforting, but as Bartlett implies, the other reason for the practice was the typical aircrew superstition requiring the correct observance of a prescribed ritual to avoid provoking fate, and hence preserve their crew from harm. After the obligatory listening to the Andrews Sisters, the next superstitious rite at 50 Squadron was the crews' 'ritual "pee"' on their own Lancaster's tailwheel before going inside and starting it up. This too was compulsorily performed in order to avoid provoking the malevolent hand of fate. Of course, such carefully observed rituals by 50 Squadron's aircrew did not in fact preserve them from harm: this hard-fighting unit lost 257 men in the course of 1943, at a monthly average of twenty-one killed – exclusive of those others who failed to return but were subsequently reported as POWs.

Even on less overtly superstitious squadrons, men tried to maintain an atmosphere of auspicious normality: at Woodhall Spa with 619 Squadron, while Ed Murrow was getting 'kitted up' in the flight office, he noted two Australian airmen who maintained their poise by whistling nonchalantly as they dressed. But for all its studied casualness, for either man this too could have been a

A Lancaster of the Australian 460 Squadron parked along the perimeter track at RAF Binbrook. Alf King described such a view of his 'big black bomber' before he boarded G-George at RAF Waddington towards dusk on the evening of 2 December 1943.
AWM Negative UK1633

superstitious ritual to ward off evil and secure his survival. As Murrow walked out to the lorry with his pilot, Wing Commander Jock Abercromby, he heard an announcement over the station's public address system, announcing a free cinema showing that evening of the movie *The star-spangled rhythm* – an escapist Paramount Pictures movie featuring a 'who's who' cast of the American stars of the era, such as Bob Hope, Bing Crosby and Dorothy Lamour. The ground crew and the off-duty aircrew would get to enjoy tonight's show, but the operating crews would miss it. Indeed, nine of the men who flew that night would never see a movie again. But it was important that 'normal life' be seen to go on.

At Skellingthorpe, Bennett's crew lorry pulled up in front of 50 Squadron's 'B-Bolty', and eight 'heavily dressed and harnessed' men clambered out onto the taxiway to face the imposing black shape of the waiting Lancaster. Each squadron maintained an inventory of twenty to thirty aircraft, and each machine was given an identifying letter as its radio callsign, normally using the military's phonetic alphabet (thus 'D for Dog' or 'G for George'); however, in some cases unapproved callsigns were chosen to grace particular machines, like 'B for Bolty', to form an association with a lucky pilot, or 'J for Johnnie Walker', to draw an auspicious association with a beloved drink. Bennett accompanied the bomb aimer, Flight Sergeant Robert Forrester, as he went underneath B-Bolty and stood within the yawning cavern of the open 26-foot-long bomb bay to inspect the bomb load. Forrester, whom Bennett found to be 'a nineteen-year-old, rosy-cheeked, enthusiastic youngster', showed him the 4000-pound 'cookie' high-explosive demolition bomb, and the tightly packed boxes of

Watched over by the squadron armament officer at left, a party
of armourers from 460 Squadron have just completed the
'bombing-up' of one of the Australian squadron's Lancasters
(the famous G-George now preserved with the Australian War
Memorial). War correspondent Lowell Bennett was given a tour
of his own bomber's cavernous bomb bay before boarding the
aircraft, and saw exactly what we see here, namely the standard
bombload of one 4000-pound 'Cookie' (top centre) plus the
incendiary bomb containers behind it. This photo was taken at
RAF Binbrook in December 1943.

AWM Negative 069821

small incendiary bombs; the young airman explained the electrical release mechanism, and clarified the function of each type of bomb: Bennett learned that the big 'cookie' was to demolish a building and also blow the roofs off buildings around the impact point, while the incendiaries were to fall inside the resultant opened-up cavities and set fire to the internal structures. Forrester was evidently very matter-of-fact in explaining to his journalist guest that this was the RAF's approved way of creating a firestorm and torching a city. The young bombardier was a charming and informative tour guide to Bennett, as befitting a man whom his friend, Les Bartlett, considered 'one of the best-liked chaps on the squadron'.

At Woodhall Spa, Ed Murrow too was deposited on the taxiway by the crew lorry, and stood there gaping at the 'big, black four-motored Lancaster, 619 Squadron's "D for Dog"'. As Murrow and the men stood around D-Dog, waiting for the time to embark, a station wagon came along the taxiway, going from aircraft to aircraft to drop off the crews' in-flight rations: Murrow was there alongside the others to take delivery of his 'thermos bottle of coffee, chewing gum, an orange, and a bit of chocolate'. Having stowed away his rations, he enjoyed the short, reflective hiatus that the take-off schedule delivered before the crewmen had to climb aboard their aircraft, start their engines and resume the war:

> Up in that part of England the air hums and throbs with the sound of aircraft motors all day, but for half an hour before takeoff the skies are dead, silent, and expectant. A lone hawk hovered over the airfield, absolutely still as he faced into the wind. Jack, the tail gunner, said, 'It'd be nice to fly like that'.

Over at Waddington with 467 Squadron, Alf King likewise disembarked from the lorry in front of his assigned aircraft, in this case 'G-for-George'[*]. Bill Forbes' crew had flown

---

[*] This is not the famed 460 Squadron's 'G for George' but a different 'G for George' that flew with another Australian squadron.

'George' through ten of their previous operations and took great comfort in the fact that she 'had not been scarred, not even scratched', despite all the 'hate' the Germans had shot at her while she went over her previous targets. Standing in front of the big black bomber, King noticed that on the side of her nose just beneath the pilot's cockpit window was a scoreboard depicting ten foaming mugs of beer, painted-on talismans of her success in getting through those ten operations. King knew that it was customary to paint bomb symbols on the aircraft to tally missions in this way, and so while waiting to board her he asked, 'Why that symbol?', addressing the question to G-George's Australian ground crew, who were also standing around waiting. He meant, 'why paint beer mugs and not bomb symbols?'. Sergeant Laurie Parker replied sardonically, with a grin, that the mugs represented 'Trips to the land of Mugs'. King evidently didn't understand, for in further explanation, Parker pointedly underlined the comment, referring in laconic fashion to the Germans as 'big mugs'. The sergeant was making his own insightful commentary upon the German people's deluded choice in electing and supporting Adolf Hitler, for in Australian slang, a 'mug' is a gullible, naïve, easily misled person.

By now, at dozens of bases across Yorkshire and Lincolnshire, airmen were boarding their aircraft and starting their engines. When the time came at Skellingthorpe, Bennett followed the other seven men up the ladder and through B-Bolty's entry door just forward of the tailplane. He left the two gunners behind to lever themselves into their hydraulically powered gun turrets, then followed the other five in ascending the sloped fuselage floor towards the

The mission log of Lancaster G-George of 467 Squadron, with each 'op' painted up on the aircraft's nose in the form of a beer mug. Alf King found his own aircraft decorated in the same way, which the crew explained as tallying the number of its 'trips to the land of mugs'.

AWM Negative UK0466

aircraft's nose section, climbing awkwardly up on top of the bomb bay and over the tall, fence-like wing-spars. Stooping and shuffling forward, he squeezed along the narrow walkway towards the cockpit, past the wireless operator's and navigator's tight workstations on the left. To the heavily harnessed, trussed-up and padded-out airmen climbing aboard a Lancaster, this progress was not straightforward: Les Bartlett, who as the bomb aimer had the longest distance to cover to reach his station in the aircraft's nose, found that he always got 'hooked up on one thing and another, climbing over the main spar getting all steamed up'.

Upon squeezing past the wireless operator and navigator in their respective cubicles and reaching the cockpit, Bennett found that once Bolton had slipped into the pilot's seat on the left-hand side, and the flight engineer bent down on his folding seat to hunch over his 'formidable array of instruments' on the right-hand side, the cockpit was crowded. The only remaining space on the flight deck for Bennett was the small area of blank floor behind the flight engineer. There was no seat for the war correspondent at all, so there he stood, with his left shoulder wedged in behind the pilot's armoured seat-back, the flight engineer's shoulders within easy reach of his right hand, and the forward corner of the navigator's chart table nudging the back of his left thigh. Comfortable it was not, but this spot certainly delivered a superb all-round view: Bennett had a good viewing angle along the leading edge of the wings to both pairs of engines, over Bolton's right shoulder to peer through the windscreen and over the bomber's nose, between the pilot's and flight engineer's shoulders into the bomber's nose compartment, with its wide fishbowl-like bomb-aiming blister; and turning around, he had the navigator within arm's reach to the left, and could bend down to look along the passageway to the wireless operator's position beyond; looking outside, he could turn around to look through the armoured-glass pane beneath the Perspex canopy roof, looking back along the top of the fuselage to the mid-upper turret and the aircraft's twin tailfins. There was also a bulbous, clear Perspex viewing blister immediately to his right, set into the starboard cockpit window, so that if he bent his head into it, he could look straight down at the ground below. This was certainly an excellent viewing platform for whatever lay ahead of him.

A 460 Squadron Lancaster damaged by a fighter attack on the night of 17 August 1943. This photo well shows the crew positions on a Lancaster's flight deck. Grinning in the background is the pilot, sitting in his armoured-back pilot's seat, alongside the flight engineer, seen at right surrounded by switches and dials. The canvas screen seen hanging over the roof at left draped the navigator's cubicle, to maintain dark conditions for his viewing of the H2S radar scope. The airman in the foreground giving the thumbs up through the broken Perspex side window is standing exactly where the journalists stood in their respective aircraft during the raid of 2 December 1943. Although hardly comfortable, this standing-room-only station was not only situated in the nerve centre of the aircraft, within comfortingly easy reach of three crewmen (pilot, flight engineer and navigator), but also offered an excellent view to left and right, ahead, behind, and even downward through the viewing blister.

AWM Negative UK0402

As Bennett looked around to acclimatise himself to the novel perspective of a bomber cockpit, the crew busied themselves with their on-board pre-flight checks. This busy, well-practised routine was recalled by Bennett's squadron mate Les Bartlett:

> Mike, our pilot, starts up the four Merlins and each member of the crew checked his equipment – our mid-upper gunner Jock and our rear gunner Fred checked the rotation of gun turrets, operation of guns, ammunition feed. Reg, our wireless operator, checked his various transmitters, receivers and other devices. Frank, our navigator, checked his set, known as 'Gee', and other items of equipment [such as the H2S ground-mapping radar] ... Finally Don, our engineer, glances at his hundred and one dials to ensure that the four Merlins are fit and healthy, while Mike tries all the controls.

This was the scene, repeated more than 400 times that evening across the bases of England's 'bomber counties', that each of our five journalists drank in as their own aircraft's systems came alive. For the bomber crewmen, immersing themselves in their start-up drills was a good way to deal with their nerves, but for each of the reporters aboard there was nothing to do to ease their pre-flight anxiety.

CHAPTER 5

A GATHERING STORM

Norm Stockton at Binbrook found himself on the flight deck of K-King, keyed up as he stood behind his pilot, his fellow countryman James English. He was pleased about being assigned to fly with an Australian outfit, and his newfound friend and fellow Queenslander, Neville Anderson, was reassuringly close by at the navigator's desk, within arm's reach behind him. But even with the unspoken uplift of camaraderie, his standing viewing position was hardly comfortable, only minutes after boarding the aircraft. What would it be like towards the end of a five-hour flight? Tightly trussed up in his unaccustomed heavy flying gear and a little bowed over in his constricting parachute harness, he had nothing to do but try to take in as many sensory details as he could for his forthcoming news report. His head was as constricted as his torso, enclosed in the leather flying helmet which tethered him to the spot once the flight engineer had plugged the reporter's helmet intercom lead into the aircraft's interphone system. The moment the intercom jack was plugged into its socket Stockton was strangely cut off from the outside world, enclosed by the metallic hush in his earphones and the oddly remote voices of the men speaking to each other only a couple of feet away. Stockton stood passively at the rear of the flight deck, trying to keep out of the way as the pilot and flight engineer went through the start-up routine.

Twenty-eight miles away at Waddington, Alf King similarly settled aboard an Australian Lancaster, in this case No. 467's G-George, similarly piloted by a fellow countryman, Bill Forbes, and with an Australian flight engineer, Pilot Officer Frank Miller from Laidley, outside Brisbane, to keep him company. Like Stockton, King was reassured by a friendly navigator close at hand behind him, in this case Pilot Officer James Robertson, whom he had found to be a 'likable young Scot from Elgin'.

At Skellingthorpe, Lowell Bennett boarded 50 Squadron's B-Bolty and was similarly left standing on the flight deck as the pilot and flight engineer worked through their practised routine of starting up each of the engines in turn. Once all four engines were running, and checks completed, the four engines were left idling 'with a full-toned, reassuring rumble'. Ian Bolton closed the bomb bay doors, and at 'exactly' 4.30 pm released the wheel brakes, signalled to the ground staff to remove the chocks, then pushed his throttles forward and turned his bomber on to the taxiway. Aware of the inertia represented by the thirty-five tons of his rolling Lancaster, Bolton carefully preserved the interval behind the aircraft taxying ahead, using dabs of brake and rudder to keep the big machine rolling along the centreline of the taxiway towards the downwind end of the duty runway. Upon reaching the end of the taxiway, Bolton applied the brakes to bring B-Bolty to a stop, waiting for his turn to take off. Bennett watched the aircraft ahead of them power up and roll down 'the long concrete strip, slowly accelerating into the distance' and then 'almost imperceptibly' rise into the air to begin its long, slow, heavily laden climb away from the earth.

Then Bolton taxied forward to take his turn at the head of the take-off queue; it was B-Bolty's turn to roll, the eighth Lancaster to get away from Skellingthorpe. A green light flashed from the control tower. Bolton gunned B-Bolty's engines and released the brakes. The engines rose to a 'higher-pitched roar' as the flight engineer pushed the four throttles forward, and the bomber accelerated down the runway under the thrust of its 6000 horsepower.

At Woodhall Spa, Ed Murrow also found that his assigned aircraft was one Lancaster in a queue of ten. Both No.s 50 and 619 had been tasked with providing the same operational commitment tonight of ten bombers to Berlin. This number was about half a normal squadron's full complement, whereas No. 460 had been tasked with a maximum effort, leaving the Australian squadron with twenty-five bombers trundling around the perimeter track to take their place in an extended take-off queue. No. 460 launched one Lancaster per minute from 4.30 pm onwards. Aboard Alan Mitchell's H-Harry, Nordahl Grieg found himself almost at the head of the queue, the third aircraft in line to take off. Whereas Bennett towards the end of the line-up at Skellingthorpe had had to drink in not only the smell of burnt 100-octane from the aircraft exhausts ahead, but also the tense anticipation of watching all those other aircraft, one by one, labour in turn down the runway, at Binbrook Grieg got it over with quickly. He was able to look over his shoulder at the queue of other Lancasters weaving along the taxiway behind him in the fading afternoon light: serried ranks of wide, plank-like wings, dully glinting Perspex cockpit enclosures, and spinning propellers. Grieg looked back ahead as Mitchell's tinny voice came over his headphones, calling to the flight engineer for full power; the engines thundered out their power, the bomber lumbered forward, the tail came up, the black tyre marks on the runway came into view through the windscreen, and the painted white runway centreline rushed by in a blur beneath the nose. H-Harry thundered down the runway, leaving the serpentine queue of Lancasters behind her standing. Now at the head of that queue, the next aircraft in line was J-Johnnie, with Norm Ginn aboard, getting ready to roll down the runway a minute later.

No. 50 Squadron bomb aimer, Les Bartlett, recalled the scene of an operational take-off at Skellingthorpe vividly:

> Lining the runway is a motley collection of ground staff, aircrew not on 'ops', the station CO, the Wing Commander with visitors and friends and, last but not least, the usual crowd of WAAFs, waving goodbye to their boyfriends ... with the mighty roar of four Merlins in our ears we give the crowd a quick wave and tear down the runway.

Bennett saw a similar scene from B-Bolty as his Lancaster thundered past the control tower, with about fifty ground crewmen standing by the side of the strip waving them off. The young war correspondent seemed to have enjoyed the thrill of his first ever bomber take-off:

> Slowly at first, then gathering speed, faster, faster, faster, the ground flooding past on each side at nearly a hundred miles an hour, suddenly a slight lift then a bump as we settled back, then another lift – we were

airborne rushing from the earth like some broad-winged bird up toward a dying winter sun.

We were aloft, rising into the cathedral of the sky, Berlin-bound for the strangest and most terrible form of battle man had yet devised.

But having only minutes earlier been given a guided tour of the contents of B-Bolty's bomb bay just beneath the floor he now stood on, Bennett was imaginative enough to perceive the cataclysmic end that awaited him and the others if an engine failed and the speeding bomber failed to get airborne or crashed back to earth straight after take-off. Despite the novelty and excitement of the take-off, he found it nerve-wracking, and afterwards reported, 'I breathed easily only after we had cleared the runway and were wheeling and climbing southeastward, setting our course for the heart of Nazi Germany.'

Once B-Bolty was airborne and safely settled into the climb, Bennett took his eyes off the scene in front, looking back over his shoulder at the airfield receding behind. 'Take a good look', he thought, 'you won't be back for many months.' The notion of the doomed flight had returned, prompted by his nagging premonition. Understandably, he had not shared this inner conviction with his similarly fatalistic, yet solicitous pilot, Ian Bolton, nor with his enthusiastic guide to the bomb bay, Robert Forrester.

Ed Murrow, aboard 619 Squadron's D-Dog at Woodhall Spa, was able to suppress any such portentous thoughts on take-off, and seems to have enjoyed the experience of flight for its own sake, as well as for its stimulation of his aesthetic sensibility:

> The takeoff was as smooth as silk. The wheels came up, and D-Dog started the long climb. As we came up through clouds, I looked right and left and counted fourteen black Lancasters climbing for the place where men must burn oxygen to survive. The sun was going down and its red glow made rivers of lakes of fire on tops of clouds. Down to the southward, the clouds piled up to form castles, battlements, and whole cities, all tinged with red.

Meanwhile at the end of the runway at Waddington, Alf King's pilot, Bill Forbes, set the most anticlimactic tone possible as he lined up 467 Squadron's G-George for take-off, announcing over the intercom, 'All set? Okay, here we go.' King had no crew duties to perform, so after take-off he too enjoyed the opportunity this gave him to view the scene in aesthetic terms as his Lancaster became airborne and climbed away into the gathering night:

> We set off with a sliver of the blood-red sun sitting prettily on top of a bank of slatey-grey clouds. We soared up over lovely English fields ...

> 'George' began a steady climb which was to take us into the high region in which the crew had been instructed to fly. There was little sensation of flying. 'George' was as steady as the deck of an ocean liner in a smooth sea.

The moon shone on a weird and wonderful cloudland far below, like a crumpled snowfield. Now and again we saw other bombers, all, like 'George', pursuing height.

Aboard 50 Squadron's B-Bolty, Bennett stood rooted to the spot in his appointed position behind the pilot as Bolton headed their Lancaster across England, slowly ascending from the 'familiar, friendly bosom of man's home' into the 'darkening void of the unknown'. Everywhere around him Bennett saw 'Lancasters, huge black birds, majestic and heavy-laden, climbing steadily'. As the 'horizon lowered' and twilight 'dimmed and shadowed the earth below', the bombers all around were swallowed up one by one in the deepening gloom, until only a few remained visible: 'The engines chanted a solemn, steady quartet of harnessed mechanical might, two bulky cowlings protruding from each sleek wing. The crew members settled to their work.' Although the bombers would not encounter German defences until they crossed the enemy-held Dutch coast, the climb across the North Sea was nonetheless an apprehensive time for the crews, who knew that each aircraft was only one of scores of Lancasters flocking together on the same course and climbing to the same height. Whereas Les Bartlett found it comforting to see other aircraft in this situation, because thereby he was reminded 'that you are not alone in your effort', by contrast, Bolton's crew remained anxious about it, keeping a sharp lookout throughout the climb, in every direction, for Lancasters drifting dangerously across their own flight path. Luckily, among the whole bomber fleet airborne that night, no mid-air collision occurred;

the first bomber to be lost would be shot down by a night-fighter over western Germany. Soon the sky was so dark that the only lights within Bennett's field of view came from the dim phosphorescent lighting on the cockpit instrument panels and the 'fiery exhaust' flare from the engines. As the climb went on, within each Lancaster the crewmen clipped their oxygen masks tightly to their faces, and reported in over the intercom, using the microphone inset within the mask to transmit their disembodied metallic voices into the earpieces of their crewmates' helmets.

In 619 Squadron's D-Dog, Ed Murrow saw a similar scene to Bennett, watching fascinated as the 'blue-green jet of the exhausts licked back along the leading edge' of the wing. With his head cleared by sucking in pure oxygen through his mask, Murrow was almost lulled into a state of reverie by the high-altitude transit to the enemy coast:

> The talk on the intercom was brief and crisp. Everyone sounded relaxed. For a while, the eight of us in our little world in exile moved over the sea. There was a quarter moon on the starboard beam and Jock's quiet voice came through the intercom, 'That'll be flak ahead'. We were approaching the enemy coast. The flak looked like a cigarette lighter in a dark room – one that won't light, sparks but no flame – the sparks crackling just above the level of the cloud tops. We flew straight and steady, and soon the flak was directly below us. D-Dog rocked a little from right to left, but that wasn't caused by the flak. We were in the slipstream of other Lancasters ahead, and we were over the enemy coast.

And then a strange thing happened. The aircraft seemed to grow smaller. Jack in the rear turret, Wally the mid-upper gunner, Titch the wireless operator, all seemed somehow to draw closer to Jock in the cockpit. It was as though each man's shoulder was against the others. The understanding was complete. The intercom came to life, and Jock said, 'Two aircraft on the port beam'. Jack in the tail said, 'Okay, sir. They're Lancs'. The whole crew was a unit and wasn't wasting words.

By contrast, Bennett was still discomfited by the presence of other unseen aircraft close by in the darkness, so did not view the scene with as much detachment as Murrow did. After two hours of anxious but uneventful climbing, B-Bolty crossed the Dutch coast at 21 500 feet, cruising at an indicated airspeed of 160 mph (equating to a true airspeed of about 230 mph once the reduced air pressure at altitude is taken into account). Bennett too saw his first flak, as shell bursts 'spattered and flecked the now dark sky, scintillant red and rose lights bursting into evanescent brilliance far ahead. They seemed quite impotent, impersonal – nothing to be feared.' But the straight-talking Ian Bolton punctured Bennett's aesthetic reverie with an admonitory observation about the flak: 'That's nothing ... Wait until we get to the Big City.'

Still the biggest fear remained air-to-air collision with an unseen bomber, as the crews knew that the bomber stream would be narrowing to cram itself into the 'cubic road to Berlin'. Visibility reduced even further as B-Bolty passed through the thick cloud banks of the forecasted weather front lying above the continent's coastal hinterland. The Lancaster's 'Monica' tail warning radar intermittently 'tinkled' its 'urgent' warnings into the crew's headphones each time some unseen four-engine fellow traveller approached too close behind; whereupon Bolton would gently swerve his bomber aside to create space for the overtaker, then resume his own course. Wordless warnings came too of bombers ahead when the Lancaster would suddenly lurch and heave as it flew through the propwash of an unseen machine in front. Again, Bolton would gently turn out of the collision path and then resume his course on track for Berlin. Every few minutes the navigator would provide a slight heading alteration to lay off the drift and stay on track, seeking to locate B-Bolty tightly if precariously within the flocking-together bomber stream en route to the target.

Aboard 467 Squadron's G-George, Alf King's crew similarly kept 'an anxious and intent watch against collision with other bombers in the cloud masses' during the climb-out from England, but by the time they were approaching the Dutch coast, King was, like Bennett and Murrow, lulled into a state of lassitude. Then the first flak bursts over the Dutch coast broke the monotony and snapped him back to alertness. By the time Bennett's B-Bolty emerged from the cloud layer into the bright moonlight and clear air above northern Germany, he too was starting to find it all routine:

> ... there was no excitement – only the steady, sonorous pounding of the four mighty engines drawing us through the night. We might have been alone, for no other plane was visible. I ate some of the concentrated food provided for a 'mission meal', lifting my oxygen

mask briefly, took occasional pictures of the moonlight gleaming all too brilliantly on our wings, watched the pilot silently, self-assuredly gripping the truck-sized wheel. There was nothing to this vaunted bombing of Germany! Where was the aerial hell that supposedly accompanied each raid?

However, as the bomber stream started to thread the gap between Bremen and Hanover, about halfway between the Dutch coast and Berlin, Bennett's mood sharpened as he perceived at some distance the ominous malevolence of the German flak which greeted off-course bombers straying too closely to those cities: 'Off to both sides, flak clawed at the sky, tearing and puncturing it with sharp, explosive bursts.' B-Bolty safely skirted Hanover's flak and searchlight zone, keeping safely to the north of that city, but close enough for him to get a foretaste of what lay ahead over Berlin: over Hanover he saw 'hundreds of searchlights aimed straight up, motionless, illuminating the thick cloud layer beneath us into a solid white blanket'. Over the intercom, the fatalistic Bolton bluntly explained what was happening without any attempt at reassurance: 'That's so we are silhouetted against the light, and the night fighters above can see us.' The pilot seems to have assumed that Bennett was as phlegmatic as he was. Similarly, Alf King aboard 467 Squadron's G-George observed the searchlights playing upon a thick cloudbank beneath:

> Fifty or 100 searchlights, ranged in rows with almost geometrical precision, probed through our protecting cover, but failed to penetrate it. The searchlights'

crests seemed to squat on top of the clouds like large diamonds on a black cushion in a jeweller's shop.

There were hazards above as well as below. Aboard 619 Squadron's D-Dog, Ed Murrow saw Jock Abercromby look up through the Plexiglas cockpit roof, watching 'a vapor trail curling across above us'. The pilot remarked over the intercom 'in a conversational tone that, from the look of it, he thought there was a fighter up there'. At that height it was unlikely to have been a night-fighter, but he was probably right about it being a hostile aircraft, as the high flyer was probably one of the observer aircraft tasked with flying above the bomber stream and radioing tracking reports to the night-fighters' control room. There was nothing for Abercromby to be surprised about; he had seen it all before, things were going just as expected. Just as surely, everything pointed to trouble ahead, once they were nearer Berlin.

As the stream of bombers winged their way across the flatlands of northern Germany, the Luftwaffe was planning to meet the raid by directing its formidable night-fighter fleet into the path of the bombers. The raiders' positions were being continuously reported to Luftwaffe air defence control rooms, with the data phoned in and radioed by radar stations, radio monitoring units, flak and searchlight posts, and airborne observers. These position reports allowed the controllers to track the bomber stream's progress across their gridded plotting boards. The early warning had started even before the bombers left England, for the Luftwaffe's *Freya* air defence radar chain along the Dutch coast could obtain radar contacts at a distance of almost 200 kilometres. This enabled the radar controllers to plot the track of the inbound bomber stream before it even crossed the coast of occupied Europe, after which German observation aircraft were dispatched to contact the bomber stream and confirm its course. These air observers accompanied the bomber stream as it flowed towards Berlin, radioing positional and directional updates to the fighter control rooms as they did so. Moreover, some of the observation aircraft dropped lines of flares to mark the bomber stream's flight path as a visual guide to the night-fighter crews, a phenomenon repeatedly observed, reported, and remarked upon by the apprehensive bomber crews. By such methods the Luftwaffe controllers at 1st Fighter Corps HQ at Zeist, outside Utrecht in the Netherlands, tracked the bomber stream as it headed inbound. Once it was plotted passing Hanover and then Brunswick without altering course, it was a safe deduction that Berlin was the target, and so at 7.23 pm the air-raid warning alarm was sounded across Berlin. With the air-raid plot now clarified, the controllers were now able to direct all airborne fighters to head towards the capital and to look out for passing trade.

And so the already battered city of Berlin had to prepare for another malevolent aerial visitation from the 'English', and much-bombed Berliners had to get ready to survive another night. On the ground in Berlin, the preliminary air-raid alarm sounded as 'three sustained tones of equal pitch and duration'. This warned the populace to get ready to move to their assigned bomb shelters. At this point they now had about three-quarters of an hour before the bombs started coming down. After an interval, the second alarm wailed. This sounded for a minute as one continuous note, warning everyone to get into their shelters at once. Most

Berliners lived in apartment blocks, and if caught by the siren in their own homes they needed to file down the stairs into the designated basement space that served as their housing block's improvised bomb shelter. After the frightening series of raids over the previous month, people were hardly likely to underrate the threat or to flout the civil defence direction to take shelter. Not heading for a shelter was not an option, as doing so was compulsory throughout Germany: failure to take shelter was an offence.

Visitors to Berlin today can still see the huge, bombproof public air-raid shelters which the Nazi authorities built after the onset of RAF raids as a passive civil defence measure – in other words, to limit the civilian casualties from the raids. The continued existence of such reinforced-concrete structures today, as massive and imposing relics of the war, might give the impression that most Berliners had access to such a shelter, but this was not the case. There were far too few of these big public shelters to protect a city population, and so most people had nothing better than the improvised bomb shelters in the basements of their own apartment buildings, office blocks, shops, pubs and factories.

The ideal shelter room was specified as being 'gasproof, blastproof, clearly indicated, clear of obstructions, and provided with lighting and seating'; and the residents were to have everything prepared for the emergency. German civilian Richard Braun recalled that the authorities instructed the residents of his city to choose as their shelter area a space in the cellar which abutted the wall to the neighbouring building's basement, and to break a small opening in that wall to enable underground escape into the next building in the event of a building collapse or fire; any windows in the basement storey were to be either walled up with sandbags, bricked up, or blocked with wooden boxes filled with sand. In the event of a building collapse, the location of the designated shelter was marked on street level with an arrow painted on the wall, to show rescuers where to dig. The shelters were moreover to be furnished with an array of survival, escape and firefighting equipment: gas masks, buckets of water, buckets of sand, a shovel, a hand pump, ladders, an axe, a first-aid kit – much of which had to be duplicated on different floors of the building. As a result of such grassroots 'Self-Protection' measures, by summer 1943 shelters of this sort had been made available for a total of 11.6 million people across Germany. Even now, this still meant that most Germans had nothing better to shelter in than their own cellar.

Once the Berlin raids escalated in November 1943, leaving the cityscape scarred by charred ruins and flattened apartment buildings, there could have been little doubt that improvised basement shelters did not offer adequate protection against a direct hit upon the building by a high-explosive bomb. A 1000-pounder would typically penetrate several floors through the building before exploding within, with catastrophic results, leaving only shattered walls standing among piles of splintered and pulverised wreckage; while a 4000-pound 'blockbuster' would flatten an entire apartment building to street level, leaving only a heap of smoking rubble. The vulnerability of Berliners who took recourse to domestic shelters is borne out by the testimony of Gertrud Kahlke, who boarded in a house close enough to the Tiergarten zoo to hear the screams of the tormented, burning animals on the night of 22 November. She recited for a friend the grisly fates of scores of people who died in their shelters in her own inner-city district of Moabit during these raids: she reported over thirty people 'buried alive underneath Putlitzstrasse No. 8', with only three survivors dug out days later, 'but by then they had gone mad'; in the house next door to her fiancé, workers dug out about thirty-five 'totally cooked corpses' from the bomb shelter 'underneath the hair salon'. In her local area, Frau Kahlke reported 'countless workers ... digging away at innumerable corpse-cellars', citing an apartment in Lehrter Strasse, where over seventy lost their lives. The official watchword was 'The air-protection room is the safest place', but it was becoming clear that this was 'no longer always the case'.

Nonetheless such basement shelters were all most people had, so they used them; it was certainly better than staying upstairs. People's belief in the protection offered by their basement shelter is shown by their nightly routine of grabbing their most valuable portable possessions before leaving their apartments and filing down the stairs into the basement, taking with them 'what needed to be saved no matter what'. Within each residential block, an air raid warden was tasked with going down last, as they went turning off the lights in the hallways and stairwells to prevent light showing in the event of a bomb blast opening up a wall or roof. There was usually enough time to go below well before the bombing started, but it was still a nerve-wracking process. One 13-year-old Berliner living in an extended family recalled how her grandmother got so flustered getting dressed before going down into the basement that she put her shoes on the wrong feet – the family 'had to laugh at her' when they spotted her error. Berliners also got into the routine of filling their bathtubs before they left their apartments, to provide water reservoirs throughout the building for firefighting, in which case the residents would form bucket brigades to pass water from the baths to the fire.

It was worse for those without their own shelter to go to, when they were caught by the sirens while out on the street, or in a place of public entertainment, away from home. Upon hearing the siren, they had to look around frantically for one of the public shelters. For most people caught by the raid while 'out and about', the available shelters were more likely to be *Splittergraben* – trenches or pits dug into the street, with overhead cover in the form of planks, iron sheeting and a layer of soil. These shelters provided protection from bomb and flak splinters and other flying debris flung about by near misses, but like the cellar shelters they could not protect their occupants from an unlucky direct hit. During the raid the frightened occupants could do little but hope for the best and listen to the 'clack clack clack' of flak splinters falling on their shelter roof. Given the limitations of most shelters, it was hardly surprising that Berliners preferred the underground U-Bahn subway stations whenever they could get to them in time.

Upon hearing the sirens most people headed to their designated shelter, but others headed for their duty stations, many of which were in relatively exposed positions above ground. For example, teenage boys in the Hitler Youth went to their assigned posts as 'Helpers' with flak and searchlight units, and with fire brigade and rescue squads. In January

1943, schoolboys born in 1926 and 1927 were drafted into anti-aircraft artillery units as Flak helper to allow soldiers of military age to be sent out of the Reich for service on the Eastern Front. The conscription of the boys was conditional upon parental consent, with limits set as to how far away from home they could serve, while their school education was officially supposed to continue. However, in effect they had been mobilised for the duration as paramilitary child soldiers, just in time to confront the RAF in the Battle of Berlin. Initially the boys' teachers visited their Flak battery locations in an attempt at continuing their schooling, but once the raids got serious the teachers stopped coming, among other reasons because of the sheer difficulty of commuting across town with so many severed tramlines and subway lines. From the end of 1943 the boys' education had effectively ended.

An example was Jochen Mahncke, a high-school student attending a boarding school in Berlin. In early 1943 the boys at his school received a circular advising that they had been conscripted as 'Flak-helpers'. The boys had already undergone basic military training in the Hitler Youth, so could quickly progress to training in their new duties with the Flak batteries. Only the physically larger and stronger boys were assigned to duties on the 88mm guns, because heaving the heavy ammunition into the gun breech was difficult work. The smaller boys were posted to less physical duties, such as operating the plotting board in the gunnery control room and working the phones to relay target information between radar, guns and control rooms. In the early days, hard-bitten Berliners had taken a cynical attitude towards the young Flak-helpers, patronising them as 'little boys' rather than proper soldiers, but after the raids got serious, they changed their attitude, expressing their appreciation by sending gifts of cake and biscuits to the boys in their local Flak battery. As the raids went on, the boys ended up becoming sleep-deprived, typically going on duty with the first pre-alarm at about 8 pm, and not standing down until the final all-clear at about 4 am. The scale of the manpower crisis the bombing precipitated within the German heartland can be gauged by the size of the flak arm defending German cities at the peak of the campaign, with 14 400 heavy flak guns and 42 000 light flak guns served by an army of 889 000 men and boys. Moreover, the flak arm was not the only avenue of pressed service for schoolboys and other civilian helpers: by 1944 Germany's fire brigade relied upon the service of 1.7 million volunteers, while there were 900 000 involved in passive civil defence tasks, including post-raid clearing-up of bombed-out blocks and districts. That makes an army of about 3.5 million men and boys serving in defence of the German cities on the home front.

Nor was that all. As thousands of schoolboys donned steel helmets and headed for their Flak or searchlight batteries, thousands of other civilians were heading to their designated posts as volunteer air raid wardens. By 1942, German cities fielded an army of 1.5 million volunteer wardens in charge of their designated building, block, or district civil defence organisation. Berlin's system of civil defence precautions was representative: it was organised into districts, each divided further into sub-groups, down to the level where every apartment building had a House Warden, and every street a Block Warden. Each of these volunteer officials oversaw their local community, leading the local group members in undertaking the prescribed self-protection measures, such as preparing their shelter room in the basement, setting out their building's emergency equipment, and attending the prescribed civil defence training courses. Between raids, the wardens went on their rounds through their community, going from family to family, building to building, and block to block to check on compliance, readiness and morale.

Those appointed as group leaders also had the task of gingerly moving around above ground during each raid, going from shelter to shelter to check on their sub-wardens and on the status of each shelter. Other wardens had to stay above ground throughout each raid, posted on the roofs as fire-watchers, to look out for fires spreading to their building from falling incendiaries or flying embers: the motto was, 'No house was to be left empty and unwatched.' Wardens had undertaken training to qualify for their duties, but once the raids started in earnest, what they had been practising seemed to be 'pointless theory' to some, rendered redundant by the enormity of real air raids: they found that 'In practice, air raids were something entirely different' from the scripted and manageable scenarios presented in training. Nonetheless, the courses appear to have become more practical, for as time went on the focus of the training shifted to firefighting and the technique of extinguishing the RAF's notorious phosphorous incendiaries.

Most wardens took up duty down below, assigned to oversee a particular shelter and to maintain order amongst the residents confined there under duress. In a situation where the male population of every local community had been hollowed out by military service, many of these wardens were women. A Berliner described the stalwart service during the Berlin raids of her local female warden, a woman who was known in the community as a housewife and mother, and who during the day was often to be seen helping at her husband's business:

> The building residents gradually collected together in the cellar, until 35 people were in there, including some elderly and sickly people. Then the questions started coming at her: 'Would it be bad today? Have you heard ...?' Etc. The Warden answered the questions, sometimes comforting, sometimes pacifying, and sometimes deflecting the question. When the first bomb fell a few women screamed. Now the Warden spoke firmly, 'Pull yourself together! What would it be like if we all screamed like that?'

By the evening of 2 December 1943, civilian Berliners had become experienced at being bombed, mostly assuming the passive role of huddling, listening and hoping, or at best the semi-active roles of watching and warning. That night they again found themselves sitting in their dimly lit shelters, listening apprehensively to the swelling rumble of aero engines up above, increasingly punctuated by the sharp staccato reports of the flak guns. Above them, the sky over Berlin had again become an active battlefield, fought out by those assigned to more active and violent roles.

While all those on the ground took their places in the shelters, Alf King, meanwhile, was up above; and he was enjoying the flight, his mind far removed from the fates and fears of the people four miles below, ruminating instead on the marvellous technology that delivered comparative comfort for him and his fellow humans breathing bottled oxygen through face masks that made them look like 'characters in a Wellsian fantasy'. It was cold at that height, but in the Lancaster, the crew heating outlet was situated beneath the pilot's seat, so where the journalist stood was more or less the warmest place in the aircraft. As the aircraft climbed, the flight engineer Frank Miller would turn around periodically to update the curious reporter on the plunging air temperature, finally confiding that the temperature outside the aircraft was −56 degrees Celsius. King was left to enjoy the thought of the protective cocoon of G-George, protecting her occupants from the deadly deep freeze beyond.

CHAPTER 6

THE RAID

But by now it was not only Lancasters that were winging their way towards Berlin. The bombers would soon be sharing the airspace with scores of German night-fighters, vectored towards the bombers' approach path. As Berlin's stoical and not-so-stoical residents headed for their shelters to await their ordeal, at Lüneburg airfield, conveniently located about 70 kilometres north of the bomber stream's track to Berlin, the night-fighters of the 8th Squadron of *Nachtjagdgeschader 3* were getting airborne, directed by fighter control to intercept the raid. Because of fog over the night-fighter airfields in Belgium and the Netherlands, only 178 fighters got airborne to tackle the raid, but even so, with 458 incoming bombers, that gave a not inconsiderable ratio of one night-fighter for every two-and-a-half bombers. The fighter control room of the Luftwaffe's 1st Fighter Corps tracked the raid's progress by monitoring the bombers' air-to-ground radar transmissions and their transponder emissions. Plotting data like this gave the German controllers sufficiently precise information of the raid's track to direct fighters on to an interception flight path. Once the fighters were airborne, the controllers broadcast a 'running commentary' to inform the fighter crews of the bomber stream's course and latest known location. The fighter crews used this positional information to navigate themselves into contact with the bombers, inserting their aircraft into the bomber stream, flying the same course and altitude. After that they could then use their on-board air-to-air radar equipment to detect and attack individual bombers.

One of these night-fighter pilots was Senior Lieutenant Paul Zorner, the CO of the 8th Squadron, who took off at 6.44 pm in his almost brand-new Me 110G-4, a modern, twin-engine night-fighter. In the German system, the best pilots got the best aircraft, and this experienced senior pilot had just received the latest model of the aircraft type, fitted moreover with the latest SN2 air-to-air radar. Zorner's radar operator, Sergeant Wilke, was enthused about the new radar because compared to the older sets it gave longer detection ranges and a wider search arc, and was easier to operate. It was also superior in providing a shorter minimum detection range, so the radar operator could track the target right up to the moment when the pilot could see it. Tonight would be the first time this already successful crew would try out this promising new equipment: the squadron CO had already been credited with eleven bomber kills. With superior equipment like this new aircraft with its latest model radar set, the expert crew had been given every advantage to add to their score, an opportunity Zorner took to the fullest. Zorner's kills that night provide not only a first-hand perspective of the raid from the German side, but also vivid accounts of the British experience of being shot down; these can be taken as representative of so many crews who failed to return from the raid, including some of those carrying our journalists.

Zorner climbed away from Lüneburg in his twin-engine Messerschmitt, following the controller's broadcast running commentary of the bomber stream's location and direction through his earphones: at that moment the British bombers were reported heading inland across the Dutch-German border at a height of 5500–6000 metres. He took a course to intercept, and only twenty minutes later saw what he thought was the first bomber shot down. In fact, no RAF bomber went down as early as this, so the burning aircraft he saw plunging away to destruction might have been the Ju 88 night-fighter which was unluckily shot down by the mid-upper gunner of a Lancaster, crashing to earth near Osnabrück. This sighting was followed five minutes later by Wilke's report of a radar contact ahead. Because Zorner's Me 110 was approaching the bomber stream almost head-on, the closing speed was too high, so Wilke directed his pilot to make a 180-degree turn and then to come back around on to the bomber's tail at a manageable closing speed. Zorner executed the turn, and as he started to straighten up, Wilke reported that he had regained radar contact at 1200-metres range, jubilant about the performance of the new SN2 radar set. After closing in a little more, the pilot spotted the bomber at 600-metres range, straight ahead and a little higher. This experienced night-fighter crew had autonomously achieved a perfect airborne interception by exploiting first the fighter controller's broadcast commentary and then their onboard radar equipment.

Although the sky was clear at altitude, a line of mist lay along the horizon, allowing Zorner to approach the bomber stealthily from out of this milky grey haze layer. As he came closer, he identified the target as a Lancaster, all the while on tenterhooks about being spotted by the rear gunner and getting blasted by the tail turret's four machine guns. Zorner almost got too nervous to go any closer to the Lancaster's deadly tail guns, but he suppressed his fear and maintained his approach, to a range of 250 metres, 150 metres ... 100 metres. Now the bomber loomed up in his windscreen, the underside of its wings illuminated by the red glow from its engines' exhaust shrouds. Centring his gunsight upon the wing, he opened fire. It was 7.20 pm, Berlin time. The 20mm and 30mm explosive cannon shells sawed through the bomber's wing, releasing a blaze of hot yellow flame to stream out of the torn-open fuel tanks. The stricken machine banked left and fell away, while Zorner pulled his fighter out to the other side to observe the result of his surgical kill.

The stricken Lancaster was 'V-Victor' from No. 97 Squadron. The crew started abandoning the flaming aircraft as it descended towards the ground, with the pilot, Squadron Leader John Garlick DFC, holding the crippled machine on an even keel so the others could get out. One of them was Flight Sergeant 'Jack' Anderson, one of two Australians in the crew, who had been on the verge of finishing his tour, but now here he was caught in the nose compartment of his blazing and doomed bomber. He had been surprised when the wing was struck by the sudden, unannounced burst of fire; he heard the 'crunch' as the shells struck the wing, felt the aircraft shudder, and through the Perspex blister in the nose saw tracers flashing past, fired from behind. The wireless operator, Warrant Officer A Dawkins, also saw 'some bright yellow streaks flying past the astrodome' (the Perspex viewing blister set in the roof of the crew compartment). He had unknowingly observed a burst of tracer ammunition from the Me 110, fired too high and so passing right over the bomber's fuselage. Dawkins 'was not unduly disturbed' at first, thinking it was 'only' flak, until he woke up to the fact that the tracers were going past horizontally.

The pilot only belatedly realised that his aircraft was under attack by a night-fighter, at first rolling the bomber into an evasive turn and calling on Dawkins for a damage report. Dawkins pulled back the blackout curtain and looked out the window of his radio compartment. What he saw shocked him: 'Below the nacelle, under the wing, was a long streamer of orange flame streaking back into the night.' He yelled over the intercom, 'Port motor on fire!' the pilot Garlick ordered Anderson to get up into the cockpit to feather the damaged port engines and actuate the fire extinguishers in the engine nacelles. Anderson heard this and bent into the nose compartment to grab his parachute pack, but by then it was too late. The whole wing was now ablaze, not just the engine nacelles. Garlick had been turning the aircraft to the left, intending to return to England, and had even asked the navigator for the course to steer for home, but now he saw that the fire was out of control. He ordered, 'Bail out, bail out!' Anderson heard this over the intercom and followed the escape drill: he entered the nose compartment, took his parachute pack from the rack on the wall, clipped it to his chest harness, kneeled by the escape hatch in the floor, opened it, and jettisoned the hatch cover into the howling void outside. With his crewmates 'on his heels', willing him to hurry up and get out of the way, Anderson got on with it: he pulled off his flying helmet so its dangling oxygen and intercom leads would not get snagged on an obstruction and strangle him as he jumped, and in the crowded seconds sat on the edge of the open hatch, facing backwards to jump out. As he sat there, the 'cold blast of air' roaring through the hatch made him 'wonder', and in the fraction of a second before he jumped a stream of consciousness flooded his mind:

> I look down, can this be possible, after all my trips, must I land in Germany, well I have to go, so here goes ... I shall never forget that awful feeling in my tummy, I have never jumped before, but this time, it's my life. I have to leave an aircraft that has always come home to base, I have to leave an aircraft that has carried me hundreds and thousands of miles, I have learned to love this aircraft, and now I have to go and leave it.

Jack Anderson jumped, holding his parachute pack against his chest with one arm, with the fingers of his other hand feeling for the ripcord. He fell away into the black night, the first man out:

> I go through space, I'm in the air now, I have no time to think, I can't. The chute opens with a colossal report, and I feel my harness jerk hard. Then I am on my way down. Visibility is nil, I have trouble to breathe, I'm not afraid ... I'm just there in space, and just as if I was on a swing, looking down, but I can't see anything ... I sail through another cloud and I see something dark under me, and then CRASH. I hit the deck in a heap, unhurt. I say my prayers. I gather up my chute, and then I see I have landed in a paddock, made to order. SO THIS IS GERMANY! Well, what next?

Meanwhile, Dawkins had turned back to his wireless set to transmit a report to base. With his set switched to wireless rather than intercom, and with his earphones filled with the static hiss of the radio frequency over the background engine roar, he missed Garlick's bail-out order over the intercom. Alerted by the blast of icy air coming from the opened escape hatch up forward, he stuck his head around his rack of wireless equipment 'to see how the rest of the crew were faring'. He was dismayed to see that the navigator and bomb aimer had evidently already abandoned the aircraft, seemingly without any thought of warning him. Dawkins switched his set back to intercom in time to hear the skipper repeating, 'Bail out, bail out!' through his headphones. The wireless operator abandoned his radio transmission, clipped his parachute on to his harness, got up to move forward through the cockpit, and ran into the navigator, Pilot Officer AG Boyd, who had remembered him after all. In what Dawkins found to be a 'very gallant gesture', Boyd had gone back aft to make sure Dawkins had heard the bail-out order. Dawkins hurried through the cockpit towards the escape hatch. As he went by, he saw that 'the skipper was straining at the controls in an endeavour to hold the aircraft in the air to give us all a chance of escaping'. Dawkins reached the escape hatch and perched on the edge: 'With my hand grasping the ripcord, I felt the rush of air sucking me out into the smoky, swirling clouds below ...' Dawkins and Boyd must have jumped at the very last moment, for by the time Jack Anderson stood up and looked around from the middle of his paddock, he could already see the 'red glow in the distance' of V-Victor's burning wreckage. He waved 'a sincere last goodbye to the aircraft', for 'so passed a good friend'. It was not only V-Victor that had passed, for Garlick was still in the aircraft when it hit the ground, sharing the fate of so many bomber pilots who were trapped onboard an almost uncontrollable aircraft, in effect obliged to sacrifice themselves so that the rest of the crew could get out. The rear gunner, Flight Sergeant Fred Edwards, also died, probably hit by the fighter's gunfire.

Zorner was watching as the blazing bomber descended more and more steeply, to strike the ground at Barenburg in Lower Saxony at 7.24 pm, marking the spot against the dark background with a blazing conflagration. This was the German night-fighter force's first shoot-down of the night. Having observed the crash and noted its location for claims purposes, Zorner had by now lost contact with the bomber stream, but by listening in to the controller's running commentary over the fighter control frequency, he headed his fighter east to regain contact. Confirmation that he was going the right way came when he started to see burning bombers going down up ahead. As he drew closer, the flashes of bomb explosions and the glow of ground fires served as beacons to confirm the bombing target – Berlin. At 8.20 pm, radar operator Wilke reported further 'trade' for Zorner on his radar set. This particular radar contact had made itself conspicuous on Wilke's radar scope by diverging from the bomber stream, veering off course to the south. Zorner followed Wilke's steering instructions in pursuit of this straggler, until at 8.24 pm he spotted it visually, by now quite close in front. Again he held his breath as he approached the Lancaster from behind, again on tenterhooks about being spotted and blasted by its rear gunner; again the Me 110 remained unseen by the bomber's rear gunner, again the pilot fired at the target's wing, again the wing burned, and again the bomber descended to crash in a burning heap. This was at 8.29 pm, near Potsdam, southwest of Berlin.

It might be considered surprising that in both of his kills Zorner was able to get so close behind without being spotted by either of the bombers' turret gunners, but RAF trials conducted earlier in the year showed how vulnerable a bomber crew was to a fighter's approach from behind and below. These trials showed that on dark nights the rear gunner would generally fail to see the fighter as it slowly loomed up out of the murky obscurity behind and below. This depressing conclusion was of course not broadcast amongst Bomber Command's crews, but Zorner's successful ambushes from close range right behind can be considered normal, typical of the way scores of bombers were gunned down by fighters in the Berlin raids.

Zorner's second victim that night was Lancaster J-Johnnie from 514 Squadron, the crew of which endured a similar ordeal to that of his earlier victim: according to the Australian bomb aimer, Flight Sergeant John Alford, the port wing was similarly set ablaze by a surprise burst of cannon fire. The Rhodesian captain, Flight Lieutenant Guy Hinde, commanded everyone to bail out, but like Garlick, he failed to get out of his own seat while holding the crippled aircraft right-way-up for the others to escape. Miraculously he was blown clear of the aircraft when it exploded in mid-air and so was able to land safely by parachute, like the others to go into captivity. Again the rear gunner died, again probably killed by the gunfire directly from behind. The turret gunners in the rear of the aircraft had the least chance of any crewmen of getting out of a Lancaster alive, exposed to the fighter's gunfire from the rear and trapped within the turret structure if wounded.

Paul Zorner's second kill was his last that night: afterwards he followed the bomber stream on the lookout for further trade, but had no joy, so at 9 pm landed at Stendal airfield, 100 kilometres west of Berlin. He went on to a highly successful career as a night-fighter pilot, surviving the war as the ninth-highest ranking night-fighter ace, with fifty-nine kills.

His shoot-down of No. 514's J-Johnnie was the eighteenth bomber kill that night by night-fighters – eighteen bombers in about one hour, while they were transiting across northern Germany to the 'Big City'. Another twenty bombers fell victim to the fighters in the hour-long period following Zorner's second kill, as the bombers bombed and then headed away from the target. The bomber stream's flight path into and out of Berlin was thus marked with the funeral pyres of almost forty bombers. This was the environment into which our five journalists were flying, and from their viewing position on their flight deck behind their pilots, wired in to the intercom exchanges amongst their crewmates, they could hardly miss the deadly import of what they were glimpsing.

The sight of blazing bombers plunging to earth was a confronting one for those bomber crewmembers whose duties allowed them to watch outside the aircraft – the pilots, bomb aimers and air gunners. However, the psychological impact of seeing all these plunging, blazing, exploding and crashing aircraft was softened somewhat by the aircrew's soothing but delusive belief in the existence of German

> This is where our journalists stood in the cockpits of their allocated Lancasters; they stood throughout the flight on the small square of free floor space between the seated navigator, seen at left, and the seated flight engineer, seen at right. The pilot's right shoulder is visible top right in the photo, as he sits on his elevated pilot's seat. The journalist could touch each crewman without straightening his arm.
>
> AWM Negative P01993.030

'scarecrow' flares, as related by 50 Squadron's Les Bartlett, who described an incident he had seen while on an earlier raid to Berlin:

> Another disconcerting sight was a 'scarecrow' fired by the German 'ack-ack' which burst about 1,000 yards starboard of us. They are supposed to represent a kite [aircraft] on fire, and believe me I was fooled, not having seen one before. It seemed to hang there. Numerous minor explosions followed and clouds of

black smoke poured out, after which it just dropped to earth a mass of flames.

He did not realise it, but Bartlett had just vividly recorded the death of another RAF bomber.

Other crewmen reassured themselves with the thought that the crashing and burning aircraft lighting up the sky around them were in fact shot-down night-fighters rather than British bombers. Aboard 619 Squadron's D-Dog on approach to Berlin, Murrow's attention was drawn to just such an encounter:

> Buzz, the bomb-aimer, crackled through the intercom, 'There's a battle going on the starboard beam.' We couldn't see the aircraft, but we could see the jets of red tracer being exchanged. Suddenly, there was a burst of yellow flame and Jock remarked, 'That's a fighter going down. Note the position.' The whole thing was interesting, but remote.

Two or three German fighters were indeed shot down that night near Berlin by bomber gunners, so it is possible that this was a night-fighter going down in flames. But meanwhile nearly forty bombers went down within the same timeframe, so Murrow and his crew had more likely witnessed the death of another Lancaster.

Journalist Norm Stockton obtained first-hand experience of just such a bomber shoot-down. He was travelling in 460 Squadron's K-King, flown by his host, Pilot Officer James English, as part of the first wave of bombers to go across the target. K-King was about twelve minutes from the target, with Stockton standing within easy reach of the navigator's desk manned by his compatriot Neville Anderson, the boy from Brisbane whom he planned to write up in his coming news story. The Lancaster was now approaching Berlin's fiery flak zone, so with all the fiery 'hate' visible in the sky ahead there was some comfort for the frightened first-trip journalist in having this experienced companion so close at hand.

If he craned his head to the left and peered behind the navigator's black-out curtain, Stockton was in a good position to see the tiny radar screen above Anderson's desk, showing the H2S ground-mapping radar picture of the earth beneath. Anderson used the radar to keep the bomber on the correct course to the target, by identifying ground features – usually lakes – and giving the pilot corrected courses to steer to take account of the wind drift and get back on the briefed approach track. The crews knew that their survival depended upon staying on track, for the essence of the RAF's 'bomber stream' tactic was to pass so many bombers through the defended area within a narrow window of time and space that the defence would be swamped: the flak defences would have enough time only to target some bombers, leaving the great majority to pass through untargeted. It was therefore dangerous to stray from the stream, or to deviate from one's allocated time-over-target, as both would make one's straying bomber more conspicuous on the radar screens in the Flak batteries' fire control centres. The crew of 514 Squadron's J-Johnnie had already found this out to their cost, as we have seen.

Therefore a lot depended upon the navigator's ability to use the H2S radar picture to orientate themselves to the ground features, and to 'map read' in the dark from radar feature to radar feature towards the target. The crews had great confidence in this equipment, believing that it was 'accurate to within a house if you got it right'. However, in reality it seems that there was a lot of trouble in 'getting it right', for un-forecasted winds on the night of 2 December were blowing K-King well to the south of track, a drift which Neville Anderson could not perceive on his radar scope. It did not help that the area around Berlin is dotted with lakes, and one lake looked much like another on a tiny H2S scope. And so, K-King's wind-induced drift to starboard went undiagnosed, so aircraft and crew diverged from the flight plan, off-track to the south. RAF research would establish that such off-track divergence would be as much as 10 per cent of the distance flown, and at that rate, a H2S-guided crew would drift 30 miles off track while flying the 300-mile leg between the Dutch coast and Berlin. This was exactly what happened to Stockton, Anderson and the rest of the crew, leaving K-King straying away from Berlin, away from the bomber stream, towards Potsdam's flak zone and conspicuously on to the radar screens of the German defenders. As K-King approached what the crew thought was Berlin, the crewmen found that the winds had blown the cloud cover away well before they reached the outskirts of the target, obliging the aircraft to traverse a wide patch of open, moonlit sky. According to Anderson's navigation plot, they still had about 40 miles to go to the target.

But suddenly one of K-King's port engines burst into flames. An unseen night-fighter had ambushed the Lancaster. And once again the attack came without any warning from the rear gunner. English threw the aircraft into a series of evasive corkscrews, still heading in the direction of Berlin, but in the course of a 'running 10 minute broken fight', the fighter re-attacked, setting fire to the incendiary bombs in the bomb bay and to one of the fuel tanks in the port wing. Flight Sergeant Alex Kan, the rear gunner (and the third Australian in the crew), was shot in the legs in the first attack, with his turret's exit doors damaged by gunfire. Finding himself trapped, unable to drag himself out of the turret to grab his parachute pack in the rear fuselage, he called for help over the intercom. Anderson was ready to move back through the fuselage to help but could not do so as he was pinned to his seat in the forward cabin because of the G-forces of English's violent evasive manoeuvres. Meanwhile, Norm Stockton must have been forced to his knees on the cockpit floor, unable to maintain his standing position through the hard pulls and pushes of the Lancaster's corkscrew manoeuvres, and was probably air sick as well.

With the fuel fire in the wing, Neville Anderson expected his pilot to order the crew to abandon the doomed aircraft, but all he heard from English over the still-functioning intercom was, 'Stick with it boys.' Despite the damaged aircraft's rapid height loss, English had edged it closer to what he thought was Berlin during the running fight with the night-fighter. With dismay, Anderson now considered that his pilot was intent upon crashing the still bombed-up aircraft on to the target. During the agonising wait for the order to jump, the alarmed crewmen took the precaution of pre-empting their pilot's command by clipping their parachute packs on to their harnesses and getting into position to go. Anderson kept Stockton right next to him, and thought the journalist seemed 'OK'; to reassure him he reached over to make sure that the journalist's parachute pack was securely clipped to his harness. Before take-off they had lightheartedly used a marker pen on the pack, marking it as the property of the *Sydney Sun*. Now the 39-year-old journalist was confronted with having to use it.

But his pilot was too late in giving the call. With the crewmen still waiting agonisingly in the passageway for the order to go, the aircraft fell into a spiral dive, still an estimated 25 miles from the target, descending out of control from 17 000 feet. The bomb aimer, Flight Sergeant Alf Catty, no longer needed instructions: now he tried to open the escape hatch in the floor of his compartment, but found it jammed. Catty's terrified struggle with the hatch release, with a queue of equally terrified airmen stuck behind him, ended with a 'mighty explosion' which shattered the whole aircraft. The burning wing tank exploded, tore the airframe apart, and blew off the nose section. Anderson, Catty and the flight engineer, Sergeant 'Dusty' Miller, spilled outside the aircraft as the cockpit section tore itself to pieces around them.

Neville Anderson regained his senses to find himself falling through space. He realised that he had been blown out of the disintegrating airframe by the explosion. As he fell, he checked that he still had arms and legs, 'unbelievably' finding that all four limbs were still attached. He fumbled for the ripcord on his chest pack parachute, pulled it, and then floated to earth under the canopy. Catty and Miller likewise took to their chutes and came to earth alive. The flaming wreckage of K-King spiralled into the ground at the small village of Paderdamm outside the city of Brandenburg, scattering wreckage over a wide area, and taking with her the lives of their other four crewmates as well as their passenger. The airframe disassembly was so violent that two bodies landed in the village of Göttin, about two kilometres west of Paderdamm, and the other three in the village of Pruetzke, a similar distance in the opposite direction.

Although Anderson afterwards conceded that his pilot 'had an outstanding fighting spirit', he was also convinced that English had 'hung on too long trying to finish the job after the time we should have abandoned aircraft'. English's fixation with getting to the target in a doomed aircraft was an extreme example of the 'press on regardless' spirit of Bomber Command. Nonetheless it was not within Bomber Command's ethos to make kamikaze-style attacks, and certainly Anderson was well justified in his critique of his captain's crew-sacrificing 'keenness' to put his bombs somewhere a bit closer to the general area of the target. And in his target-fixation, English had disregarded the presence onboard of his civilian, non-combatant guest, Norm Stockton. Like the other four crewmen who did not survive, the reporter was either killed in the airframe disintegration or trapped within a section of wreckage as it plunged to earth. Jack English had been appointed to the role of Stockton's host because of his status as an experienced, dependable pilot, and hence a safe pair of hands to look after his assigned pressman. Yet his extreme determination to put his bombs on the target in a doomed aircraft had killed most of his crew as well as his guest.

If the crew had bailed out earlier, as soon as it became clear that the wing fire was out of control, Stockton's survival chances would have been good, for besides English he was probably the only other uninjured crewmember who failed to get clear of the exploding wreck. Everyone else left aboard had already been hit: the wounded Alex Kan was trapped in the tail turret, while Catty considered that both the mid-upper gunner, Flight Sergeant Ivan Rodin, and the wireless operator, Sergeant George Cole, had been killed by the gunfire. Anderson afterwards expressed his surprise that Stockton had not 'gotten away with it' by escaping the aircraft, but in the harsh reality of that cataclysmic airframe dismemberment, his failure to get clear can hardly be considered surprising. Norm Stockton never did get to file a first-hand bombing story, as his American press colleagues had done back in the Australian theatre; nor did he get to write up Neville Anderson, the Brisbane boy bringing his bomber to Berlin; nor did he get to publish his memoir. English's K-King went down at 8.12 pm, forty-eight minutes after the first bomber fell to Zorner's guns; it was probably shot down by Senior Sergeant Walter Kammerer from Night Fighter Wing 5, and was the ninth bomber shot down by fighters en route to the target.

Ed Murrow's aircraft, D-Dog from 619 Squadron, could not have been far behind Stockton's K-King, and Murrow may have witnessed his colleague's fiery descent. Piloted by Jock Abercromby, D-Dog had similarly lost its cloud cover at 30 miles out from the target, and like Stockton's aircraft had to fly out into the open to be confronted by Berlin's defences, a moment described vividly by Ed Murrow:

> ... suddenly those dirty gray clouds turned white and we were over the outer searchlight defenses. The clouds below us were white, and we were black. D-Dog seemed like a black bug on a white sheet.

The flak began coming up, but none of it close. We were still a long way from Berlin. I didn't realize just how far. Jock observed, 'There's a kite on fire dead ahead'. It was a great, golden, slow-moving meteor slanting towards the earth. By this time we were about thirty miles from our target area in Berlin. That thirty miles was the longest flight I have ever made.

Time also slowed down for the people caught on the ground, stuck in the path of the bombing. Léon Butticaz, a Frenchman who had been forced into service as an impressed labourer for the Nazi war economy, was caught in a Berlin *S-Bahn* train station during one of these raids. He described listening to the 'sinister sound' of the raid, which sounded like a 'long, slow, gloomy throbbing noise, like organ crescendos'. As the doom-laden cacophony rose, he and the others in the bomb shelter were reduced to waiting passively 'in a perpetual torment of anxiety'.

Grete Freytag from the Berlin suburb of Wilmersdorf described her experience of a near miss while in a shelter during the Berlin raid on the night of 26 November 1943:

> Boom! ... Have our hearts stopped? Are we still here? What a stroke of hell! We're still here. Grab someone's hand. But what an impact! For a second it went right through bone and marrow. And then the uncanny silence – darkness, the fumes from the bomb explosion, dust, and the debris of pulverised mortar. Now it's completely quiet outside. But inside our cellar there come the sounds of footsteps, murmuring, quiet whimpering. The strip of light against the cellar wall

allows a little illumination, and people are turning their flashlights on. In their light we see that the vaulted ceiling is still there and that all of us are still here also. The warden, who had just started climbing the cellar stairs at the moment the bomb hit, has been flung back against the wall. He won't be giving any more directions.

Another perspective from the ground comes from an air raid warden, Otto Krause, who worked as the head waiter in the Pilsator pub on Alexanderplatz, recalling his experiences on one of the preceding raids, on the night of 22 November. He was an area leader for the local air-raid precautions organisation, so had to do his rounds during the raid, visiting each of the shelters in his area and checking in with their wardens. Before going below into the shelter, he got everything organised in his own pub: 'Lights out, everyone down into the cellar-shelter, and the guests into the public shelter.' Having sorted things out at the Pilsator, he then made his way to another pub close by, the Bierkeller von Borchardt, to check on the basement shelter there. But by the time he walked in, 'The raid was getting worse and worse, and all of us inside owe our lives to the fact that at the last moment I was able to close the cellar door.' Just as Krause closed the door behind him there came a thunderous crash from outside; it shook the ground like an earthquake. This was probably the detonation of a 4000-pound 'blockbuster'. Having survived this close detonation thanks to the shelter, he went back outside to head for the next shelter on his rounds. Emerging now into the fiery night, he saw that 'The railway station was hit!' and heard bombers rumbling past in the darkness overhead. Then he walked back out onto Alexanderplatz, previously a bustling shopping precinct and public transport interchange, but no longer: 'what devastation – I don't want to describe what I saw, but it was only ruins that were staring back at me, burning houses and burning shops'.

Another air raid warden, Irmgard Häuser from the up-market residential district of Charlottenburg, described the night of 23 November from her vantage point as a firewatcher up on the roof of Wormser Strasse No. 4, not far from the Kurfürstendamm, Berlin's most famed shopping street. She found the raid to be 'a storm that couldn't be withstood'. First, she saw an incendiary bomb fall on the house next door, which started burning straight away. She ran downstairs to warn the people in the cellar, but they had neglected to prepare water for a bucket brigade and so had to stand by and watch their house burn down, 'right down to the cellar'. The occupants only just had time to save their most precious things. Frau Häuser recalled that, 'so it went with innumerable houses'.

As people huddled together in the shelters in districts throughout the Berlin area on the night of 2 December, one of the approaching bombers they could hear, with mounting apprehension, was Lowell Bennett's Lancaster, 50 Squadron's B-Bolty. Like Ed Murrow's D-Dog, it was in the third wave, and on its approach to the target it too ran its own gauntlet through wide open, backlit skies, in the broad battle arena four miles above the huddling masses down below. As B-Bolty approached the outer edge of Berlin's defended area, Bennett found that 'the flak became sharper, clearer, and much more personal':

Here, from the outer ring of defences, heavy blots of light checkered crimson in the sky, scores of ghostly searchlights swept and fingered across the backdrop of night, and fighter flares hung everywhere – a surrealistic display, lighting the world to an unnatural day.

Not far ahead, the Path Finders had already arrived and dropped the target indicator, a chandelier-like cluster of red and green flares ...

Explosions from light guns flecked and ruptured the sky below us; heavier bursts rent the air above us. But there was no noise above the steady, vibrant pounding of the engines ...

I was not frightened; I was far too impressed for any other emotion to register. The display ahead, and now behind and on both sides – for we were coming over the city – was spectacular without comparison with any previous experience ...

Below, fires had already been started – blood-red patches splashing and heaving in a Dantean hell on earth. I counted five areas that were glowing and trembling, cadmium crimson enshrouded by billowing masses of flame-lit smoke ...

Suddenly, not far ahead, a bomber was directly hit. A tremendous explosion, though inaudible to us, rocked the sky. Flaming fragments tumbled and drifted downward like crimsoned autumn leaves ...

Almost immediately there was another explosion and a searing gash of light. Another bomber had been hit, and it swirled earthward like an immense firebrand. We watched it strike the ground with a yawning, gushing explosion and its fiery incendiaries spew out about it in a solid ring.

With such confronting proof that the unseen German night-fighters were wreaking deadly execution all around, Bennett was alarmed to perceive that B-Bolty herself was now perilously poised in a pool of light: 'Night-fighter flares hung everywhere as if suspended, and – with the searchlights and flak – lit the sky into a fantastic arena for twentieth-century struggle. The moon still shone with a shameful brilliance, and the stars looked down on the greater light below.'

Caught thus within a floodlit arena, there was nothing B-Bolty could do to avoid herself becoming the object of the night-fighters' malevolent attentions. The mid-upper gunner reported over the intercom, 'Fighter climbing ahead on starboard'. To evade, Bolton rolled the Lancaster into a 'violent' corkscrew, made up of alternating climbing and diving turns left and right. But despite the vigorous evasive manoeuvring, the gunners then reported two more fighters behind. Bennett heard the 'metallic stutter' of machine-gun fire from the two turrets as the gunners tried to put the fighters off with bursts of tracer. Having seemingly given them the slip, Bolton sought to re-establish B-Bolty on its bomb run into the target. But as soon as he did so Bennett saw 'jets and bursts of light' flashing past – tracers from one of the night-fighters, still behind. Again, Bolton rammed the control column forward and reefed the bomber over into another corkscrew. In the negative-G of the sudden dive, Bennett had to hold on tightly to avoid being thrown up against the cockpit roof. As the bomber straightened out from this series of turns, the gunners again gave 'curt, clear warnings' over the intercom of two fighters astern. Then Bennett's deceptive-seeming, oxygen-breathing, metallic-voiced cocoon of safety was torn apart:

> Disaster struck with terrifying abruptness.
>
> Our world burst into an inferno of flame. The plane shuddered, then heaved and rocked violently. A long burst of cannon fire had slashed into our right wing and both engines had exploded into a furious fire.
>
> We could see the metal twisting, melting, and tearing away from the wing with the intensity of the heat. Flaming strips of fabric flashed past. A solid panel of fire blocked vision on our right side.

Bennett had had his premonition, of which he had felt the pangs repeatedly both during the pre-flight process and after take-off, but now that it was actually happening there was no comfort in it: 'the realization that we were lost – on fire and going down over Berlin, six hundred miles inside Germany – was panic-striking'.

He overheard a series of orders from Bolton to the flight engineer: to feather both starboard propellers, cut the fuel to those engines, and activate the fire extinguishers; and he watched the flight engineer right next to him bending over his control panel to carry them out. Listening to and watching the precise actions of the busy cockpit crew allowed 'momentary sanity' to return to Bennett's mind, but seconds later he heard Bolton announce that he could not jettison the bombs because the gunfire had smashed the jettison handle. Now Bennett remembered that he was standing right on top of a 4-tonne load of high explosive, phosphorus and magnesium.

And then the unseen fighter struck again:

> A roar drowned even the noise of our two remaining engines and of the fire ... Cannon fire smashed into the bomb aimer's compartment, missing his head by inches, disintegrating his instrument panel.
>
> The fire had spread to the wing fuel tanks and flames enveloped us, a whitish red sheet which swamped and covered the entire right side of the plane. Its heat penetrated the cabin in a wave of furnace-hot breath ...
>
> In frenzied urgency I reached down, snatched up my parachute, and buckled it to the chest hooks without awaiting instructions. I knew without being an airman that this Lancaster would never carry us home.

Then came Bolton's just-in-time announcement over the intercom, 'Okay, boys, bail out. Sorry.' Bennett saw the other crewmen hurry to attach their parachute packs to their harnesses, noticing too that the previously unruffled flight engineer was in such a panic that he was having trouble attaching his chute with trembling hands. Bennett stood out of the way as the crewmen went through the intricate choreography of the bail-out drill, queuing up in the narrow corridor leading down into the nose compartment while the bomb aimer unlatched and jettisoned the escape hatch in the floor. This queue left Bennett still standing in the cockpit next to Bolton, which gave him a good view of the latter as he struggled to hold the aircraft straight enough for the other men to get out – the pilot's standard self-sacrificial task in a doomed and crippled bomber. Bolton's previously splendid Lancaster was reduced to what Bennett now saw as a piece of 'shattered machinery', 'surging and bucking like a wild horse'. Bolton yelled, 'Hurry, boys, can't hold it much longer.' As the escape hatch fell away, a 'torrent of cyclonic wind rushed through the pitching plane, like a flood of stabbing ice water'. In those overloaded microseconds, mental impressions flashed past Bennett's mind, 'crowding each other with unprecedented speed'. One of these thought impressions was, 'This is a helluva way to get a story.'

Bennett felt the Lancaster 'shaking and shuddering as if it would tear itself apart', and he now saw that it was doing just that: he 'glanced at the starboard wing. It was melting away. Both engines had torn loose. Large sections, glare-red with fire, were breaking off and flashing backward'. He turned back to Bolton, watching him 'fighting desperately, silently' to keep the wrecked bomber flying right-way-up for a few seconds longer so that the men could get out. The bomb aimer shouted, 'Bye, skipper. Good luck,' and jumped. In accordance with the escape drill, the next man in the queue was the flight engineer, who was still struggling with his parachute clips even as he fell through the hatch. Bennett was next, jostled from behind by the increasingly anxious-to-get-out navigator and wireless operator:

> I heaved myself forward, weighted down with parachute, life belt, musette bag, and trench coat, and fell over the steps leading into the bomb aimer's compartment. My borrowed flying boots both came off. But there was not the slightest desire to stop and collect them. For all five senses there was only one sensation and one command: 'Get out of this plane alive'. I tore off the oxygen mask.
>
> ... I crouched by the hatchway with a wild wind pounding my face, thinking suddenly and quite coldly, 'Should've doubled my insurance. This is no good for a family man', grabbed at the parachute's rip cord, and hunched forward through the opening.
>
> ... We were four miles up, over twenty thousand feet above the center of Berlin, in that vast, unearthly void. Below, just as I jumped, I could see the fires and the flak, the flares and the search-lights. It was a kaleidoscopic nightmare.

Bennett dropped through the hatch into this yawning pit of pyrotechnic fury. Unseen by him and the others who flung themselves through the hatch after him, B-Bolty plunged away into a spiral dive, utterly unresponsive to Bolton's heaving upon the controls. Now with only his own life to save, the pilot wriggled out of his seat and crawled forward along the cockpit floor towards the howling open escape hatch in the nose. Bolton later recalled that:

> Something fell on me and I was pinned against the hatch. Then there was an explosion and I was hit on the head. Next thing I knew I was dropping into the darkness. I vaguely remember pulling the ripcord.

Like Guy Hinde only minutes earlier, he was only saved by the fortuitous structural disintegration of his Lancaster, his still-living body spilled into the air as one random component in a spray of aircraft wreckage.

Exactly as Bolton's air gunners had reported, B-Bolty seems to have been attacked by two or three night-fighters, those of Captain Leopold Fellerer of Night Fighter Wing 5, Captain Erhard Peters, from Night Fighter Wing 3, and Corporal Andreas Hartl, piloting a single-seat FW 190 from Fighter Wing 302. Their attacks on the Lancaster started at 8.12 pm, and the bomber was shot down by 8.22 pm – giving a ten-minute interval for the events and impressions Bennett experienced and described.

CHAPTER 7

'ORCHESTRATED HELL'

While some crews, like those of Stockton and Bennett, were suddenly confronting the horrifying and fiery doom of their Lancasters, others were slipping past in the darkness unmarked and unmolested. Some of these crews were even spared the trauma of having to observe their comrades' mid-air destruction. One was Alf King's G-George from 467 Squadron. On approach to Berlin, King's view outside was obscured by cloud, as his aircraft luckily flew through weather conditions different from the wide open sky Bennett's B-Bolty and Murrow's D-Dog experienced – undoubtedly because 'George' flew a different track into Berlin. All crews sought to keep on track and on time, flocking together within the prescribed flight corridor of the bomber stream, but in practice the further they flew the further the bomber stream diverged and spread out. As we have seen, some strayed into danger, drawing themselves conspicuously to the attention of the German fighter controllers, while others fortuitously found safer patches of sky to fly through – or by virtue of better navigation remained within the relative safety of the herd, as Bomber Command tactics intended. Either way, Alf King got a dream run across northern Germany during G-George's approach run to the 'King of Targets', as he reported afterwards: 'Cloud protected us practically the whole way. Then, 10 miles from the target, it became wispy. Visibility

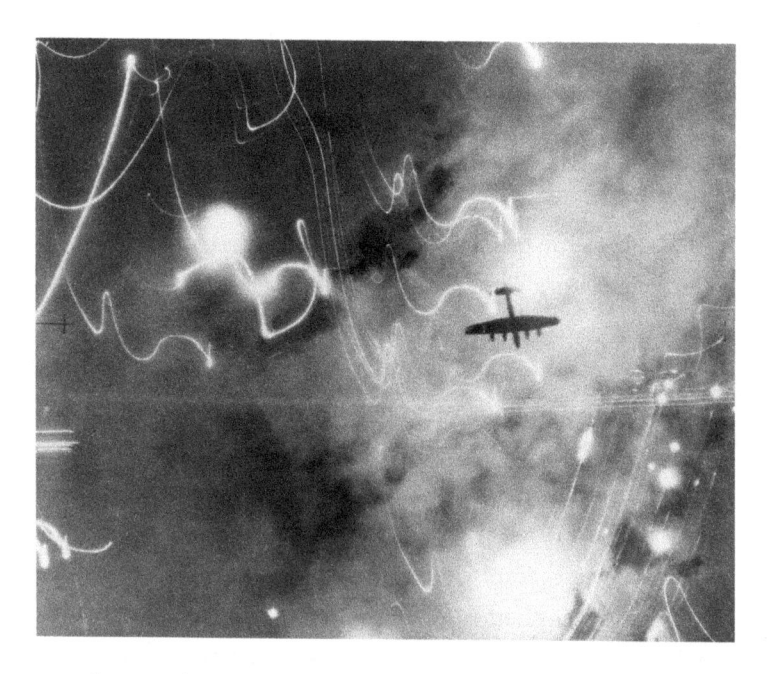

Each journalist risked his life to see this scene from the cockpit of a Lancaster: the flare and flak filled the sky over a German city at night, with other Lancasters passing through the maelstrom on their bombing runs.
AWM Negative SUK11190

was perfect over the target itself.' Clear air was, as always over Germany, a very mixed blessing, because straight after King's Lancaster arrived in the band of clear air over the target, the journalist was treated to the sight of 'hundreds of searchlights and light and heavy flak' concentrating against the bombers as they went across the target. Berlin was defended by thirty-five heavy searchlight batteries, deploying a total of 420 searchlights, each of which threw a beam powerful enough to brightly illuminate a bomber at 20 000 feet. That night this formidable array of searchlight batteries would successively hold seventy-seven 'targets' in their beams as the bombers passed by overhead, flying through the Berlin flak zone. Sometimes the searchlights locked on to a bomber for up to four minutes, designating it as a target for both the anti-aircraft guns and the night-fighters: the guns would engage targets below 5000 metres (16 400 feet), while the fighters hunted above that, safe from 'friendly fire' accidents with their own flak. This night, a total of about 100 fighters would enter Berlin's flak zone and hunt for the bombers as these passed like moths through the bright matrix of searchlight beams swinging through the sky over the city.

This was the environment King was trying to take in as he stood perched behind his pilot Bill Forbes with his left hip and shoulder jammed in between the edge of the navigator's chart table behind and the pilot's armoured seat-back in front. Through the cockpit windscreen he saw the surreal sight of a bomber up ahead, 'perfectly coned in searchlights without fighters attacking it or flak directed at it'. He also saw the Pathfinder crews' target-marker flares going down ahead, as well as, more ominously, lanes of red 'fighter-flares' laid by high-flying German aircraft to mark the path of the bomber stream for arriving night-fighters.

Alf King's G-George was part of the second wave, and so flew ahead of Bennett's B-Bolty and Stockton's K-King. These two Lancasters were at that time somewhere further back, probably to the southwest, in the process of being stalked by night-fighters, as we have seen. By 8.17 pm there were already about fifty night-fighters in the sky roundabout, all operating within the flak zone over Berlin, having been summoned there by the fighter controllers' 'running commentary' broadcasts. Fortunately for his peace of mind, King did not see any of them. But meanwhile, out of sight and so mercifully out of mind, Stockton's K-King was getting shot down at 8.12 pm, and Bennett's B-Bolty at 8.15 pm. King's G-George went over the target to bomb only five minutes later. All three of these machines were thus approaching the target area just as the fighters started arriving there in numbers. Two of the three were unlucky, found by fighters, while the third was lucky enough to squeak through without attracting the fighters' attention. For those crews who survived the early round of ambushes to reach the target area, these early arrivals found the target less cluttered and obscured by light pollution and visual distractions, for as the raid developed the bomber crews' target picture became increasingly distorted and confused with fires, smoke, bomb flashes, and a multiplication of target-marking flares.

The early-arriving G-George thus presented Alf King with a target 'defined with remarkable clarity by the Pathfinder force a few minutes earlier with target-indicators of different colours. The bomb-aimers' particular objectives stood out like beacons amid a confusion of colours.' Despite the pyrotechnic panorama veiling the earth and sky ahead, as he followed the intercom chatter King believed he could perceive the crew's aiming points on the ground:

> From the time we sighted them, about 10 miles out, until we passed beyond them was the most exciting ten minutes through which I have lived. The two central figures in that brief period were Forbes and the bomb-aimer, Pilot-Officer William Grime, of Ealing,

London – two 'Bills' who co-operatively directed and instructed each other over the intercom phones. I stood behind the imperturbable Forbes and watched the fascinatingly fantastic scene over his shoulder.

As soon as he sighted his target indicators [ie pathfinder flares], for which he was on the lookout, Forbes asked Grime whether he had seen them. Grime answered confidently in the affirmative and then gave the pilot a slight alteration of course, adding: 'You can weave a bit, Bill.'

Bill Forbes weaved to lessen the danger from flak, but it was only for seconds. Then Forbes settled down to hold his plane to the level, undeviating run so essential for accurate bombing.

Flak poured upwards, though none burst close enough to 'George' to threaten the crew's safety.

But these were those few seconds which bomber crews dread and against which they must summon up all their courage, determination, and imperturbability – a few seconds in which they never know whether the next flak-burst is going to extinguish their life, smash their limbs, cripple their plane, or whether they will slip past the German gunners.

The flak, to the uninitiated reporter, seemed desperately dangerous, but according to 'George's' veteran crew of youngsters, it 'wasn't much'.

With his vision perhaps over-stimulated by the awesome light display out in front – a composition of flak explosions, triangulated searchlight beams, drifting flares and pulsing bomb bursts – the journalist retained enough sharpness of hearing to keep monitoring the intercom exchanges between pilot and bomb aimer: Grime reported 'Bomb doors open', acknowledged by Forbes with 'Okay'. Despite the laconic response, King commented that these were 'magic words that thrill even the most hardened crews', because everyone knew that the aircraft could only resume evasive manoeuvring once the bombs were gone. Seconds later Grime's still 'unruffled' voice crackled over the intercom with the 'even more magic words', 'Cookie gone'. Another 'Okay' came from the undemonstrative Forbes. At this, the by-now keenly apprehensive King started counting slowly to himself; upon his silent count of five Grime's voice came through again, 'Incendiaries gone', followed by another 'Okay' from Forbes. They bombed at 8.20 pm.

The 4000-pound 'Cookie' plunged away from G-George's gaping bomb bay, swaying into the abyss below, followed by the shower of incendiaries: 1200 4-pound magnesium rods and sixty-eight 30-pound phosphorous bombs. A relieved King had an opportunity to reflect on what they had just done:

> We had delivered, free of charge, to Hitler and company, a 4,000lb building-blaster and morale-shaker, and many fire-raisers.
>
> This was the climax of the flight. Almost four hours from base to target.

> Down below – four miles below – early comers had already started fires, and our waves stoked them thoroughly.
>
> As they lightened 'George', I – the spare part on the plane – had the best opportunity to watch those fires increase in numbers, and from a band seemingly join in an immense conflagration. Amidst them glowed 'cookies', angry explosions like boils on white flesh. Some billowed and grew in volume above the flames.

As 'George' hurried away from the target area, seeking to regain the obscurity of night beyond the lit-up area, from his perch behind the captain's seat Alf King received ongoing impressions of the still-malevolent sting of the defences:

> Below 'George' another Lancaster nosed forward, silhouetted sinisterly against the flaming background like a shark in an aquarium pool.
>
> It was not without cost that the inferno in Berlin's heart was lit. Three flak bursts seemed simultaneously to hit one Lancaster and it burst into flames.
>
> Another seemed to get into difficulties and later several parachutes could be seen floating down.

Newly operational crews flying their very first operation to the 'Big City' were as overwhelmed as King was by the fantastic scene which such a raid presented to an airborne observer. Norman Wells, the rookie rear gunner aboard

9 Squadron's veteran thirty-two-trip Lancaster, 'J-for-Johnnie Walker', similarly found the scene he saw over Berlin shocking and overwhelming:

> ... when we got there, God, it was horrendous. We all thought, we can't get through this. It was a mass of searchlights, and with the flak and the photoflashes going off and the bombs exploding, it was as bright as day. Nothing hit us but we could see plenty of other aircraft going down, plenty.

Even seasoned combat aircrew found the scene of a big raid almost overwhelming, if they could find a spare moment from their in-cockpit tasks to look around them and take it all in. A German night-fighter pilot, Wilhelm Johnen of Night Fighter Wing 5, described the diabolical scene Berlin's flak zone presented during one of these big raids:

> What was now taking place over the city surpasses any human imagining. Hell is let loose! A sea of searchlights illuminate the night, thousands of flak gunners unleash a magic fire of inconceivable fury. The English 'Master of Ceremonies' has already marked the aiming point with fire-bombs ... Berlin defends herself mightily. The brightly illuminated night is saturated with thousands of little cloudbursts reaching up to 8000 metres. I fly directly into one flak salvo and am flung by the air pressure to a lower altitude ... Right and left, over and under me aircraft are burning and plunging away. Numberless fires cover the earth. Night fighters getting shot at by flak are shooting out burning

flares as identification signals, enemy bombers explode in the air and shower a rain of colourful, glowing confetti upon the city. A magnificent fireworks-display! The ceaseless flashes of the flak explosions sap the nerves. Bitter powder smoke is sucked into the cabin.

The night fighters go for the enemy. Here over Berlin we no longer need radar devices; with the naked eye we can see the English planes as they pass across the city. Everyone shoots at someone. Red, yellow, and green tracer ammunition saws through the night and flashes past over my cockpit roof.

Alf King was lucky enough for fate to give him a less action-packed passage through Berlin's aerial maelstrom, but the feeling of sensory overload was similar. While King's G-George was heading away from the fiercely lit target area to escape into the night, Ed Murrow's D-Dog was entering the same demented theatre of light and flame. Like Bill Forbes had done, Murrow's pilot, Jock Abercromby, looked ahead to see the target indicators, seeking to line up on them while hopefully also avoiding the searchlights. Murrow recorded his crowded impressions:

Dead on time, Buzz the bomb-aimer reported, 'Target indicators going down.' At the same moment, the sky ahead was lit up by bright yellow flares. Off to starboard another kite went down in flames. The flares were sprouting all over the sky, reds and greens and yellows, and we were flying straight through the middle of the fireworks. D-Dog seemed to be standing still, the four propellers thrashing the air, but we didn't seem to be closing in. The clouds had cleared, and off to starboard a Lanc was caught by at least fourteen searchlight beams. We could see him twist and turn and finally break out. But still, the whole thing had a quality of unreality about it. No one seemed to be shooting at us, but it was getting lighter all the time ...

... And then, with no warning at all, D-Dog was filled with an unhealthy white light.

I was standing just behind Jock and could see all the seams on the wings. His quiet Scots voice beat into my ears, 'Steady lads, we've been coned'. His slender body lifted half out of the seat as he jammed the control column forward and to the left. We were going down ... And then I was on my knees, flat on the deck, for he had whipped the Dog back into a climbing turn. The knees should have been strong enough to support me, but they weren't, and the stomach seemed in some danger of letting me down too. I picked myself up and looked out again. It seemed that one big searchlight, instead of being twenty thousand feet below, was mounted right on our wingtip. D-Dog was corkscrewing. As we rolled down on the other side, I began to see what was happening to Berlin.

The clouds were gone, and the sticks of incendiaries from the preceding waves made the place look like a badly laid-out city with the streetlights on. The small incendiaries were going down like a fistful of white rice thrown on a piece of black velvet. And there below were more incendiaries, glowing white and turning red. The cookies, the four-thousand-pound high explosives, were bursting below like great sunflowers gone mad. And then, as we started down again, still held in the lights, I remembered that Dog still had one of those cookies and a whole basket of incendiaries in his belly, and the lights still held us, and I was very frightened.

Abercromby's violent manoeuvring finally broke the Lancaster out of the searchlights' malevolent apex of light. He plunged D-Dog into the comparative obscurity of the flare, flak, flame, and flash-lit sky beyond, before rolling wings-level to resume his bomb run. Murrow clambered to his feet and looked straight down out of the starboard viewing blister, to see that the white fires in the city far below had turned red: 'They were beginning to merge and spread, just like butter does on a hot plate.' As the aircraft stabilised on to its bomb run, like King he intently listened in over the intercom to the pilot and bomb aimer's discussion about which green target-marking flares to line up on:

The bomb doors were opened. Buzz called his directions: 'Five left, five left.' And then, there was a gentle, confident upward thrust under my feet and Buzz said, 'Cookie gone'. A few seconds later, the incendiaries went, and D-Dog seemed lighter ...

Just as Murrow and the crew were breathing a sigh of relief, Buzz came back on the intercom to report that one 'can' of incendiaries had failed to release from their bomb shackle. The horror scenario that flashed into Murrow's mind was the possibility that Wing Commander Abercromby would feel obliged to set a good example to his men by going around again to deliver this last munition. However, the CO took a pragmatic line, asking the bomb aimer to check if it was in fact a bundle of small (4-pound) or large (30-pound) incendiaries that had hung up. Buzz used a torch to peer into the bomb bay through the small, clear Perspex inspection panel at the rear of his compartment. He reported back that the incendiaries that had failed to drop away were only the small ones. Now Abercromby announced the decision everyone was yearning for: 'well, it's hardly worth going back and doing another run for that'. A still nauseous Murrow 'began to breathe, and to reflect again – that all men would be brave if only they could leave their stomachs at home'.

Although D-Dog did not have to run the gauntlet of a second bomb run, she still needed to get clear of the defended area. Threats emerged from every side, unexpectedly: firstly, two aircraft appeared to port, one of which was identified by the mid-upper gunner as a German fighter crossing the Lancaster's track close overhead. And then:

> ... there was a tremendous whoomph, an unintelligible shout from the tail gunner, and D-Dog shivered and lost altitude. I looked to the port side and there was a Lancaster that seemed close enough to touch. He had whipped straight under us – missed us by twenty five, fifty feet ...

D-Dog survived these near misses, and the navigator 'sang out the new course and we were heading for home'. As Abercromby turned the Lancaster on to the new heading, at once he 'flew straight into a huge green searchlight'. Such specially coloured beams were believed to be radar-guided 'master searchlights', so in haste the pilot 'rammed the throttles home' to roll into another evasive diving turn. Bluntly, he told the crew, 'We'll have a little trouble getting away from this one.' After executing another series of nauseating corkscrews, Abercromby got D-Dog clear of the searchlight, rolling out again wings-level to put some distance behind him to the target. Then he headed away west into the dark night for home.

When the corkscrews stopped Murrow got up off the floor once more and looked out to port, past the pilot's head and over the top of the wing, towards the target area, finding it lit with a 'red, sullen, obscene glare'. As they headed away, the crew saw further air battles in the darkness around them, including another aircraft going down in flames. D-Dog was not out of Berlin's defended area yet, dogged by flak whenever she flew straight and level:

> ... a great orange blob of flak smacked straight in front of us, and Jock said, 'I think they're shooting at us'. I'd thought so for some time. And he began to throw D for Dog up, around, and about again. When we were clear of the barrage, I asked him how close the bursts were and he said, 'Not very close. When they're really near, you can smell 'em'. That proved nothing for I'd been holding my breath.

Ahead of Murrow's D-Dog, Alf King was similarly exiting the area aboard G-George, but he enjoyed an easier run out of the target area than did his American colleague. As 'George' extended its progress beyond the defended area after bombing, King's view of the fires, flashes and flares in the target area became increasingly obscured as these drifted into the blind spot beneath and behind the bomber's belly. However, King could still turn around to look back over the wing. What he saw seemed to confirm his impression hitherto of a devastating raid: 'For many miles beyond Berlin's outskirts the flames and their reflections in the sky could be seen. The later waves had done their work as efficiently as the early comers.' While D-Dog and G-George headed for comparative safety of the darkness beyond the target area, Murrow's colleague and compatriot, Lowell Bennett, was at that time still airborne, albeit suspended beneath a silk parachute canopy. He floated down alone through the frigid air from 15 000 feet, having been the third man to escape through the cockpit floor hatch of his blazing Lancaster:

> It was cold ... biting, numbing cold. I had pulled the rip cord almost immediately ... We had parachuted right over the target area, and the flak was vomiting lustily into the sky, choking the air with a crimson cordon of death ...
>
> Almost immediately there was a back-twisting jerk and I thought my arms and legs would be torn away. I glanced up to see a white sheet billowing out

reassuringly above, and at the same time saw the flak and flame framing a fantastic background ...

At that point there was a sort of lifting of the eyebrows, an idiotic thing to do coming down over Berlin ... I said aloud, 'You wanted a big story. Well, here it is. Goddamnit'.

Flak spangled the blackness around me. My ears rang with the concussion of explosion and the change of air density. My lungs ached for oxygen in the bitterly cold, thin air and my head whirred with the wildness of this nightmare.

There was an annoying, biting realization – even in all this madness – of my own appalling insignificance: dangling up there, impotent in that vastness, alone and helpless against the jagged streaks of light which filled the icy void. A man-made sheet of silk, and a woman-made man suspended and swinging beneath it – an animal intrusion, an atomic impertinence in this infinite wilderness of the unearthly.

It was not only Bennett, suspended so vulnerably beneath his parachute, who was struck by the puniness of his life when measured against the enormity of this new form of warfare. For very different reasons, Wilhelm Johnen, a German night-fighter pilot, had in an earlier Berlin raid been cut to his heart as he looked down from his aircraft upon the stricken city below, which lay burning despite all his efforts and those of his colleagues:

I circle over the burning city, waiting for a straggling bomber. The flak is falling silent. But still the huge fires eerily illuminate the night. My crew goes silent over the intercom. We simply do not want to believe that the Reich's capital, Berlin, should be doomed to die. In the course of this battle in the heart of Germany, it is becoming clear to us all that victory has been gambled away, that Hitler can at best only win a bit more time. I wonder whether it makes any sense to ponder this, and then we cast a last glance at the burning city and set course for base.

The enormity was felt too by those down below, caught in the path of the bombs. Even for those Berliners ensconced deep underground, the bombing was terrifying. The 19-year-old Ellen Slottgo had gone out with friends to see *Tosca* at the opera but had been caught by a raid while changing trains at the Nollendorfplatz underground railway station. Even though the passengers were ushered to shelter on the lowest platform, once the bombs came down, 'The room was shaking; it was almost like sitting on a swing.' For French forced labourer, Léon Butticaz, even within the relative safety of a public bomb shelter, it seemed as if there could be no escape from the seismic violence outside. The bomb explosions came as 'a crushing sensation', then as 'a series of heavy blows' which hammered the ground 'just like an earthquake'. Then, 'Blasts of hot air struck us, whipping our faces, blowing our hair about and going up the legs and sleeves of our clothes.' People in the shelter trembled with fear, some sobbed, and others were 'overcome with a sudden bout of diarrhoea'.

By now seasoned Berliners could recognise the different kinds of bombs dropped by the British, and had developed a 'great fear' for both of Bomber Command's favoured munition types: the 4000-pound high-explosive 'blockbusters', the blast of which flattened whole apartment blocks and 'could crush the lungs' of those near-missed; and the phosphorous incendiary bombs, of which the people were 'terrified', because the burning phosphorus 'could not be put out by water and the burns from which were almost impossible to treat'. The RAF's smaller 4-pound incendiaries could ignite a building if they fell inside an already broken roof, while the 30-pounders were heavy enough to penetrate intact roofs, smashing through several floors to ignite fires deep within a building.

It was of course worse to be caught out in the open. Heinrich Möller, a schoolboy who served as a Flak helper with the local Flak battery, described the experience of being caught on his flak observation tower underneath the bombs during one of these Berlin raids. He heard 'this horrible shrieking, the like of which I have never heard before, as the hail of bombs came down on to us', and then a hail of thousands of incendiaries smacking into the ground all over his battery position. Two gunners were killed on the gun tower: 'One had his head bashed in by an incendiary bomb falling right on top of his steel helmet; that scattered his brains. The other was hit by an incendiary bomb on the shoulder ...' After that the suburb roundabout caught fire, blazing so fiercely that a 'hurricane of wind' blew across the battery position so violently that Möller and his comrades 'had to tie ourselves to the rails to avoid being thrown over the edge'.

For those members of the German ground defence organisation who were similarly placed on duty at above-ground posts, but whose positions luckily stood aside from the bombs' impact zones, they could obtain spectacular views of the awesome fireworks in the sky around them. In this manner a contingent of boy auxiliaries obtained an immediate view of a Lancaster's airborne destruction above the southwestern outskirts of Potsdam. In the town of Michendorf, Sergeant Major Hans Kresten was at the head of a Hitler Youth fire brigade troop posted on lookout duty at an observation post, when he saw horizontally fired tracers in the sky, marking a bomber under attack from a night-fighter. After only a few seconds, he saw a bomber revealed against the obscurity of the night, lit by a fire glowing in its body, a fire which quickly burst into a blaze. The crippled bomber fell into an uncontrolled dive, circling in a tight spiral as it descended rapidly towards the ground beyond the outskirts of the village. At an altitude of about 1000 metres the doomed bomber disintegrated in an explosion so powerful that it ignited the bombload, and with almost 5000 pounds of incendiary bombs in her bomb bay, the resultant cascade of burning phosphorus showering out of the broken bomber's belly was so brilliant that one of the watching boys later recalled that, 'In my life I have never again seen such fireworks.'

Bennett's B-Bolty was destroyed in a very similar fashion, and indeed not far away from where Kresten's boys were standing. Exploding just like the bomber described above, B-Bolty came to earth in a spray of airframe components, the pieces scattering on to the ground south of Caputh, and into the woods near the Flottstelle road, close to the adjoining Schwielow Lake. As we have seen, Bennett's pilot Bolton had self-sacrificially stayed at the controls to let the others bail out, and then was miraculously ejected from the wreck in mid-air. Having been blown out of the nose compartment of the disintegrating bomber, Bolton found himself descending beneath his parachute, fleetingly sharing the sky with the blazing, tumbling wreck of his aircraft as it hurtled towards the ground:

> When the parachute opened, I remember nothing more until I noticed trees below me. Then a crashing noise and a very abrupt stop. I swung against the tree trunk, loosened my harness, and slid off and fell to the ground.
>
> At the same time there was a terrible roar. It seemed to fill the whole world. I saw a flaming aircraft coming down – straight for me, it seemed. It struck a few hundred feet away with a terrific crash, sending debris far over my head. I rolled over and watched it for a moment in the distance. I felt pretty badly about it, as I lay there on my side watching it: a bright burning circle that was our bomber's funeral pyre.

Unmarked by Bolton, passing overhead B-Bolty's crash position at that time was yet another Lancaster, on approach to the target. Like many other bombers that night, and just like B-Bolty, this Lancaster had drifted to the south of the bomber stream's prescribed track into Berlin, and it thereby drew upon itself the attention of the Flak batteries around Potsdam which guarded the southwest approaches to the capital. It was Alan Mitchell's H-Harry from 460 Squadron, carrying Nordahl Grieg. At this point the Lancaster was evidently crippled by either fighter attack or radar-directed flak, for it descended precipitately while still 20 kilometres from the target area, and then jettisoned its bombload from low altitude. As we have seen, captains could be surprisingly tenacious in retaining their bombloads, even in a crippled aircraft, so this jettisoning shows that the bomber had by now sustained significant damage: the captain now got rid of his bombs in a desperate bid to save the aircraft. The jettisoned 4000-pound 'cookie' fell into the Teltow Canal, while 100 incendiaries fell across the nearby small town of Kleinmachnow, hitting forty buildings and starting serious fires.

The third salvo that came crashing to earth near Kleinmachnow was not more bombs, but a shower of sundered components of the Lancaster itself. As we have seen, shot-down bombers often ripped themselves apart in mid-air from the violent stresses of an uncontrolled descent. Straight after jettisoning its bombs, Mitchell's Lancaster suffered violent mid-air disassembly, much as Bennett's B-Bolty had done. The severed right wing of Grieg's Lancaster sailed into Lake Machnow, which lies along the canal marking the southern outskirts of Kleinmachnow. This was the fifteenth bomber to go down that night, only a minute after B-Bolty, which had been the thirteenth victim of the night. H-Harry did not fall far away either: Bolton's bomber fell to earth on the western outskirts of Potsdam, while Mitchell's bomber went to ground on the opposite side of that town, on the eastern outskirts.

Grieg's doomed bomber might have been one of five claimed shot down by Berlin's flak gunners that night.

Although it was the night-fighters that did the great bulk of the killing in the flak-free zone above 5000 metres altitude, the flak was also a killer. By January 1944, Berlin's flak defences comprised 124 batteries of anti-aircraft guns spread right around the circumference of the great city. Of these, 75 batteries were equipped with the heavy guns of 88mm, 105mm and 128mm calibre, all able to engage Lancasters at their bombing height of 20 000 feet. On the night of 2 December, for one hour and seventeen minutes as the bombers fought their way overhead across Berlin's flak zone, a total of thirty-five batteries of heavy anti-aircraft artillery took part in the battle, firing 14 032 rounds ranging in calibre from 88mm upwards. Two-thirds of these rounds were fired under radar control, and yet despite the use of this state-of-the-art gunnery technology, it seems that only four bombers were actually shot down by flak. On that basis it had taken more than 3500 rounds of heavy AA ammunition for each flak-kill scored. But flak's primary effect was to push the bombers higher, too high for effective target identification and bomb-aiming – and hence causing them to miss the target. Although the great majority of shot-down bombers were victims of the night-fighters, the gunners exacted an additional deadly tithe, particularly when already-damaged bombers passed overhead through their engagement zones. This is likely what happened to Alan Mitchell's crew, with their machine crippled by a fighter attack, forced to turn for home and descending inadvertently into a flak zone, where the gunners delivered a rapid-fire *coup de grâce*.

While Nordahl Grieg's Lancaster tore itself apart over Kleinmachnow, the night air over the Berlin flak zone was still being ripped and scorched by flak-shell detonations at the rate of three explosions per second. As Grieg and his host crewmen died, Bennett was still descending by parachute through that fiery night, having pulled the ripcord at high altitude, as soon as he abandoned the bomber. This gave him a descent to earth lasting fifteen frigid minutes. He had almost been strangled by the twisted strap of his musette bag pulling tightly across his face in the parachute deployment, and the pain and discomfort of this injury seems to have prevented his consciousness being dulled by the incipient hypothermia and hypoxia of the deep-freeze descent from altitude. Instead, this slow descent gave him a thinking interval in which to take in the fiery scene he was dropping into. His acute imagination was not dulled by the oxygen deprivation, for on the way down he started becoming hypersensitive to the 'creaking, straining' sounds of the parachute shrouds by which he was suspended beneath the silk canopy. Terrifyingly, he could not escape the notion that those sounds signalled the taut cords breaking under the strain and pitching him to his death in the abyss below. Swept along by his speeding train of thought, he saw that his premonition had come shockingly true: 'I found it hard to believe that the shadow of suspicion had become the terrible substance of reality: it was a one-way flight to Berlin.' Also rushing through his mind came rueful thoughts that his present, self-inflicted predicament was ill-fitted to his supposedly responsible role as husband to a 'young British wife', and father to his two-year-old son. But outside and beyond the conflicted inner life of the precariously dangling parachutist, the sky battle raged beyond:

Beneath me, as much as I could see with the strap cutting into my mouth and throat, the fires spread larger and clearer. I was coming down right into the target area and a new fear, that I would drop into one of the fires, rushed through my brain, elbowing out all other thoughts.

A burning plane screamed past below, so close there was a momentary rush of hot wind on the bootless feet. A nearby shell-burst rocked the parachute and for a frantic moment I thought it had been pierced. Then, in the space of a few short gasps for breath, I counted three stricken bombers, careening like flaming meteors toward the ground. A gust of wind caught the parachute and I twirled and spun as helplessly as an untended marionette ...

The descent was desperately slow and deathly cold. Fifteen or twenty minutes had elapsed since I had left the plane; it seemed eternal hours. I felt myself drifting away from the city and the fires. My eardrums were now so swollen inward with the air pressure, I could no longer hear the planes and guns clearly. Deep anger began to replace fear and excitement.

A lone searchlight swung onto me, its glaring whiteness eating through closed eyelids. I waited for a moment for it to swing away, and when this did not happen, was overwhelmed with fury ... after a moment the search-light moved off through the sky.

Suddenly, off to the side and below, there was a glint of light, sparkling and reflecting on water. I tugged desperately at the shrouds on one side of the chute, to veer off landwards, but to no avail, for the lines were ice-coated and stiff.

Almost immediately I struck, smashing through thick reeds, plunging waist deep into mud and chest deep into water. Its frigidity brought quick sanity. I twisted the release apparatus on the chute harness, punched it, and felt the sail fall loose and drift away. Then I seized the life preserver and tore down the handle which automatically inflated it.

I was down safely. Worst damage, as far as I could make out, was a badly cut lip, two scratches on my ankle from flak or plane fragments, and awfully cold arms and legs.

Bennett's account of his shoot-down and parachute descent typifies the spatial and geographical disorientation of the bomber crews that night, caused by the flak, fire and searchlight-blinded scene all around. He thought he had come down over the target – Berlin – and that the fires he saw below from his parachute were those of the great capital city itself, whereas in fact his Lancaster had actually come down near Potsdam, more than 35 kilometres southwest from the centre of Berlin, and therefore about ten minutes' flying time short of the real target.

Potsdam and its environs formed part of only the outer ring of Berlin's searchlight and flak defences; such navigational misapprehension was common that night, particularly as the elite pathfinder crews themselves had been led astray by the un-forecasted winds en route to the target. Many of their navigators failed to diagnose the strength of the crosswind, so that the pathfinders' flight paths drifted southward of the bomber stream's intended route into Berlin. The result was that instead of the bomber stream tracking as planned into Berlin from the northwest, via the towns of Stendal, Rathenow and Nauen, it tracked much further to the south, via Genthin, Brandenburg and Potsdam. The airmen mistook the latter places for the former, the province of Brandenburg being so studded with lakes and towns that the radar echoes became indistinguishable on the navigators' tiny H2S radar scopes. So instead of crossing into Berlin over the northwestern suburbs as intended, the bomber stream had entered Berlin's defended zone from the city's southwest corner, with many crews mistaking satellite towns like Potsdam for the Big City itself.

B-Bolty crashed to earth on the eastern shore of Lake Schwielow, while Bennett landed only a short distance to the west, in the lake itself. This district was semi-rural, so the fires he had seen were either the result of wayward RAF bombing of nearby Potsdam, or decoy fires set in open country by the Germans to deceive the bomber crews. Such decoys had been a standard passive-defence tactic used to confuse night raiders for years, and the RAF knew it, for from 1941, crew briefings had included identifications of such decoy sites and warnings not to be fooled by them. In the ongoing game of deception and counter-deception between the RAF and the Luftwaffe, the Germans gave their fake fires a further appearance of authenticity by surrounding them with a ring of searchlight and Flak batteries, just like a real target. The final touch was the launching of fake parachute marker flares into the sky over the decoy target area, fired into the air by rockets, as well as the ignition of fake marker flares on the ground. A June 1943 report by Bomber Command's Operational Research Section concluded that German decoys had contributed to about half of the RAF's failed raids, noting with concern the appearance of decoy 'sky marker flares' which replicated even the RAF's most recently introduced red target markers.

Berlin's 1st Flak Division had a unit specifically tasked with setting these decoy fires in the countryside and firing fake target-marking flares, and on the night of 2 December this unit set seventeen large decoy fires to simulate large urban fires, as well as seventeen 'success fires', representing smaller, fresher fires recently ignited by incendiaries. In addition, they fired 170 fake marker flares from flak guns and rockets, these replicating the appearance of pathfinder target markers so as to draw bomber crews away from the real aiming point. Mistaking such plausibly located dummy fires for burning buildings and suburbs remained an easy mistake for frightened and disorientated bomber crews, and on this night these various ruses seem to have had some success, as the decoy sites attracted twelve 4000-pound blockbusters, thirty-eight other high-explosive bombs and more than 12 000 incendiaries. Given the location of their crashes, and their misidentification of their bombing targets, it is possible that both Bolton's and Mitchell's crews had been misled by fake ground fires around Potsdam. They were certainly not the only ones to do so.

Another crew that had taken off from Binbrook that evening, 460 Squadron's J-Johnnie, flown by 26-year-old Flight Lieutenant Tom Alford, from Sydney, also fell prey to navigational misadventure and resultant wayward bombing. Alford was a 'cool', mature, experienced pilot who had previously flown fourteen operations at the head of his crew. On the run in, Alford and his bomb aimer, Flight Sergeant Laurie Leask, identified the target, opened the bomb doors, and stabilised the aircraft on to its bomb run. Scarcely had the crew heard in their earphones Leask's welcome announcement, 'Incendiaries gone' than their Lancaster was struck from behind by fighter gunfire. Startled by the gunfire, the pilot pushed, pulled and swung upon the control yoke to heave the damaged Lancaster through a sequence of violent evasive corkscrews. But after that the bomber was struck again: the night-fighter had managed to stay behind the corkscrewing bomber, waiting for it to resume level flight and then attacking again.

In the second attack, the fighter's explosive ammunition sawed through the Lancaster's fuselage and starboard wing, igniting the fuel tanks. Alford warned the crew, 'prepare to abandon aircraft', and when the fire extinguishers failed to put out the flames called, 'Abandon aircraft!' Laurie Leask, closest to the emergency exit in the nose compartment, jettisoned the hatch immediately and cleared the way for the others by jumping out first. Meanwhile each of the others had grabbed his parachute pack, hooked it on to his chest harness and stepped past the pilot, following Leask out one by one while Alford held the aircraft right way up to enable their escape. Last in the queue exiting through the nose hatch was the navigator, Flight Sergeant Eric Daley, who by now could see the starboard wing 'blazing furiously'. As he reached the hatch to jump, he saw that Alford was getting ready to leave his seat to follow him out.

The wireless operator, Flight Sergeant Norm Ginn, had gone aft to exit the aircraft via the crew entry door on the starboard side of the rear fuselage. On the way past the mid-upper turret in the bullet-torn centre fuselage, he saw that the parachute pack of mid-upper turret gunner, Flying Officer David Hore-Browne, remained in its storage rack. Looking inside the turret he saw that Hore-Browne was dead, hit by the second fusillade of cannon fire. Hurrying past, he arrived at the open rear hatch, where he found the rear gunner, Warrant Officer Mason, hunched by the exit with his parachute pack already clipped to his harness, but seemingly too fearful to jump. The only thought in Ginn's own head was, 'Get out!', so he set Mason a good example by stepping straight past him and leaping into the void. Unseen by Ginn, Mason snapped out of his stupefaction and followed him out.

Ginn coolly free-fell for some thousands of feet before pulling the ripcord. Although this was his first parachute jump, he had such complete confidence in the parachute that he 'just accepted it' when the canopy and shroud-lines tumbled out of his chest pack and brought him up with a wrenching jerk. Now descending quietly and slowly beneath his canopy, Ginn heard the engines of the other bombers 'going back home' and felt 'a bit sad' to be left behind. Meanwhile his parachute drifted him with the wind out of the well-lit searchlight zone and out into the dark sky beyond the edge of the defended area. Thanks to his freefall, he had seen no other parachute since leaving the aircraft and had also not seen what happened to his Lancaster. Looking below, he saw a white expanse beneath him which he took to be a lake. He was at once seized with fear of going into the freezing water, but before he could do anything about it, 'Bang!', hit the hard ground and tumbled over to sprawl upon the frozen earth. Luckily it had not been a lake after all, but a snow-covered paddock.

As Ginn scrabbled in the snow, the bombers' engine noises must have been coming mostly from the sky to the north, because unknown to her crew J-Johnnie had overshot Berlin and gone on to a misdirected bomb run far beyond the city's southern outskirts, nowhere near the prescribed target area in the centre of Berlin. J-Johnnie was shot down by Corporal Heinz Oberheide from Night Fighter Wing 3 at 8.33 pm, the defences' twenty-fifth bomber victim that night. Oberheide's crew noted their victim as going down in a position estimated as between 10 and 35 kilometres *east* of Berlin. A flak unit also claimed this kill, noting that the bomber came down near the small town of Märkisch Buchholz, a location more than 50 kilometres south-southeast of the centre of Berlin. Once again, an experienced and competent Lancaster crew had believed that they were over the target when they had in fact skirted it far to the south and completely overshot the city, bombing the forests, lakes and meadows of the Spreewald district by mistake. It is likely that this was another crew deceived by a decoy site.

The pilot, Tom Alford, did not survive, as was more or less usual for the pilots of doomed aircraft. It was well understood that it was almost impossible for the pilot to get out, as the crippled aircraft would somersault on to its back as soon as he relaxed his pressure upon the controls. In fact, he had gotten out but had not survived the jump: Norm Ginn would later be told by German interrogating officers that Alford's body was found beside the burning wreck: the pilot had somehow wrestled himself out of the escape hatch, but only just before the tumbling bomber speared into the ground, too late for him to deploy his parachute before striking the ground right alongside. On average a mere 10 per cent of Lancaster aircrew escaped alive from their shot-down aircraft, and the crewmen with the best chances of getting out were those who shared the forward fuselage with the ill-fated pilot, as their work stations were close to the escape hatch in the floor of the nose compartment: namely, the bomb aimer, flight engineer, navigator and wireless operator. So it proved in this case, and those airmen thus selected by fate and circumstance to survive the destruction of their aircraft, like Norm Ginn, found themselves on the ground and alive. And if they had come to earth uninjured, their next duty was to evade capture. Ginn knew the drill: he gathered up his parachute and harness and started digging in the snow to hide these giveaway items from the inevitable German ground pursuit.

CHAPTER 8

SURVIVORS

Bennett would have envied Norm Ginn his chance to dig a hole in the snow to hide his parachute, for at about the same time he had splashed down up to his waist in freezing water. The young American reporter found himself mired in a shallow, reed-filled lake, and immediately saw that there were other ways for airmen to die than by fire and explosion. Ill-dressed for the occasion, he was dragged into the icy water by the sodden, absorbent mass of his trench coat. In his attempts to stay upright his bare feet slipped from beneath him in the mud as he vainly clutched at yielding 3-metre-high reeds. The only slightly solid footing he found was that provided by the root mass at the base of each clump of reeds, but even so he kept slipping into the deeper water, saved from foundering only by the buoyancy of his life preserver. He was going nowhere, and getting colder and weaker:

> The coat and musette bag were becoming heavier all the time. I was dully aware of a terrible coldness throughout my body. The exertion of each step was a tremendous physical effort. I had only managed to take about twelve steps, and had no idea if I was going in the right direction. My watch had recorded 8:35 after I landed, and by 10:30 I had covered less than twenty feet from the harness, behind which stretched the parachute, limp, deflated, ghostly white.

> I could feel my legs freezing in the mud and water;
> my fingers were already numb and helpless. I knew
> I would have to reach dry land soon or freeze in the
> black solitude of this lake.

The exhausted Bennett stopped his energy-draining floundering through the mud and stood on a reed-clump as high up out of the water as he could, reduced to shouting for help into the night: 'Komm hier. Help. Godammit, get me out of here.' Soon his voice became too weak to shout, and in his frozen, exhausted state, he 'reached the stage where it no longer mattered if I were saved'.

While Bennett struggled for his life in the icy lake, Alf King's G-George had at last got clear of the flak and disappeared into the darkness of the night, escaping the vast upended cone of tremulous luminosity that sat so malevolently over Berlin. Luckily, King's pilot, Bill Forbes, found a welcoming bank of cloud hovering beyond the city outskirts, allowing the Lancaster to complete the return journey to the enemy coast in the safety of 'complete cloud'. Hidden thus from the attentions of both flak and night fighters, it was a relieved journalist who regained his view of the earth only in the last half hour of the flight, while descending over the North Sea en route for home. His relief was complete when Forbes lined 'George' up on Waddington's flarepath and put the wheels gently down upon the runway for a perfect landing. King 'breathed a sigh of happy relief, despite the thrills of the experience he would never have missed'.

Murrow's D-Dog too flew home safely:

We began to lose height over the North Sea. We were over England's shores. The land was dark beneath us ... We were over the home field. We called the control tower and the calm, clear voice of an English girl replied, 'Greetings D-Dog. You are diverted to Mulebag [RAF Coningsby]'. We swung round, contacted Mulebag, came in on the flare path, touched down very gently, ran along to the end of the runway and turned left. And Jock, the finest pilot in Bomber Command, said to the control tower, 'D-Dog clear of the runway'.

Due to fog at Woodhall Spa, all of No. 619's operating aircraft were diverted to RAF Coningsby, home to the famous No. 617 'Dambusters' Squadron. After landing, Jock Abercromby taxied D-Dog along the perimeter track, parked the Lancaster on the indicated hardstanding and shut down the engines. In the sudden silence the crew collected their flight gear and waited for the van to come by to deliver them to the station ops room. The returning crews assembled one by one in the ops building for debriefing, where the staff chalked each crew's landing time onto the ops board. As time went on, Murrow noticed that two of the ten aircraft dispatched by No. 619 that night had still not returned. Nonetheless, the other crews reported themselves satisfied with their bombing; the squadron recorded that the raid had been 'a good one', with 'fires seen burning when 150 miles away on return journey'.

Far from the hot cocoa, sweet buns and pent-up nervous banter that Murrow found in the Coningsby ops room, Bennett was still freezing to death in his lake. It was Berlin in December, when night-time minimum temperatures get down to -1 degrees Celsius, with water temperatures only a few degrees warmer. By this time, the night sky was silent, the bombers having long since departed German airspace: 'The sky had grown completely dark except for a vivid reflection in one direction, and the water no longer mirrored the vivid hues of explosions and fires as when I had first landed.'

By now he was close to collapsing into the freezing water from exhaustion, there to succumb silently to hypothermia. But then he heard men's voices. Bennett summoned enough strength, and enough schoolboy German, to resume shouting, 'Ist kalt hier ... Komm hier, bitte'[*]. He heard the voices shouting back, and then the sounds of creaking oars, water washing against wood, and 'the rhythmic breathing of men'. A boat finally hove into view above the reeds. He saw two men aboard, one of them heaving on a long pole to punt the boat through the shallows. Finally, it was close enough for that man to reach the pole out to the swamp-mired survivor, to give him a handhold so he could be dragged aboard. But Bennett's hands were too numbed for use: he eagerly grabbed the pole, but his frozen fingers just slid off when the boatmen tried to pull him in. The rescuers punted laboriously forward another couple of metres, rearranged themselves in the boat, and reached over the gunwale to get him. Each of them took an arm and pulled together. Bennett felt like the catch of the day as he was pulled aboard, wet, cold and slippery as a fish. He had feebly shouted from the water that he was 'Amerikaner', and the two men now

---

[*]   'It's cold here ... come here, please.'

pulled him to his unsteady feet and looked him up and down. One of them confirmed to the other, 'Ja, Amerikaner.' Bennett lost his balance and fell on his face in the 'shallow mud and water' that sloshed about in the boat's bilges. One of the Germans then pulled him back up to sit on the wooden thwart, and then kneeled by him, trying to restore Bennett's circulation by rubbing his legs:

> First one man worked the pole while the other rubbed my legs – then they changed places. I could not help thinking how decent of them it was to do that for me …
>
> Finally, we broke free from the reeds, out into clear water, clear moon and starlight, and I saw we were on a fair-sized lake. Some feeling was coming back into my legs and arms, and morale was returning.

He was saved.

While Bennett was mired in the lake, his pilot, Ian Bolton, was not far away but on dry land, trying to make distance from the crash scene. Initially stunned by the blow to his head and overcome by the shock and adrenalin of his near-death experience and miraculous escape, Bolton had succumbed to momentary unconsciousness as he lay on the ground at the base of the tree in which his parachute had snagged. When he got up, he found the night 'bitter cold' despite his flying kit: the pilot's seat in a Lancaster was the warmest place in the aircraft as it was adjacent to the cockpit heating outlet, so pilots flew only in woollen battledress uniform (albeit with woollen underwear underneath) – unlike the gunners, who in their freezing cold turrets flew in all that plus electrically heated sheepskin flying overalls. To warm up a bit and to get away from the tell-tale wreck, the inadequately dressed Bolton started walking, taking a path through some woods. Coming to a track, he saw that some buildings loomed up against the darkness ahead, and to avoid them took a path around them through the fields, using a few bushes for cover. 'Suddenly a shadow detached itself from the darkness and I saw a gun glinting. I was on a flak site and a sentry challenged me.' The 'bushes' had been sandbagged defensive positions! He blurted out, 'That's it; here I am. What's next?' Bolton was captured.

Another would-be evader, Norm Ginn, was on the ground at the same time, but about 50 kilometres to the east, on the far side of Berlin's southern suburbs. As we have seen, this Australian airman had parachuted from Tom Alford's 460 Squadron Lancaster after it was clobbered by a fighter at the end of its bomb run. Having come down heavily in a field, he hastily stuffed his parachute underneath an unconvincing mound of snow and then set off, trying to remember what he could of the escape and evasion routine he had been taught during training. Confronted now with the necessity of applying it, he decided that the training had been very poor, as about all he remembered was the injunction to keep off the roads. As he walked uncertainly into the night, he took stock of the contents of the aircrew escape kit issued to each man before take-off: a chocolate bar, a tube of condensed milk, water purification tablets and a silk map. He risked turning on his torch to try to orientate himself to the map but quickly decided that the map was not fit for purpose, being too small, at too great a scale, with minimal geographical detail.

Despite his dissatisfaction with his resources, he persisted, heading south with the ambitious intention of walking across Germany to the south of France and thence neutral Spain. In the distance he saw car headlights stabbing the horizon and supposed it was a German military vehicle picking up the other members of his crew. Avoiding the roads, his improvised route took him through a pine forest, but he found the undergrowth so thick that he could not help making a racket as he crashed through the branches. While Ginn was bashing self-consciously through the undergrowth, afraid of the noise he was making, his fellow countryman and crewmate, Laurie Leask, was moving through the same forest, similarly walking south away from the crash site. Leask heard someone crashing clumsily through the forest and went quietly to ground to let him pass; he assumed the noisy walker was a clumsy German soldier on the hunt for RAF aircrew on the run. The two crewmates thereby missed a chance to reunite. But Leask's instincts were good, as he successfully dodged several German patrols during his evasion. By sun-up on 3 December, Ginn and Leask were still at large, separated, but both successfully on the run.

At the same time as the two Australians were heading away on foot, Bennett was still in the boat with his rescuers, suffering from hypothermia in his heavy, saturated clothing. However, now that he was no longer immersed in near-freezing water, his frozen legs were slowly warming up, and he felt some strength returning. He watched as the boatmen rowed the boat towards a now-visible 'blurred, darkened shore'. After that he felt the keel ride up onto a beach. By now Bennett was keenly aware of the pistol sitting in its holster, hidden beneath his coat. The boatmen had not frisked him for weapons. One of the men jumped ashore and pulled the boat further up the beach. The other man took Bennett's arm to help him off the boat. With a rush of animal instinct Bennett made his move:

> Now or never, I thought. We had taken a few steps up the beach. My legs were not steady, but I felt I could stand on them alone.
>
> I shook the man's hand from my arm, swung away from him and turned to face both of them. The other was scooping up the oars in the boat, and looked up at the noise. In the bright third-moon, I could see their faces and felt sure they could see the gun which I pointed and waved at them, motioning the one on shore back toward the boat. He hesitated.
>
> *'In dem Boot'*, I ordered, as softly as possible, in case there should be others nearby, and pointed the gun towards the row-boat. Both men looked stupidly surprised. I honestly felt very badly about it. They had been kind to me, much kinder than I would have been to them under opposite conditions.

Having run out of German, Bennett continued his instructions, somewhat apologetically, in English. His plan, such as it was, conceived in the milliseconds between impulse and action, was to send his captives back out on to the lake in the boat while he made his escape on foot:

The man on shore stepped back into the boat ... The other man stood stock-still, balancing the two oars and looking more than somewhat confused. Neither of them made any move to sit down and row.

Then I made the mistake. I had been standing in water ... I felt my shoe-less feet becoming numb again. I moved sideways out of the muddy hollow, still facing the boat ... The second step was into a hole ... I fell sideways, the gun spilling out of my hand as I clutched for something to keep me on my feet.

I didn't see him, but I felt him coming, one of the men from the boat. He hit me in the back with his shoulder like a football tackler and I thought my leg was broken. The air went out of me as into a vacuum.

Bennett tried to get out from under his tackler and get back to his feet, but the man pinned him down. Between the frantic physical effort and the adrenalin, Bennett ended up lying 'alone on the ground, panting as if I had been wrestling for hours'. By then his assailant had let him go: 'I looked up to see the other man, holding my gun and pointing it at me, motioning me to get up.' His impulsive escape plan scotched, Bennett allowed his opponent to grab him by the arm, pull him to his feet, and lead him along a path, covered by the man with the pistol, who now followed more warily behind. Bennett would be going into captivity after all.

He was led to a cottage by the shoreline, evidently the home of one of his rescuers, and whom he had gratuitously antagonised by threatening with his pistol. Once inside, they let bygones be bygones, stripping him of his sodden outer clothing, heating a basin of hot water, placing his numbed feet into the basin, and making him a *Leberwurst* sandwich, served with a cup of hot coffee:

> The actions were quick, decisive; they seemed not at all interested in the personality of their prisoner, only in his immediate physical needs.
>
> Both bread and coffee were *ersatz*. But after the experience of four hours in a lake, both were eminently acceptable. No fine brewed coffee has since been as welcome even though this drink seared a dangling, badly cut lower lip.
>
> With the food, the light, and the decreasing numbness of brain and extremities, sanity returned slowly. I looked about the room and at the two strangers who had saved me.

He saw that one was young and 'pleasant', a junior noncommissioned officer (NCO) in the German army, and that the other was older and harder, a civilian. Perhaps to make amends for his bad behaviour, Bennett pointed at his musette bag, intending to offer them a smoke from his stash of 200 American cigarettes. Unfortunately, the cigarettes' cellophane wrapping had failed the immersion test, for when one of the Germans drew out the packet it turned out to be a sodden, melted mess of paper, tobacco and wrapping. The disappointment of all three men was no doubt partly assuaged when the older man reached into his own pocket and offered Bennett what proved to be a 'tasteless German cigarette' instead. Bennett found that the 'ersatz' cigarettes, 'dung-filled' or not, lightened the previously strained atmosphere, for some broken banter ensued in 'hybrid' English-German about Mrs Roosevelt and about Bennett's ludicrous escape aspirations.

After an hour a civilian woman arrived, evidently tipped off to the presence of a real-life prisoner in her neighbourhood. About 40 years old, she spoke 'reasonable English' and had moreover brought a 'tremendous' English-German dictionary to help make up for any mutual linguistic limitations. She was Margarete Thurnhofer from the nearby village of Flottstelle, which lay on the eastern shore of Lake Schwielow. With the help of the dictionary, Frau Thurnhofer and Bennett conversed about the war. He discovered that her husband was an infantry sergeant on the Eastern Front, and that she had not seen him for seventeen months. He found that his female interlocutor was a Berliner, that she had been evacuated from the city only days before, along with her 12-year-old daughter, and that her only other child, a 7-year-old son, had been killed during one of the RAF raids. Putting aside any understandable animosity, the woman's maternal instincts must have been aroused by the boyish, injured 23-year-old American before her, for she wrapped him in the blanket she had brought with her, and darned his badly torn sock. Bennett questioned her about the air raids as she went to work with needle and thread, and she surprised him with her vehement response, 'They are hard. But we will not capitulate.'

By the early hours of 3 December both Bennett and Bolton were in the hands of captors, but a number of other survivors remained at large. Neville Anderson, the navigator in Stockton's aircraft, whom Stockton was going to write up in a local-interest story for the benefit of his fellow Queenslanders back home, made a safe parachute landing in the darkness, as we have seen. Examining himself, he found he had suffered only superficial wounds and bruises on his right foot, so he set off at once, trying to get away from the crash site. En route he met up with both the flight engineer, Dusty Miller, and the bomb aimer, Alf Catty, who had come down in the same 'stick' of parachutists. Miller was also slightly injured, having been nicked on the leg by a bullet from the night-fighter. The party split up, with Catty going off alone in one direction, while the other two men walked together for nine hours, moving northwest in a direct line away from the wreck. They rested up in the small hours in a deserted pigsty, and then resumed their walk, covering about 12 miles before dawn. Trying to take advantage of a layer of light mist in the predawn darkness, they passed directly through a small village, but the gamble backfired, for there they were seen and quickly apprehended. Thus they passed into German military custody, where they were joined by Catty, whose evasion attempt had likewise come to nothing. Although Anderson had identified the place where he was captured as 'Groningen', the village's name was Mahlenzien, in the Havel region of the province of Brandenburg, far to the west of Potsdam.

While these three survivors entered the Luftwaffe POW processing system, their five crewmates would be decently buried in the villages where they fell. The bodies of Alex Kan and George Cole were interred in the cemetery at Göttin, in the village where their bodies had come to earth, while the remains of James English, Ivan Rodin and Norm Stockton were put to rest in the cemetery at Pruetzke, within the municipal bounds of which they had plunged to the ground. A local woman, Frau Thiele, afterwards continued to look after the airmen's graves in Göttin, and on 22 November the following year decorated them with flowers according to the local observance of *Totensonntag*, the annual Lutheran day of remembrance for the dead. Another pious woman performed the same service in Pruetzke, for the graves there were also 'tidily kept' and similarly decorated on the holy day.

While the bodies of their comrades were being collected from their wrecks and prepared for burial, the survivors had lived to see the next day, albeit in German custody. Lowell Bennett was luckily numbered among them, processed alongside airmen survivors and would-be escapees like Neville Anderson, Alf Catty and Dusty Miller. Bennett officially entered the POW system when two 'impressively military' sergeants arrived at his hosts' lakeside cottage just before dawn, to take him into military custody. The men were from a local searchlight battery, and these two soldiers were tasked with escorting the prisoner back to the battery command post. No doubt warned about Bennett's oppositional tendencies, one of the sergeants carried a revolver, and the other a sub-machine gun. The former was as belligerent in his own way as Bennett had been on the beach the night before, intimidating the captive by a close-up staring contest, followed by a volley of accusatory facts – his wife had been caught up in the previous RAF raid on Berlin, and was still in hospital with two broken ribs. 'What did I think of that?', he barked into Bennett's face. Although intimidating, the dramatic effect was lessened somewhat by the pause while Bennett's 'not unattractive' female interlocutor laboured to render a version of the sergeant's speech into English. Bennett could see the man's point, but did not allow himself to empathise:

> What the hell could I think? First of all, I was too cold to think. And if I was doing any mental work, it was about my own seemingly pathetic condition – about a wife and son and the absence of a bank account – and not about some comic opera sergeant's rib-less wife. What did I think about broken ribs? Too bad, that's all. I drove an ambulance during the blitz on London, and picked up a lot of good people whose bomb-authored injury was far more severe than broken ribs. War is obviously hell. But his wife's ribs were hardly my concern. Those things, however, must not be told to an armed German sergeant, when your marrow imitates an icicle, and you're wrapped in a blanket with no pants. So I tried to register deep sympathy, and asked the woman to translate, 'It's a difficult war'.

This seemed the right answer, for the gruff sergeant softened and held out 'another of those tasteless, but warming, cigarettes' as a peace offering. Then the two soldiers marched him off on the first leg of his journey through the POW processing system. Bennett was still barefoot, so before setting off on the walk to the command post, the boatman who had saved his life, and whom he had threatened with a pistol, generously 'loaned' him his own pair of carpet slippers. They were too big, but better than nothing. Thus shod, Bennett set off 'through the sharp, sobering morning air, in half-dried clothing and with half-warmed legs'. The revolver-armed soldier led the way, and the other one walked behind, with the unseen sub-machine gun pointing at Bennett's back. As he 'stumbled along slowly and awkwardly' on the hard, icy road in his rescuer's ill-fitting slippers, Bennett was struck by the melodramatic ludicrousness of his situation, by the shocking egotism of his escape attempt the night before, and by the beauty of the morning, as they walked through a forest of 'pine trees, silvered with frost and rooted beneath virgin snow': 'There was no war in the crisp invigoration of the air, nor in the white-mantled fields stretching away on either side. The only war here was in the sergeants and in myself.'

Arriving at the searchlight battery, the German sergeants brought him inside a hut and presented him to a 'youthful, dapper lieutenant', who greeted him politely in German with, 'How do you do? You speak German? Your papers, please.' The sergeants handed Bennett's identification papers over, and the officer perused them while considerately allowing Bennett to sit down and warm himself by the stove. Straight after, another soldier knocked, entered, gave a stiff 'Heil Hitler' salute, and brought in a captured RAF airman. It was none other than Bennett's pilot, Ian Bolton. Bolton's sudden appearance came as a pleasant surprise to Bennett, who had last seen him struggling at the controls of B-Bolty and who had given him up as lost in the spinning, burning wreck of their Lancaster: 'Now, he walked into the room looking just as neat and composed as he had on the airfield in England. We greeted each other as reunited brothers.' Taking Bolton's identity papers, the

German lieutenant obligingly permitted the two men to talk while he completed the paperwork.

Bennett discovered that Bolton had had a better night than he had: having been apprehended when he blundered into the flak site in the darkness, Bolton too had been taken into a hut, and had also been gawked at by curious local civilians who came in to view the captive; but his clothing was dry, he retained his footwear, and he had been conveyed by car to another location, rather than walking there; he had even been granted a few hours' sleep on a hard bed. But on the other hand, Bennett thought Bolton still seemed a little concussed by the blow to the head he had suffered as the aircraft came apart; he also found him 'heavily weighed down with the responsibility' for the other six men in his crew, constantly interrupting himself with agitated questions about 'what had happened to his boys'. But both men were greatly bucked up by the meal of coffee and brown bread that was brought in for them, and they 'ate as starved men'.

As the morning went on, other RAF survivors straggled in under guard; the 'miniature headquarters' of the searchlight unit was being used as the collection point for all POWs taken in the area. Soon there was a group of airmen sitting in a semicircle around the heater stove in the centre of the room, 'each enveloped in his own personal bewilderment, his ideas of escape, his half-dazed post mortem of the mission which had brought him here'. Like Bolton, each was weighed down by thoughts of lost crewmates. The facts bear this out: of the almost forty heavy bombers shot down over Germany that night, in only fifteen cases were there any survivors at all to be taken prisoner.

Of these fifteen 'lucky' crews, in only a single case had all seven men survived. Besides those few, every other man was bereaved. Bennett described the resultant mood:

> None of us talked much. What conversation there was came in sporadic bursts. Each tried hard to be brave and nonchalant and unruffled, although his own disaster filled his consciousness. The RAF boys, with a self-disciplined British background, held themselves well. One Canadian boy, however, represented another reaction to the situation. He was also the sole survivor from his plane, and cursed abruptly and violently every few moments, ... 'These goddam krauts' ...

Another exception was a 'small, bony Scotsman with a fiercely dirty face and a broken kneecap who had to be supported as he hopped painfully along'. As another sole survivor, this man was filled with grief, not only for his crewmates, but for his wife: they had married only two days before, and now he repeatedly asked himself out loud, 'What was his lassie thinking now?' Indeed, within just a couple of days she would be receiving the 'We regret to inform you' telegram from the Air Ministry, as we will see.

Bolton's agitation about the fate of his crew was justified, for two of his men had failed to get clear of B-Bolty before its cataclysmic destruction at 3000 feet: the navigator, Pilot Officer Alex Watson and one of the air gunners, Sergeant Ron Moody. The remains of both men were buried afterwards in Caputh. Despite the distance of rank (for Bolton was a flight lieutenant, Moody a sergeant) these crewmates had been good 'pals', and Bolton would be so 'terribly upset' by his friend's death that he never got over it to the end of his life. In the random manner of war, Moody had not gotten out, whereas by a pure fluke of circumstance Bolton had been flung clear in the explosion, miraculously still alive.

Life and death in the air war upon Germany's cities was random whether you were in the air or on the ground. Indeed, fate was as blind for the frightened civilians caught in their shelters as for the airmen and journalists caught by night-fighter gunfire in their aircraft as they passed overhead. Just like the airmen crouching within the illusory shelter of their bombers' aluminium fuselages, many of the civilian shelters down below provided protection that was part-illusory. A 13-year-old boy described his ordeal on one of the Berlin raids:

> It's not the first time that the sirens got us out of bed, and perhaps it will be the last time for many. Bombs scream ... dust whirls, and smoke comes into the cellar ... We hold onto each other fearfully. The light goes out. Flashlights turn on. The Colonel calls out that Mühlenstrasse 3 is burning ... Everyone has their gasmask on or wet towels over their noses and mouths. A yell frightens us all: 'The house is burning!' It was set alight from the house next door. The stairwell is already burning, so we can no longer save our building. Look out for the burning phosphorous [sic]! We can't stay in the shelter any longer. It's already burning too. We have to go outside onto the street, to take shelter in the public air raid trenches along the street. When

we emerge from the cellar, there is fire everywhere, everything is burning. Yells are ringing out and the fires are crackling. Everything gets lit up in green, from the phosphorous bombs. The trench is already quite full, but more and more people keep coming in.

By the cold grey dawn of 3 December, the same perverse process of arbitrary chance which had doled out to some German civilians the fate of personal survival but confronted them with the smoking ruins of their homes, had likewise doled out to two Australian airmen, Laurie Leask and Norm Ginn, the fate of having their aircraft reduced to a smoking hole in the ground, while they themselves still lived. And both men were still on the run to escape capture.

Leask applied the textbook evasion technique of walking through the night and resting up in a hiding place during the day, to avoid being seen. Ginn tried to do this too, and so when the sun started to rise on the morning after the raid, he found a covered position in which to lie. However, upon lying down to get some sleep, he found that it was just too cold to do so. Giving up on the sleep, he broke cover and resumed walking, just to stay warm. When night fell on the evening of 3 December, he was by then so tired that when he found a good, dry spot under some bushes, he successfully fell asleep, and slept through, despite the bitter cold. Resuming his walk in the morning of 4 December, he found that the extensive pine forests continued to provide cover from observation, but that his path was nonetheless taking him back towards settled districts: he had to cross a railway line, he skirted roads and villages, and he spotted people and avoided them. He even had to go to ground in the foliage while a soldier walked past.

Towards the end of that day, Ginn was hiding near a village and its outlying fields and farm buildings. When darkness fell, he hid in a haystack in a field outside the village to sleep, but it was so cold that he got little sleep. He persisted nonetheless, and got up at dawn, cold, tired and hungry. Besides the chocolate bar in his escape kit, his last meal had been the pre-mission lunch of 2 December, more than 60 hours earlier. Trying to take advantage of the early Sunday-morning quiet, this time he took a shortcut straight through the village, but unfortunately, the villagers turned out to be industrious early risers: he was discomfited to see a young girl out of doors, delivering milk to their front doorsteps. He managed to stifle his panic enough to give her a casual wave as he went past. As Ginn made his way down the street, he passed by a baker's shop. Being a Sunday, it was shut, but he could see some of yesterday's loaves in the shop window and was by now so famished that he even considered breaking the glass and stealing the bread, despite now being under observation from a few more early-rising village children. With his heart in his mouth and a growling stomach under his ribcage he walked beyond the village and just kept going, with as inconspicuous a gait as he could manage, and made it unmolested into the cover of the next forest.

Later that day (5 December), Ginn found his path blocked by a river, and cautiously made his way along its bank. Coming to a bridge, he saw it was overseen by a guard on the near side, who had stopped a group of about half a dozen people passing across the river and was questioning them at length. Trying to take advantage of this distraction, Ginn summoned up all his courage and nonchalance, skirting the press of people and crossing the bridge. As he neared the far bank, only now did he see that there was a guard on that side of the bridge as well. Ginn turned aside to avoid him, seeing as he did so that the soldier was an old man. The soldier called out a challenge, and Ginn ran for it. Even in his malnourished state he outran the older man, who did not fire either – perhaps this 'Dad's Army' type had not been issued with live ammunition?

By the end of that day, after three days without food, hunger was becoming such a big problem that in his fatigued and frozen state Ginn's resolve was weakening. This time he walked right through the night, perhaps so overcome with hunger pains and nausea that sleep was out of the question. He was crossing an open field in the darkness when he felt movement nearby. Assuming it was soldiers pursuing him, he stopped and turned to give himself up, only to realise that it was a herd of cows. Afterwards he skirted some houses, and then came to another river. Moving along its bank to another bridge, too late he perceived the outline of a man in the darkness. Ginn tried another nonchalant wave, then kept walking. But the man followed, and as he loomed out of the darkness, Ginn saw that it was a dog-handler with an Alsatian dog. He was caught. The dog-handler marched him to a nearby hut, where he was delivered to a young officer who questioned him politely. Ginn was surprised that the German officer spoke English 'as good as I could'. After a creditable evasion attempt, Ginn now joined Bennett, Bolton, Leask, Anderson and the other lucky survivors for a year-and-a-half stint in captivity.

Norm Ginn was apprehended on the night of 6 December, by which time the Berlin raid of only four nights before had already become old news in the newspapers back home. After his initial, rather genteel interrogation, he was taken by car to another location and placed in a cell. There he received 'quite a nice meal', his culinary appreciation no doubt sharpened by the fact that it was his first in almost five days. The next morning, he was put once more in a car and driven some distance away to another location, where he again was kept alone in a cell overnight. The next day (probably 8 December) he was taken by an officer and two guards on a train trip to the POW holding facility at Tempelhof, Berlin's pre-war civil airport in the southern suburbs of the city. Travelling on the above-ground S-Bahn line, Ginn had the novel experience of being stared at by the curious civilians who shared the carriage as they went about their daily commuting. However, this sign of normal life continuing was belied by the view out the train window of the bomb-damaged city.

Ginn was so struck by the extent of the devastation that he started to get worried that the civilians in the carriage might assault him as an act of vengeance. He could see that building after building had been 'flattened' by the bombing. Judging by his shocked response, it appears that Ginn had retained some scepticism back at Binbrook about the claims the RAF was making about its bombing results, because now that he was confronted with this sight of the target area close up, he was stunned to see that Berlin could actually look so 'awful'. As shocking as the sight was when viewed from ground level, bomber crewmen like Norm Ginn could have been neither ignorant nor naïve about what they had been doing to German cities in the course of their raids: crews would see their own bombing photos, and those of the other crews, pinned up in their operations room, showing the fires and flashes below, light scars set against the discernible grid-pattern of the cities they were attacking and setting ablaze. Now he got to see what this looked like up close.

After his short but harrowing train journey Ginn spent a night in a cell at Tempelhof, before being conveyed by train again the next day to Frankfurt. So far from being lynched by civilians in this much-bombed city in western Germany, upon arriving at Frankfurt *Hauptbahnhof* and being marched along the street to catch a tram, he was given some bread by a sympathetic civilian who evidently felt sorry for him. Indeed Ginn must have looked a particularly pitiable sight due to the burn injuries on his face, inflicted during his exit from his blazing Lancaster almost a week before. Nonetheless he was perhaps lucky not to be confronted with more hostility: after the sad carnage among the animals of Berlin Zoo during the raids of 22 and 23 November, the lamentable effects of which included the jarring sight of four dead crocodiles flung into the street in Budapester Strasse, one five-year-old boy had solemnly told his mother that he wanted to 'shoot dead all the English, but only when I'm old enough'.

Similar to Norm Ginn's experience, on the morning of 3 December Lowell Bennett with his party of captured RAF airmen had been given a similar tour of Berlin's bombed-out districts, when they were taken from their initial collection point at the searchlight command outside Potsdam, and driven to their next overnight stop at Tempelhof, where they would be processed at the same POW holding unit to which Ginn had been taken. The nine captives were conveyed in the back of an old truck with a tattered canvas cover, and although their guards dropped the canvas sides, evidently to prevent the prisoners from orientating themselves to the ground or gleaning intelligence along the way, there were so many holes in the old canvas screen that there was 'a crack for every eye'. Bennett peeked out enough to see that they were following a route along Berlin's east–west arterial road, then along the *Unter den Linden* boulevard through the very centre of the city, and then via an axial road out to Tempelhof in the southeastern suburbs.

Throughout the journey, the guards watched impassively as the POWs peeked out through the holes in the canvas. The tension in the truck was so palpable that no-one said a word the entire trip: perhaps the guards were embarrassed about their wrecked Reich-capital, while on their part the airmen might have been shocked to see the effects of their handiwork close up, just as Norm Ginn was, and perhaps rendered a little sheepish about what they had done.

Bennett certainly was as taken aback as Ginn was. Having seen artillery-ruined villages in 1940 France and 1943 Tunisia, and having driven ambulances around London during the 1940–41 Blitz, he considered himself a seasoned observer of wrecked buildings, but Berlin was something else:

> London had sections of gutted and gaping ruins, block-square fields of smashed debris where buildings had stood. But here was a city that had been killed,

hammered and pulverized, burned out and blown up with a completeness defying description.

… In that drive we saw very few glass doors left in the remaining buildings – and not one whole glass window.

The bulk of the damage seemed to have been caused by fire, as the RAF's Bomber Command had planned. Block after block, as we drove along, contained only shells of buildings, scorched black and half-molten with the heat of tremendous fires which had devoured them. Occasionally, there were evidences of the terrible 'blockbuster', and here, ten-story apartment houses were telescoped into ten feet of rubble.

Householders and shopkeepers in the less damaged areas were sweeping a harvest of glass off the streets and into neat piles along the gutters. Everywhere squads of khaki-clad Russian prisoners of war struggled to clear the wreckage. For every fifty prisoners there was a German guard …

Todt workers (of the German labor corps) were also to be seen in profusion. These men too were uniformed in khaki and worked, much like the Russians, to clear debris from the sidewalks, load trucks with removable salvage, tear down partly destroyed buildings, and return what was left of the city to a semblance of orderliness.

Other than the two groups of workers, very little civilian interest seemed focused on the awesome wreckage. Berliners hurried along the streets, some carrying suitcases and boxes, possibly carrying their last worldly possessions. Others moved along much the same as people on business in New York or London.

Bennett was witnessing the cumulative effect of the whole series of raids in the 'Battle of Berlin' so far, not just that inflicted in his own raid on the night of 2 December, but that had been the fifth in a series of raids starting on the night of 18 November, and the cumulative damage from all these raids had evidently become devastating. The second and third raids, on the nights of 22 and 23 November, had achieved concentrated bombing right in the central government district of Berlin, which bears out Bennett's observations of severe bomb damage even in the central district around *Unter den Linden*.

Descriptions of the devastated state to which Berlin had been reduced by the morning of 3 December can be corroborated from the German side. The Luftwaffe's 1st Flak Division, deployed to defend Berlin from air attack, counted the bombs which fell within Berlin in this five-raid series: 475 'blockbusters', 3000 smaller high-explosive bombs, and 770 000 incendiaries. Despite Berlin's strict imposition of civil defence measures to minimise civilian casualties, the detonations of these weapons during these five raids had killed 3801 people and wounded 16 041. Most people had died in building collapses: of these casualties, an estimated 4500 people had been buried in the rubble of collapsed buildings, of whom only 1202 were dug out alive.

In terms of material damage, hundreds of public buildings and industrial facilities had been bombed, an estimated 6000 private dwellings had been destroyed, plus 7000 heavily damaged, and another 57 000 with less severe damage. This left 510 000 people who had lost their homes and needed to be rehoused.

Confronted with such numbers, it is perhaps too easy to see the damage in abstract terms, but one woman in Berlin-Spandau has described her reaction to returning home after one of these Berlin raids:

> My eyes look for the old, well-known shop window frontage of my own apartment building, but the glance returns unanswered. Comically tiny appear the piles of wreckage that now lie between the high walls of the neighbouring apartment blocks. Do the 50 apartments of the building's residents and the strong walls of a giant apartment block really lie here like this? Did it really take only minutes, or even seconds for everything to be cracked and splintered and burst apart like this? Like a giant's fist the bomb crushed everything and anything.

Another Berliner, Luise Siedel, described in forensic detail what she saw of inner Berlin while seeking shelter from the 22 November raid. She had been caught by the raid while heading home from the People's Opera House in Charlottenburg, and was forced to endure a frantic night trying to find a shelter:

> The opera was over and I was heading for the underground railway when suddenly the air raid siren

sounded. Now I had to find a shelter, but where? I tried the Kaiser Wilhelm Memorial Church, but the shelter there was already over-full, so I had to go on further. Finally in Budapester Strasse I found a public shelter. After I had sat inside for some time, I noticed that there was smoke throughout the cellar. Luckily there was a water tap at hand. I wet my handkerchief, as I had no gasmask with me ... After a short time, they said that everyone in the cellar should get out, but not to panic. As I stepped out onto the street, my eyes were met with a sight that made me tremble. Everywhere I looked there was nothing but fire, fire and yet more fire. I took off, I wanted to go home. Yes, but no! I tried to go along the *Kurfürstendamm*, but there it was all fire, smoke and dust. I saw that Joachimsthaler Strasse was burning as well, but I really did want to get to the U-Bahn station. But when I finally reached the entrance to the U-Bahn, I couldn't get in as it was already packed with people. I started looking around the area, seeing that the Wilhelm Hall [a café and cabaret venue], the Ufa Palast am Zoo [an adjoining cinema], and the whole row of houses there were now a sea of flame. I went back into the *Kurfürstendamm*, seeing that the Kaiser Wilhelm Memorial Church was also burning. Then I ran further, along Tauentzien Strasse, and that was burning fiercely too. I tried to escape the fire by turning into small side streets, but the British had dropped their incendiary bombs into those as well. Wherever you went it was burning. Finally I reached the Wittenberger Platz, where a storm of wind suddenly came out of nowhere, blowing flames flat upon the ground; it looked like it was raining fire. But I really wanted to get home, so ran further, along Kleist Strasse. But there too it was all flame, as far as Nollendorf Platz. Along Bülow Strasse I stayed underneath the overhead railway as I went, as even in that street there were many houses burning. Finally I reached Potsdamer Strasse, thinking that here it would be better and safer, but it was exactly the same, just wreckage and fire. As I went across the Potsdamer Bridge the warning siren sounded a second time. I couldn't find shelter inside any of the houses, so went on, running as far as Potsdamer Platz, where I waited in the U-Bahn underground shelter until the all-clear. Then I went out again and saw that the Potsdamer railway station was in flames. I went along Leipziger Strasse as far as Charlottenstrasse, but couldn't go any further as it was blocked, because even there everything was burning. So I had to go further, as far as Hausvogteiplatz. From there a side street led to the Pleasure Garden, past the City Palace and into the Neue Königstrasse. By the time I reached City Hall, the *Haus des Zentrums* had been consumed by flames.

Frau Siedel's distressing journey home on one of the worst raids of the war provides testimony of how severely hit the centre of Berlin was on that night.

From accounts like these from German civilians, it is clear that Bennett and his companions were by no means the only people to be shocked at seeing the harrowing destruction of Berlin close up.

Although many shot-down Allied flyers found the devastation their work had wrought sobering, just as Bennett and Ginn did, some remained callous when confronted with the city's suffering. During the drive through the city to Tempelhof, an airman in Bennett's party looked up into the sky, observed the cloudy weather and then remarked with unconcealed glee, 'Looks like another good night for a raid.' Bennett found the man 'over-garrulous' for favouring his small band of survivors with his tactless and 'frequent comments on Germany's unhappy situation'. But the rest showed sensitivity and kept their mouths shut.

Arriving at Tempelhof airfield at the end of their eye-opening road journey, Bennett and his party were disembarked and marched into the administration block to begin their official induction into the POW processing system. They lined up before 'efficient' but 'somewhat officious' clerical sergeants from the Luftwaffe, who took down their identification details. There were also female soldiers, about whom the new POWs amused themselves by referring to them as *Luftwaffettes*. The captives willingly gave their names and numbers, for they knew that it was in their own interests to have their identities registered by the Germans, for only thus could their families and squadron mates receive confirmation that they were alive. They knew that the RAF casualty system would already have declared them 'missing', and that in Bomber Command that usually meant killed. Indeed, they could correctly suppose that their families were already being informed by telegram of the brute fact that they'd failed to return, and they knew that families were apt to fear the worst. So, having your name and number recorded by the Luftwaffe was the first step to their suffering loved ones receiving the joyous news of their survival.

Having had their identities inscribed in the roll of prisoners, the captives stood before a lieutenant and surrendered their personal effects, such as watches, pens and papers. 'You get everything back later', the lieutenant explained to Bennett 'in laborious English', 'eager to assure us that we would be well treated'. It took half an hour for this processing to occur. After that they were marched to a cell block, and each of them was locked into a tiny cell, nine feet by four. Each prisoner had thus been placed in solitary confinement. This was a standard protocol during interrogation to prevent the prisoners conferring and colluding, but to the gregarious Bennett, it was a torment. He found his cell so 'colorless, barren, lifeless' that his 'reaction was an overwhelming sense of hopelessness, friendlessness, and weariness'. After a few hours the door was unlocked, and an armed guard passed in a plate containing Bennett's 'first substantial food for more than twenty-four hours'. It was only 'a plate of thick barley soup', but in his reduced condition, he found it 'perfectly delicious'. The guard returned to collect the plate, leaving Bennett to resume his contemplation of his fate in the disquiet of isolation. Bennett found that 'Singing and whistling were no time-passers; the noise rattled off the walls and only re-emphasized the personal misery of such solitude.' In his desperation, he tried reciting all the poetry he knew, and 'then the Gettysburg Address and some of the Rubaiyat'.

Fortunately, the trial of social deprivation suddenly and unexpectedly ended that night when 'a guard swung open the door' and led him out of the cell. He and the others were brought into an anteroom, to be told they were being moved to another camp. But before they could be moved the air-raid siren sounded: it was the night of 3 December, and Air Marshal Harris had sent 500 bombers to Leipzig, with a few Mosquitos to raid Berlin as a diversion. No-one on the ground knew the raid was only a decoy, so with the sirens moaning their insistent warning, Bennett noticed the guards becoming 'hurried and jittery' as they ordered the POWs into their assigned shelter room. The prisoners were led in single file through the main shelter area, watched inhospitably as they passed by 'hundreds of scowling, anxious German faces' who had already assembled in their shelter. As he followed along, Bennett ruminated on his situation and rediscovered some humour: 'Go through every Goddamn *Luftwaffe* raid on London, then come to Berlin and be bombed by the goddamn RAF.' The prisoners, injured and able-bodied alike, were herded together into a too-small room, then the door was shut and bolted. With the 'indistinct coughing of the guns' and the 'hollow thumping of bombs' coming from the distance, the overcrowded room became hot from the press of men, and the air stale and humid from their massed, anxious exhalations. Finally, a 'red-faced Australian gunner' banged on the door and shouted, 'No air, mate. Leave the bloody thing open a bit. No air.' An annoyed guard appeared and reluctantly left the door ajar. With the slightly improved ventilation, Bennett found that at least the air inside the crowded room 'did not worsen'. After that the sirens blew the all-clear, the guards re-emerged from their own bunker and chivvied the POWs out of the underground shelter, back out to ground level, and onto a bus, for a 'several hour' trip to an anonymous depot, where each man was again placed into solitary confinement.

About noon the next day (on or about 4 December), Bennett's batch of POWs were driven back into Berlin in two trucks, one for the able-bodied and one for the wounded. Reaching the centre of Berlin, they were deposited in front of the Anhalter railway station, which connected Berlin to destinations in the south and so was regarded as the city's 'Gateway to the World'. There the twenty-nine prisoners disembarked, watched over by their seven assigned guards, each 'armed with an efficient-looking machine gun'. Bennett described the scene:

> While we stood in a loose group at the back of one truck, as the wounded were helped down and brought from the other truck, a crowd of citizens began to collect in a half-circle around us. There were housewives, with their laden shopping baskets and one with a bawling baby; there were boys, dirty-faced little urchins who stopped their street playing for a moment to watch the strange procession; and there were old men, who watched us as they might watch any other street spectacle.
>
> And we were a spectacle! With myself as an exception, everyone wore the blue battledress which was RAF flying uniform. But many of the jackets were torn; all were by now unpressed and dirty. Every one of us had at least two days' beard. Most of the boys still had on their flying boots; I was clad in carpet slippers. A third of us were wrapped in bandages, many standing on one leg

and leaning an arm around a companion's shoulder for support. We must have looked slightly deranged, like Dead End kids, and like the gangsters Dr. Goebbels had been describing to his readers – all at the same time.

But one of the English sergeants said something as the crowd thickened into a sizable group of sullen, curious spectators. He said something that made me think suddenly of Elgar's *Pomp and Circumstance* ... I had been watching the British boys more than the crowd. I wanted to see their reaction to the crowd. I noticed the sergeant looking around. He said, suddenly, without any apparent forethought: 'Chaps. Remember we're soldiers. We're British.'

And everyone strengthened a little: the British, the Australians, the Canadians ... and the American. Such a gesture meant nothing to the crowd, for it was busy inspecting our uniforms, our faces, our boots, our wounded, but ... at least one non-British witness was proud of him for it.

The guards formed us into a column, four abreast, and we marched into the station. 'Marched' is the wrong word, for two-thirds of us carried the other third and after the first few steps were well spread out. In the station, up the long sweep of stairs and onto the train platform we straggled, the guards hovering about us, their tommy guns slung within easy reach should any one of the unwounded try to leave in another direction.

Bennett himself helped carry a man with badly crushed legs, finding it 'hot, tiring work' despite the winter temperatures. As he sweated beneath his trench coat at his labour, he retained the presence of mind to take in the scene, finding Anhalter Station comparable in architectural grandiosity to New York's Grand Central or London's Victoria Station, and with 'the same thousands of hurried travellers, the same teeming confusion'. Witnessing these almost 'peacetime conditions', he was perplexed to see that the station building itself was undamaged, in contrast to the 'destruction outside'.

However, it seemed that beyond the confines of the undamaged train station, peacetime conditions no longer pertained to the German railway system, for when their train arrived, it was not even a German train, but a French third-class train (evidently requisitioned by the *Reichsbahn* for the German war economy), and it was half an hour late in departing the station. Once aboard and underway, the prisoners pestered their guards with questions, eliciting the admission that they were headed for Frankfurt-am-Main, to undergo formal interrogation at a processing camp, before onwards allocation to POW camps. The prisoners were confined to their own segregated carriage, but it was unlighted and unheated, and the trip was slow, with frequent stops at stations en route, at which Red Cross girls offered coffee and biscuits to the travellers. At each such stop, the passengers opened the windows on the station side of the carriage and leaned out, calling out to the girls to refill their cups from urns of hot ersatz coffee. Recognising that the POWs had no cups and so could not get the coffee, the guards relaxed their severe attitude by filling their own, military-issue water bottles with coffee and then passing these around for the prisoners to drink from.

The guards loosened up even further as the halting journey went on: when the trip started the guards would accompany each prisoner if they needed to go to one of the toilets at each end of the carriage, and then waiting outside to walk him back to the central seating compartment; but evidently fed up by this repetitive chore, the bored guards then started to permit the prisoners to go to the toilet without close supervision. Observing this and the disorder and distraction of the station visits, for a second time Bennett conceived the idea of escaping. He had been trying to get friendly with one of the guards by conversing with him in his 'execrable German', and now he exploited the resultant relaxed atmosphere by asking if he could visit the toilet. The guard gestured 'all right' with a wave and let him go by himself. Thus encouraged, Bennett 'decided to capitalize upon his unsoldierliness' when it got dark. When that time came and the train started slowing to a stop at the next station, and with his tame guard distracted by the need to get his canteen ready for another refill of coffee for the prisoners, Bennett seized the moment, asked the same question and was given the same casual 'all right' wave.

He made his way up the central aisle of the 'pitch-black' carriage but went straight past the toilet, instead passing through the communicating doors into the next carriage. He found it was a second-class carriage with an aisle going along the side, past a row of closed-off seating compartments. He walked to the far end of the carriage. However, there was a cluster of people at the exit door, readying themselves to step down from the carriage once the train came to a complete stop, and even with the dim lighting from the station lights, he dared not try to squeeze past them, knowing that the 'bright' military-style tunic buttons and 'US' insignia on his uniform could scarcely go unnoticed. In desperation, he entered the toilet of this second carriage and tried to get out through the window. But it was too small, so there he was, stuck with his feet on the toilet pedestal, his body contorted into an arch, his shoulders against the wall and his head out the window. In that vulnerable pose, 'I felt a hard knob press deeply into my stomach'. Bennett 'jumped a foot' from fright, slipped down, stood on the floor, and found himself face to face with his 'friendly' guard, who now held the barrel of his sub-machine gun 'buried hard' into the would-be-escapee's stomach. Then the soldier cocked the gun 'noisily' to emphasise the point. Bennett raised his hands above his head in submission, but his mind was still a whirr of wild, disordered impulses. The guard reached behind, opened the toilet door, stepped out, beckoned the prisoner out, told him to put his arms down, then walked him back to the POWs' carriage, following behind with the unseen menace of the 'Tommy gun' pointing at the prisoner's back. As he was marched down the aisle, Bennett felt 'terribly foolish, terribly frustrated', and these feelings were only sharpened by hearing what the guard said to him in German as they went. As far as Bennett could decipher, the guard was saying, 'You must not try to escape. You will freeze in this weather. And if you get away you might be killed.' The guard's restrained and measured response only made Bennett angry. Grinding his teeth together, he thought: 'You bastard, what are you being nice to me for? If I caught you trying to escape I'd probably kick your teeth out. Skip the advice and the condescension. Next time there will be no recapture.'

Needless to say, after this near-miss the guards did everything by the book for the rest of the trip: now they withheld themselves from conversation with their potentially devious charges, took it in turns to sleep, and were seen 'diligently counting heads' at every stop. By now it was 4 am, and with another three hours to go before arriving in Frankfurt, the prisoners too fell silent, worn out by the distress, discomfort and drudgery of their first two days' captivity. Exhausted, they succeeded in sleeping through the rest of the night journey 'despite the hard seats and cramped quarters'. The train arrived in Frankfurt in the predawn darkness, and at the *Hauptbahnhof* they were bundled out of the train and onto another one, a local train taking them on a half-hour journey to the outlying village of Oberursel, where the POW interrogation centre was situated. Arriving there with the 'first hints of gray light ... beginning to streak the sky', the men were herded out onto the street to form up again, 'shaking with cold' in the 'frigid pre-dawn air' at a tram stop. Standing in line with the others, Bennett found during the transfer from station to station that he had singled himself out for special attention, for 'During the entire time a guard stood beside me'. With the cold and exhaustion, the mood of the captives was subdued: 'None of the boys talked; no one had anything to say, or could or wanted to say anything if he had.' After waiting half an hour in the freezing cold, a three-car tram arrived. The guards ushered the other passengers out of one of these carriages, so that the POWs had a carriage to themselves. The tram even had electric lighting, quite a tonic after the unlit train trip, and in the warm electric glow Bennett saw that they were in a non-smoking car. He occupied his mind reading the advertisements posted on the walls of the car's interior; they boasted of 'German hair tonics, German toothpastes, German stockings'. Nationalism worked in advertising. The tram conductor came in and amused the watching and listening Bennett by discussing with one of the guards whether the prisoners needed to have tickets or not.

Bennett found the whole scenario 'fantastic'. Barely able to process the enormity of his experiences over the previous three days, his eyes 'swam with the sheer idiocy and tragic hilarity of the whole panorama, today's, yesterday's, and guesswork as to what would be tomorrow's':

> It was pure, out-of-this-world madness. It was like a movie or a book. Only it wasn't. Because you can put down a book or walk out of a movie. And here you were one of the chief actors in this crazed play.
>
> It was only seventy-two hours old, this episode, this personal melodrama. But the vortex of sudden change, of emotional and physical antithesis into which we had been flung, or flung ourselves when we had jumped from our planes, this confused, exotic lunacy was overpowering and uncontrollable.

CHAPTER 9

THE DEAD

While would-be evaders like Lowell Bennett and Norm Ginn were being trucked to Berlin and inducted into the German POW system, their dead comrades were being processed for burial. We followed Nordahl Grieg's Lancaster, H-Harry from the Australian 460 Squadron, to the point where it was shot down in the 'orchestrated hell' over Berlin's satellite city of Potsdam. We will now return to that location to see how ordinary German civilians experienced the 2 December raid, and what happened to the airmen who did not survive the destruction of their bombers. Potsdam was often overflown by bombers intent upon hitting Berlin and was routinely hit by wayward bombs intended for the capital. Formerly the royal residence for the kings of Prussia until the abdication of Kaiser Wilhelm II in 1918, its location on the southwestern approaches to the capital frequently placed it right on the bombers' approach path. For example, when the raid alarm sounded in Potsdam on the night of 2 December 1943, that was the 158th such alarm for the satellite city and its environs.

Just like the inhabitants of the much-bombed capital city to the east, the residents of such frequently overflown towns and villages on the outskirts of Berlin had to take cover in improvised bomb shelters whenever the raid alarm sounded. For example, the Sander family in the village of Kleinmachnow outside Potsdam had turned their house's cellar into a bomb shelter, with the floor overhead reinforced by tree trunks cut to size and propped up beneath the floor joists. This family shelter was used by the Sanders' neighbours as well; the man of the house, Eugen Sander, alerted the neighbours to the raid alarm by sounding his bugle. Any residents of these satellite communities who flouted the air-raid regulations to leave the shelter and steal an illicit look outside were well placed to witness fiery confrontations between British bombers and Berlin's defences during the bomber stream's contested passage across the flak zone. For example, from the gloom of the blacked-out village of Flottstelle outside Potsdam, the Thurnhofer family had a viewpoint eastward towards Berlin, and during the 2 December raid one of them risked leaving the basement bomb shelter to look outside: to the northeast this daring eyewitness was confronted with the awesome sight of a wide inverted cone of 'blood red' sky hanging over the capital, the pyrotechnic amalgam of searchlight beams, flak bursts, parachute flares, and fires.

During such raids the sight of blazing British bombers plunging to destruction became almost routine for those whose duties kept them above ground at posts around Potsdam, such as the thousands of men and boys serving in the numerous flak, searchlight and fire brigade crews. For these people, it was so common to see a flaming British bomber arcing downwards through the night sky somewhere out towards the horizon that such an event was scarcely worth recording. On the other hand, the destructive arrival of a shot-down bomber within one's own locality was sufficiently rare for each such incident to be vividly remembered. For the inhabitants of the usually tranquil village of Kleinmachnow, situated on the banks of the Teltow Canal, about 10 kilometres beyond Potsdam on the way to Berlin, one such memorable event in the repetitive series of Berlin raids was Nordahl Grieg's bomber crashing on the evening of 2 December 1943.

That evening the raid alarm sounded at 7.27 pm. The night sky over Potsdam was once more riven by the deep rumble of bombers trundling past in the darkness 4 miles overhead. As usual the British were seemingly using the Prussian royal city as a navigational waypoint en route to Berlin, despite its off-putting array of searchlights and Flak batteries. The citizens of nearby Kleinmachnow once again took shelter in their cellars, listening to the sharp crack of flak guns and the whistle and crump of wayward bombs, as the British bomber stream battled its way through the defended airspace overhead, doggedly heading towards Berlin. This was the bombers' fifth visit to the Reich capital since the RAF launched its winter Berlin Blitz on the night of 18 November. Small municipalities like Kleinmachnow were too insignificant to be directly and knowingly targeted by the RAF, but the surrounding fields, woods, marshes, canals and lakes nonetheless took their random share of wayward, misdirected bombs, and of crashing bombers.

Just outside the village that night, a detachment of SS soldiers was on duty at the 'Hakeburg', a grand country home on the southern edge of the built-up area. These soldiers stood guard duty at the building's resident radio research institute, an organisation involved in developing radio systems for guided bombs – a program which in typical organisationally incoherent Nazi fashion was run by the Reich Post Office. Nearby was a detachment of the volunteer auxiliary fire brigade, staffed by men too young or too old for service in the *Wehrmacht*. Among their number was 62-year-old local gardener and grandfather, Franz Marz, who earlier that year had along with a number of his peers been obliged to 'volunteer' for the local fire brigade. These newly conscripted men had thus 'volunteered' their time on weekends to undergo training in the fortress at Spandau, while during raids they stood duty in their home village, standing by to attend to any fires. On this night Marz had put his family to bed and then hopped on his bicycle to ride the short distance to join his colleagues at their duty station.

Men such as these, whose duties necessarily posted them at ground level rather than permitting them to take refuge below ground in bomb shelters, were positioned to see the tracer ammunition from the local Flak detachments firing at any low-flying bombers going past en route to Berlin. On the night of 2 December 1943, they could see the angry red bursts of the flak shells exploding around a single bomber that came on, approaching Kleinmachnow from the north, having turned off its Berlin-bound flight path. It then descended to an unusually low altitude, hotly engaged as it went by the rapid-firing Flak batteries emplaced round about. Back at home, Franz Marz's two grandsons had their sleep disturbed by the approaching battle in the sky; as they lay in bed, they were jolted to apprehensive wakefulness by heavy explosions which came and went from not too far distant.

These explosions came from the burning bomber which now passed over the village at an altitude estimated as 400 metres, jettisoning its bombs as it went. There came the shrieking of a salvo of bombs, followed soon after by the vast, earth-shaking explosion of a 4000-pound 'Blockbuster', and then the cracking and fizzing of the small incendiaries, a shower of which rained down, banging, thumping and clattering upon the roof tiles, chimneys, gutters and cobbles of the village. The bomber had turned around by the time it flew over Kleinmachnow, seemingly having abandoned the mission and trying to limp back home to England. By now it was coming in from the southeast, heading roughly homeward. It was obviously crippled, indicated by the crew getting rid of its bombload, the munitions of which had just randomly fallen across the village beneath. But almost simultaneously with the arrival of these bombs came the stricken bomber itself, unable to escape the fire of the local Flak batteries. The Lancaster exploded in the air right overhead, then the sundered airframe tore itself apart and scattered its pieces all over the countryside and waterways south of the village. As the burning, disassembling wreck tumbled earthward, the Hakeburg castle lay below, directly in its plummeting path.

The Hakeburg castle was a romantically conceived *Schloss*, the equivalent of a French *chateau*, built in neo-Roman style, and set in a stately forest park wherein grew some ancient trees claimed to be as old as 1300 years. These leafy grounds were pleasantly set on the northern shoreline of Lake Machnow, a small kidney-shaped lake, 600 metres long by 250 wide, set along the otherwise straight course of the Teltow Canal. Now the blazing aircraft wreck came crashing down within this noble park, shearing tree trunks and littering the lawns and shrubberies with a spray of twisted, torn and scorched airframe debris. The impact was so violent that a severed wing splashed into the lake 200 metres beyond the impact point.

The stricken Lancaster's bombload had come down within Kleinmachnow itself, falling in the residential street, *Im Tal*, so Franz Marz's firefighting detachment now had some real fires to put out. Indeed, before the blazes were extinguished, four residential buildings were partly destroyed, including the one housing the village school, as well as another forty houses lightly damaged. With a local fire emergency to attend to, the party of apprehensive volunteer firemen soon got underway through the darkened streets to lend a hand to the householders in the bomb-hit street, but as they passed the entrance to the Hakeburg, soldiers flagged them down, directing them instead into the Hakeburg grounds, and leading them to the bomber's burning wreckage. The auxiliary firemen were instructed to extinguish those fires instead of attending to the fires in the village, guided in the task by SS soldiers from the Hakeburg's guard detachment who had arrived at the burning wreck straight after the crash; the aircraft had come to earth right inside the grounds they were guarding. In the light of the flames, just-arrived volunteer fireman Marz could see enough of the bomber's crew amongst the burning wreckage to know there was nothing he or anybody else could do for them: he remarked of the British airmen, 'None of them are getting out of that.' Some of the flyers had evidently been ejected from the disintegrating fuselage in mid-air, falling to earth by themselves, while others came to earth within the sheared fuselage. Now Marz and the other first responders found the bodies scattered among the torn-up aircraft components across the debris field. The fires

Representing all the men in our story who did not survive their shoot-down, this photo shows a dead RAF rear gunner by the wrecked tail section of his Halifax bomber, shot down in one of three Berlin raids in January 1944. The wrecked tail gun turret is evident middle right, with belts of .303-inch ammunition strewn about. The dead airman has been extracted from the ruined turret and has undergone the initial search for identification material and intelligence, as shown by his opened-up flying suit. After this his remains will be transported to the mortuary complex at Döberitz for official identification, record-making and burial, all conducted by the Luftwaffe.

AWM Negative 128254

at length abated, allowing the mixed party of firemen and soldiers to get closer to the wreckage and to drag away from it the remains of eight men – more than the British bombers' usual complement of seven. All eight bodies ended up lying on the grass in a row. By the time the bodies were removed they had become 'badly charred' by the intense fire, with two of them 'completely burnt'. Marz thought the dead airmen looked like 'huge puppets' as they lay there with stiff arms outstretched, and afterwards described some of the bodies as being so badly burned up that the carbonised remains measured only 60–80 centimetres long.

After this gruesome work, the civilian firemen did not need to hear the SS men announce authoritatively that all eight airmen were indeed deceased, but the soldiers made the ponderous pronouncement all the same. With the human remains recovered, it was now a military responsibility to process them for burial. The SS soldiers began the process by opening the dead airmen's clothing to try to find any identifying materials. Some of the firemen who were watching the soldiers conduct this examination saw that one of the bodies wore a decidedly non-military checked shirt beneath the flying kit. This unusual fact triggered a round of authoritative and not so authoritative commentary from the onlookers: the pundits in the group decided that the wearer of the 'unusual uniform' was an Irishman flying with the RAF (having presumably mistaken checks for tartan and Irish for Scottish).

While the bodies were undergoing this initial inspection of their pockets' contents, there was still much work for Marz and his party of firemen to do, and by the military personnel who had come to guard the wreck: the smaller fires needed to be extinguished, a safety watch had to be maintained over the larger fires until they burned themselves out, and the hazardous live ammunition, pyrotechnics and flares scattered amongst the wreckage needed to be secured and safeguarded. It is salutary to consider that this whole process – the arrival of first responders at the crash scene, the clean-up of the debris field, and the retrieval of the bodies – was repeated about forty times in various local communities across northern Germany on that night alone, for on that single raid, that many bombers fell violently to earth, as we have seen. And that was only one raid, in only one series of raids, in only one bombing campaign.

At 9.31 pm, the all-clear sounded in Kleinmachnow, allowing the residents whose houses remained unscathed to go to bed. But Franz Marz and his comrades had stayed on duty at the crash site all through the night; he himself did not get home until 'towards morning' (dawn came at about a quarter past seven). His grandson, Günter Käbelmann, who was only seven at the time, was woken up by the commotion of his grandfather's arrival home at the end of a long, hard, memorable night. Sneaking out of bed, Günter saw that his grandfather's work clothing was blackened by soot, and the boy stood in the shadows eavesdropping on the adults' conversation, hearing gory descriptions of scorched and incinerated bodies, and of the torn airframe components of a ripped-apart bomber. Marz had returned home with two burn blisters on his hand from getting too close to the flames.

It was the bomber's sundered fuselage which had ploughed into the pleasant woodlands within the grounds of the Hakeburg, falling to earth in the green belt along the northern shore of Lake Machnow. If the trajectory of the wreckage had kept it in the air only a second longer, it would have plunged hissing into the waters of the lake and buried itself in the absorbent mud of the lakebed. Indeed, a section of the bomber's left wing followed this trajectory, splashing into the water 200 metres further on, directly opposite the Hakeburg crash site and at the foot of the lake's southern shore. The snapped-off right wing, meanwhile, remained largely intact, and with both engines still attached it had sailed away through the night sky, surfing the cold air along a flatter trajectory to crash down within the village of Teltow, 3 kilometres east of the fuselage's crash site at Hakeburg. But it was the Hakeburg crash site that held particular significance because of the identity of one of the men who fell violently to earth inside the leafy grounds of that estate – the mysterious civilian who had died in the checked shirt. This was the body of the war correspondent who in death would become canonised as a Norwegian national hero.

In bomber-scarred Kleinmachnow, daylight on 3 December brought not only welcome sleep for worn-out middle-aged firemen like Franz Marz, but the removal of the airmen's bodies to the military barracks at Döberitz, a jolting 34-kilometre road trip for the insensible airmen in the back of the truck. The men's bodies were taken to *Reserve Lazarett 101*, the military hospital that had been set up on the site of the nearby 1936 Olympic village to service the adjoining military barracks complex. Ironically, the bodies were placed in the makeshift morgue set up in the Olympic *Haus der Nationen* (House of the Nations), within which now lay together without discrimination the bodies of young men from Britain, Canada, New Zealand, Rhodesia, Poland, Czechoslovakia – and from Norway and Australia. There lay the eight bodies of Nordahl Grieg's crew and those of scores of other RAF airmen killed in the bombers that had crashed in and around Berlin that night. The Luftwaffe was responsible for processing the bodies of Allied airmen, and so undertook the mortuary process of collection, examination, and preparation for burial. Perhaps the most important task here was that of identification: military personnel examined each body's clothing, harness and pockets for any sign of the dead man's identity, such as name, initials, rank, service number and service (namely, whether a member of the British RAF itself, or one of the sister air forces from the dominions, like the RAAF). Because the RAF-issue identity tags were easily rendered illegible by exposure to fire, the difficult task of body identification often depended upon finding an unburnt name and number written with marker pen on the inside of a battledress collar or flying helmet, or upon the webbing strap of a parachute harness.

In due course, having made what identifications it could, the Luftwaffe would advise Germany's OKW, the military high command in Berlin, of the names and numbers it had identified as 'confirmed killed', after which the OKW would advise the International Committee of the Red Cross (ICRC), so that the ICRC could pass on the identification details to the British Red Cross, thence to the Air Ministry, who would notify the next of kin. In this way, enough identifications would be made for families to learn that their sons, brothers and husbands were dead, while for the other bodies classified as 'unknown airmen', the families would in due course be advised that their loved ones were 'presumed dead'. Of the eight men killed in the Hakeburg crash, one of the bodies was found with a pendant inscribed 'Nordahl'. This body was therefore incorrectly recorded as an unknown airman of unknown rank, but with the surname of Nordahl.

The dead airmen from the 2 December raid were processed in this by-now routine manner: after conducting the identification and intelligence examination in the hospital morgue, the Luftwaffe had the bodies transported in batches to the nearby Elsgrund cemetery for burial. This place was the POW annex to the nearby Döberitz cemetery, the annex having been specifically set up to accommodate the hundreds of RAF bodies that had been coming violently to earth during the 1943 air offensive. There was no room for numbers like these in the original Döberitz graveyard, and so the RAF dead were interred in the newly extended British plot at Elsgrund instead. The burials were conducted by six Russian POW forced labourers working under the supervision of Herr Lippold, the cemetery supervisor. Prayers were said over each grave by a military padre; the interments were conducted with as much dignity as could be mustered in a mass-burial process involving scores of bodies.

After identification processing in the morgue, the bodies were placed in plain wooden coffins, to be interred in numbered plots at Elsgrund, evidently placed in the earth in the order in which they were lifted off the back of the truck. After all the recent raids, featuring scores of crashed bombers, there had been so many bodies to be processed in the morgue and then buried by the truckload that bomber crews were often inadvertently split up in the administrative confusion: thus, instead of all men from one crew being buried together, as intended, they might be buried apart, in random groupings. Between the Luftwaffe supervisors and the civilian staffs, firstly in the morgue and then at the graveyard, the administrative system often lost track of which body went with which others. In this manner the eight men from the Hakeburg crash were buried separately from one another. At the time the German cemetery staff had recorded that four of these bodies were buried together side by side, but after the war the British reinterment teams discovered these records to be incorrect. Indeed, they found that 50 per cent of the grave sites were incorrectly recorded by the German authorities, not helped by a mid-course change of system in the numbering of the rows. Given the decency and correctness of the Luftwaffe's handling of RAF dead earlier in the war, it appears that the RAF's Berlin raids were killing so many Allied airmen that the responsible authorities had lost the administrative capacity to efficiently process and accurately record such a large number of burials – in amongst all the other galloping demands and administrative crises imposed by a bombed capital and a deteriorating war. In this rising fog of clerical confusion, the German authorities were content to accept without further investigation that one of the bodies from the Hakeburg crash was an otherwise unknown Allied military flyer with the surname of 'Nordahl'.

Two months after the raid, a Norwegian-speaking radio operator at Wannsee, just outside of Potsdam, tasked with monitoring 'London Calling', a Norwegian-language news program from the Norwegian government-in-exile in London, heard the official announcement of the death of the famous poet, Nordahl Grieg, while participating in an air raid. The radio operator was Antonie Sander, a 20-year-old translator and stenographer from Kleinmachnow who, thanks to her professional qualifications and aptitude for foreign languages, had found a good job only 10 kilometres from home at the top secret Interradio wireless facility set up in the old Swedish Pavilion at the fashionable lakeside resort of Wannsee. The Interradio facility for which she worked was run by Goebbels' *Reichspropaganda* Ministry; it was tasked with monitoring wireless news and information broadcasts round the clock in thirty-six languages, listening out for significant items of interest to the department, for advice to the German government. On this occasion, Frau Sander had identified the item as significant, so completed her translation of the text into German and handed it on for the information of her departmental superiors. As this report ascended the chain of command, only now would the realisation start to dawn amongst the German military authorities that the unidentified dead airman whom they had recorded as surnamed 'Nordahl' had in fact been no airman but the national poet of Norway and inspiration to the Norwegian resistance movement.

By the time Grieg's death was publicly announced two months after the 2 December raid, at the Hakeburg crash site torn pieces of aluminium were all that remained of the broken Lancaster he had died in. By then the debris had been cleared from the grounds by a Luftwaffe recovery unit, destined like all other Allied aircraft that fell in enemy territory to be recycled into new Messerschmitts, Heinkels and Junkers. But Kleinmachnow locals had also been raking over the Hakeburg crash site for souvenirs almost as soon as the fires had stopped smouldering. An 11-year-old boy, Heinz Ortleb, who lived in a house close to the crash site, had on the night of the raid heard the 'fearful crash' nearby, and although strictly kept at home by his parents throughout the first night and day, remained full of curiosity to see the wreckage. Two days after the crash he somehow managed to evade parental observation long enough to sneak out through the fence with two friends to see it for

A portrait of Nordahl Grieg which captures something of the intensity of the man who became a Norwegian patriotic icon. He wears the insignia of a captain in the Norwegian army, in his capacity as official war correspondent.
Thorsten Perl

himself. Scouring the field, Heinz claimed to have found a uniform jacket and a signal pistol, both of which were later taken from his possession by adults. He also claimed to have seen a complete case of incendiaries lying on the ground, flung from the bomber's bomb bay. The crash site made a deep impression on him, and even sixty years later he would walk the banks of the nearby canal thinking of the violent event that had happened that night and of the men who had died. Long after the site was restored to nature, small fragments remained scattered around, hidden amongst the vegetation; some of these relics were still being discovered and recovered as late as 2011.

CHAPTER 10

REPORTING THE RAID

While Lowell Bennett was getting extracted from the lake, while Norm Ginn was going 'on the run', and while the bodies of the dead airmen were getting retrieved from their smoking wrecks, the surviving crews were arriving back in England and getting debriefed. A journalist had been present in the Binbrook briefing room on the night of 26 November, reporting upon one of Bomber Command's most charmed aircraft, No. 460's Lancaster G-George, which had miraculously completed seventy missions without getting shot down; he described the scene after the return of the bombers:

> Soon after the plane had landed that night airmen from all parts of Australia began finding their way to the interrogation room in flying kit. Padded with enormous white sweaters, they looked as bulbous as Arctic sailors, which is natural enough considering they had been flying for six hours. Most of them had been over Berlin four times in the last eight nights. But it was rare to see fatigue lines on any one's face. The tall grave faced Australian VC, Group Captain Hughie Edwards, quickly cross-examined aircraft captains as they led their crews into a brilliantly lighted interrogation room, on the wall of which was a map of Europe. An RAF padre and two WAAFs offered the

The crew of 460 Squadron's famous G-George, jubilant at their safe return. The electrically heated flying suits for the turret gunners, and the crammed-full 'gen bag' of the navigator, show that they have come back from a mission.

AWM Negative UK1304

airmen huge mugs of heavily sweetened rum, which night fliers now get after a super cold mission, with biscuits and cigarettes. A black and white cat named Hyso belonging to the squadron's photograph section sat purring round the airmen, licking the rum from the empty cups.

No. 460's charmed 'G-George' flew to Berlin again on the night of 2 December and returned safely just as she had in the earlier raid. But on the latter night five other crews from No. 460 did fail to return, their callsigns tallied on the ops board as missing by the early hours of 3 December. It was unlikely that the atmosphere on that occasion was quite as upbeat as that described above, although the same basic routine applied.

On that night, even with the names of the five missing crews still chalked up on the board, with ominously blank spaces left in the 'time landed' column, the rigours of the night must nonetheless have been softened a little for those who survived by the ritual smoking of cigarettes, with the chill of spending six hours at 20 000 feet thawed by the hot rum and sugary tea. As the men soothed themselves in the surety that they themselves at least had made it back to live another day, each crew was interviewed by an intelligence officer, to produce a raid report on what they had done, and what they had seen.

One of 460's pilots, Flying Officer Ron McIntyre, blurted out his impressions of Berlin's flak to the waiting reporters in the Binbrook ops room: 'There were blocks of searchlights, hundreds of them ... The flak was pretty solid ... It gives you the impression that it is impossible to get through it, but you do somehow ...' For 20-year-old McIntyre, new to ops, this introduction to Berlin had clearly been both an intimidating and a stimulating experience. He would be dead by the end of the month, shot down on the night of 29 December, on a return visit to the Big City – the fatal ninth op for him and his crew. After debriefing, the survivors went off to bed for a well-earned rest. Sadly, in so

A bomber crew from 460 Squadron undergoing debriefing in the ops building at RAF Binbrook after returning from a raid in 1943. The only man not wearing aircrew brevet above the breast pocket of his tunic is the intelligence officer, third from left, who is asking the crewmen proforma questions about what they observed and experienced, jotting the details down for inclusion in a squadron intelligence report for submission to HQ. Sweet tea with a jot of rum soothed the men's nerves and thawed them out from the six-hour night flight. Note the map of Germany on the wall, for clarification of locations.

AWM Negative UK0401

many cases, such as McIntyre's, it was the sleep of the soon-to-be dead.

However, for Ed Murrow at Coningsby and for Alf King at Waddington, there would be no rest for now, despite the fatigue of a noisy, uncomfortable, frightening and cold night flight: they had to compose and file their reports – the whole point of the entire costly exercise. The time pressure was particularly unforgiving for Murrow, who had to compose the text for his radio broadcast and then hurry back to the CBS studio to deliver it live on-air, after rehearsing his delivery on the return train to London.

As Murrow waited at Coningsby for his transport to Lincoln railway station, he collected his thoughts and made his notes for the broadcast. As he waited, alertly absorbing the experience, he was the only journalist to witness 619 Squadron's crews file into the ops room one by one, and in a position to overhear the debriefings. Each returning aircraft reported in by radio as it entered the circuit area, and then the waiting base staff chalked its landing time on the ops board. Once the time passed for the aircraft's maximum time airborne, Murrow could see blank spaces beside the names of two crews from No. 619 who had still not returned. Initially he could not have known about any losses other than those of his host squadron, but evidently soon heard about those three missing Lancasters from the other squadrons which had conveyed his colleagues, Grieg, Stockton and Bennett. The phone in Coningsby's ops room was connected to those at Binbrook and Skellingthorpe, and it seems that soon the news of the three missing correspondents was phoned through. Murrow was a 'close friend' of Bennett and Stockton, so the news must have hit him hard. Now Murrow had an additional moral purpose for his broadcast, as well as another news angle for his story.

His report went to air the night following the raid as a 'Special Broadcast from London' at 6.45 pm, US Eastern Standard Time, as a nineteen-minute program entitled

'Orchestrated Hell'. He prefaced his on-air report with a spoken tribute to his missing friends and colleagues:

> Yes, Lowell Bennett, of International News Service, Norman Stockton, of Australian Associated Newspapers Service, and a third unidentified correspondent, wherever you are, your stories came through.
>
> They are in print, perhaps not just as you would have written them, but in print they are.

Describing the raid itself, Murrow summed up the experience of the night by an explanation of the title:

> Berlin was a kind of orchestrated hell – a terrible symphony of light and flame. It isn't a pleasant kind of warfare ... Men die in the sky while others are roasted alive in their cellars. Berlin last night wasn't a pretty sight. In about thirty-five minutes it was hit with about three times the amount of stuff that ever came down on London in a night-long blitz. This is a calculated, remorseless campaign of destruction.

He also identified by name only two of his missing colleagues, as the news of Grieg's participation and non-return was for now suppressed:

> There were four reporters on this operation. Two of them didn't come back. Two friends of mine, Norman Stockton of Australian Associated Newspapers,

and Lowell Bennett, an American representing International News Service. There is something of a tradition amongst reporters, that those who are prevented by circumstances from filing their stories will be covered by their colleagues. This has been my effort to do so.

Murrow went on to describe his flight, recalling the moment when D-Dog had recrossed the German-held coast on the way back to Lincolnshire, recalling the reason for his personal commitment to this work:

Dave, the navigator, said, 'We're crossing the coast'. My mind went back to the time I had crossed that coast in 1938, in a plane that had taken off from Prague. Just ahead of me sat two refugees from Vienna – an old man and his wife. The co-pilot came back and told them that we were outside German territory. The old man reached out and grasped his wife's hand. The work that was done last night was a massive blow of retribution, for all those who have fled from the sound of shots and blows on a stricken continent.

Although Murrow's account of his purpose was authentic, he was mistaken about the retribution exacted by the Berlin raid in which he had participated. As typified by the wayward crash locations both of Bennett's B-Bolty and of Alford's J-Johnnie, the un-forecasted winds across northern Germany on the approach to Berlin had blown the bombers badly off course and dispersed the bomber stream away from the target. As we have seen, these aircraft had drifted far to the south of the specified approach path and their crews had badly mistaken their targets.

The navigational disarray that night is shown by Luftwaffe tracking of the incoming bomber stream's progress across German airspace, which plotted the passage of the bombers towards the capital not as a narrow bomber stream pointing like an arrow towards Berlin, as intended by the RAF planners, but as a broad front stretching 40 kilometres in width from Potsdam in the south to Oranienburg in the north; by the time it neared Berlin it was more of a wave than a stream. In Luftwaffe operations rooms, the right flank of the vanguard wave of pathfinders was plotted missing Berlin itself and overflying the southern outskirts of the city, while the left-most pathfinders were plotted overflying Berlin's northern and northeast edges. As a result, the pathfinders' target markers were scattered widely from one end to the other of Berlin's vast and sprawling urban area. Although some of the pathfinder crews had managed to correctly identify the southward drift and make enough course corrections to find and mark locations in the central parts of Berlin, most of the follow-up main force veered even further south than the straying pathfinders had done: the Luftwaffe controllers plotted the main body of the RAF bomber force getting lost over southern and south-eastern Berlin, with only a few individual bombers reaching the actual city area in the centre, where their bombloads fell in haphazard fashion.

Such deflating details were of course unknown to the RAF at the time, but the disappointing bombing pattern was clear enough from the returning crews' bombing photographs, which showed that bombloads had been dropped 'over a wide area of southern Berlin and the countryside south of the city'. But any such ambiguity was skipped over in the bland official communique issued by the Air Ministry and obediently repeated in news stories throughout the world, according to which in the 2 December raid 'very heavy fires were started' in Berlin by a 'great force of our heavy bombers'. Dodging any question about the specifics in favour of sweeping rhetoric, Air Marshal Harris himself declared that his command would continue pounding the German capital, 'Until the heart of Nazi Germany ceases to beat'.

The optimistic gloss in Murrow's reporting was perhaps influenced by repeated official statements of this kind, but it was also derived from his own eyewitness view of the fires below, as well as from the optimistic perspectives of the returning crews whom he saw and overheard during the debriefings. Judging from the testimonies the airmen gave to the interviewing officers, most participating crews believed they had bombed the briefed target and that the target area had been hit hard. For example, of the twenty crews from 460 Squadron that returned to base, most thought it had been a 'good attack', that the target had been 'well marked' by the pathfinders, and that the resultant bombing had been 'well concentrated'. There was some critical dissent, however: Flight Sergeant Merv Stafford reported the pathfinder marking to have been 'scattered', and that as a result the 'Area covered by bombing [was] more extensive than last time' – in other words, that the bombing had been distributed widely rather than concentrated. Warrant Officer Dick Power and Flight Sergeant Bob Baker agreed, reporting the bombing as scattered. Flight Sergeant Ken

Godwin's impressions were similar, reporting that the resultant fires were also scattered, and that it was 'not such a good concentration as the last attack'. He was one of the last to bomb, at 8.49 pm, so was well placed to assess the overall pattern of the fires below. Similar variation was evident amongst the crew reports at 619 Squadron. Clearly, Murrow had taken his version of the bombing results from the majority opinion of the returning crews at Coningsby; as this opinion was optimistic, he omitted the discordant complication of the dissenting perspectives for public consumption.

Despite the wayward target marking and scattered bombing, the RAF had nonetheless inflicted damage upon industrial facilities within Berlin's sprawling urban area, in the potluck manner of 'strategic bombing'. In the 2 December raid, German authorities counted a total of thirty 4000-pounder blockbusters and 201 other high-explosive bombs that fell inside Berlin, as well as 22000 small incendiary bombs. Although the resultant bomb damage was less than that of the preceding raids, it was hardly insignificant, with 340 buildings destroyed, another 3001 buildings damaged (including 464 severely); and with ninety-nine people killed on the ground and 151 injured, and 8862 people rendered homeless. This was the measurable, physical impact of the 1600 tons of bombs that the RAF had released upon and around Berlin in the three-quarters of an hour following 8.04 pm that night, at the cost of 230 aircrew killed, as well as another sixty who escaped death and were captured. As usual with raids on the German capital, the bombing had been scattered by the vast area of Berlin's conurbation: at 2330 square kilometres, it was so big that even veteran crews in the Pathfinder Force had difficulty finding a particular aiming point within the city. In this raid, it is clear that the crews which had found their way to the general proximity of the urban area had mistaken for the briefed aiming points diverse locations through the suburban outskirts, as well as the satellite towns and villages beyond Berlin's urban fringe.

The RAF did not know the real results on the ground in any detail at the time, so used the optimistic crew reports as the basis of the media reportage the next day. Such factual imprecision was standard practice in a war with new battles and new stories on the front pages daily. Any factual quibbling about the raid would be swamped by succeeding stories: there would be another raid the next night for the media to report on, and another Berlin raid soon after that, so any inconvenient details specific to the 2 December raid were unlikely to be raked over in public in time to affect the story. The initial reporting set the narrative, that narrative became the official version of what had taken place, and there would be no time in the middle of a busy war for subsequent historical revisionism in the public sphere. The resultant tone of the media reportage was correspondingly upbeat, and this positive standpoint was not dented by the admitted heavy losses of crews and aircraft. Nor did the shocking loss of three out of five accompanying journalists do anything to shake anyone's resolve in pursuing the bombing campaign upon the German civilian population.

Alf King's eyewitness reporting of his experiences aboard 467 Squadron's G-George did not depart from the expected script about the RAF's bombing accuracy. He declared that when he arrived over Berlin, the aiming point 'had been defined with remarkable clarity' by the target indicator flares laid down by the preceding pathfinder crews, such that the 'bomb aimers' particular objectives 'stood out like beacons'. The reader was left in no doubt that the bombers had hit the aiming point with surgical precision. But neither did he disguise the awful brutality of the bombing; indeed he seemed almost to revel in the apocalyptic destruction he reported. Determined to view it through an aesthetic framework, he described the 'devastation by explosive and burning' of Berlin to be 'Superb in the savage beauty of its light'. He painted the 'turmoil' of the city below as 4000-pounder 'Cookie' blockbuster bombs 'smashed amid the built-up area and thousands of incendiaries cascaded down and took hold among the blocks of buildings in fantastic alphabetical designs ... The cookies exploded in seemingly mushroom-like glows. They then died in plumes of smoke.' King observed that strings of the small incendiary bombs had ignited on the ground to form 'i's, t's and l's', with one string forming 'an almost perfect V-for-victory'.

The human cost of the raids, in terms of fallen Allied airmen, was not hidden from the public either. On the day after the 2 December 1943 raid, newspapers truthfully reported that forty bombers had been lost that night, as well as quoting German radio communiques that so far 'the bodies of 146 British airmen had been recovered from wrecked planes'. Nor did the media shy away from reporting the carnage inflicted upon German civilians. In articles published on 4 December 1943, the Battle for Berlin was characterised for the Australian public as 'the most dreadful air attack in the history of the world', causing up to the

Ed Murrow described the scene as 'Orchestrated hell'. This is a photo of a raid on Duisburg in February 1945, but this extraordinarily well composed shot offers a vivid impression of what any big raid must have looked like to the aircrew passing over the destruction they caused below: evident is a section of streetscape at top right, another Lancaster at a lower altitude, the pinprick lights of bursting incendiaries, the huge, bright orb of an exploding 'blockbuster' upper centre, burning streets at centre, billowing black smoke clouds at right, and the white-seeming puffs of flak bursts closer up beneath the photographer's aircraft.

AWM Negative P00811.024

time of writing more than 40 000 deaths, severely injuring more than 40 000 people, and injuring another 100 000 less severely:

> ... the heart of the Nazi Germany has been described as a battlefield, with the day and night echoing with the explosions of delayed bombs, of falling buildings, and the cries of the injured. By night it is an inferno of flame, with the probability of more bombers dropping their deadly loads to add to the panic and confusion. Nearly half a million citizens are homeless.

While the statistics cited above were inaccurate, and the lurid details exaggerated, the overall gist of the commentary was a reasonably unalloyed admission of the brutality of Bomber Command's methods.

Judging by the candid remarks about fire-raising that returning crews made during debriefing, there can be no doubt that the aircrews who had to carry out this work understood their commander's apocalyptic intentions: aircraft captains implicitly acknowledged the purpose of the raid as being to ignite widespread conflagrations across entire city districts. Some examples at Waddington will show the general tenor of the crew reports that Alf King must have overheard about the effect of the bombing. No. 467's Pilot Officer Bert Jones reported that because the bombing concentration was poor, the city 'did not burn as expected'. Flight Sergeant Stephen Grugeon conversely remarked that it had been 'rather a concentrated attack', but that nonetheless there had been 'no apparent fires', as he had expected. Flying Officer Colin Reynolds took a halfway position, noting that despite 'scattered' target marking by the pathfinders, the bombing had still caused a 'good concentration of fire in one area' of the city. Pilot Officer Henry Crouch reported similarly, noting that despite a lot of crews dumping their loads well short of the target, the bombing had been 'very well concentrated in one area' and that the resultant fires were seen 'increasing in intensity'. Even so, he observed with evident regret that the fires had not been 'as impressive' as those in the preceding Berlin raids – an accurate observation, as we have seen. Crews were in the habit of reporting approvingly of any blazes large enough and bright enough to be seen from a distance, measured according to the distance at which they could be observed from their bomber as it headed home across Germany – on this raid, Pilot Officer Milton Smith reported with satisfaction that his rear gunner could still see the fires of Berlin from 60 miles away.

At Coningsby, Ed Murrow overheard similar terms of reporting by the crews from his host No. 619 Squadron. Wing Commander Jock Abercromby himself noted that he had observed '2 areas of fire' in the city below, while Pilot Officer JWE McGilvray reported in more detail that he had seen 'two large areas of fire which seemed to be spreading. Large pall of smoke – glow of fires seen for 50 miles.' Pilot Officer RM Rumble saw something similar, but upon arriving over the target ten minutes later than McGilvray, saw that the conflagration had developed to the extent that the fires' glow remained visible against the eastern night for 100 miles during P-Peter's retirement across northern Germany. When Pilot Officer GS Stout went over the target the ground was obscured by cloud, but he was encouraged by the glow of fires visible underneath the cloud.

At Skellingthorpe, the men of 50 Squadron too reported having looked down upon the city in hope of seeing it flare up into a city-wide blaze like Hamburg had done several months earlier. As his Lancaster departed the defended area, Pilot Officer WG Smith's crew reported seeing a 'good glow' beneath the clouds, with smoke rising to 15 000 feet. For his part, the more experienced Flight Lieutenant RF Burt was disappointed that there were 'not many fires' evident, correctly deducing that most aircraft were bombing the wrong target. Pilot Officer HA Litherland was also disappointed, being able to report 'only 2–3 medium fires', contrary to his expectation of a major blaze. Flying Officer AS Keith saw some more encouraging evidence, however, reporting a 'large concentration of fires'. The details reported differ, but the normative expectation was the same: that the objective of the raids was to burn the whole city down in a vast firestorm.

There was of course a very pragmatic reason why the crews hoped to see such widespread conflagration: simply put, if they torched Berlin as they had done Hamburg, then the Battle of Berlin would be over, and they would be able to stop flying these long, dangerous missions to the most heavily defended target on earth. Successfully bludgeoning and scorching the city into rubble and ashes would bring an end to their ordeal of repeat visitations to the 'Big City', and hence a better chance of staying alive to finish their tours. To illustrate the logic of this incentive to hit Berlin hard, it is instructive to note that of the twelve RAAF captains from 467 Squadron who returned safely from the

2 December Berlin raid, four would die the following month during repeat visits to this formidable target. But whatever the reasons, it seems that most airmen had come to terms in matter-of-fact style with the brutal and indiscriminate intent of the campaign they had been committed to by their governments and commanders. It helped that the damage and mayhem the bombs unleashed remained an abstraction when viewed from 20 000 feet.

Fed by optimistic crew reports like many of those above, upbeat war news about the raid was disseminated throughout the English-speaking world and beyond, through syndicated copy composed in London. Stories were teletyped throughout the global cable network and written up into stories by news editors far and wide. We can take as an example of this reiterative, officially sponsored reportage by the *Danville Morning News* from Pennsylvania, which not only printed the text of Murrow's broadcast the previous night, but editorialised in truculent tones: 'Tonight we can tell you how Berlin burned, we can tell you because we get a vivid picture from a man who saw death raining down out of the skies over the Nazi capital.' The editorial relished 'the fiery Holocaust that hit the German capital last night', and 'the enormous destruction which has turned Berlin into a city of horror'. *Danville*'s editor laid the rhetoric on even more thickly by alluding to lurid reports from neutral visitors to Berlin:

> ... there are stories of the frantic and bewildered people of Berlin, a people wandering about the city without homes, without gas, light, or electricity, a people with

the ever constant fear running through their minds
that the bombers, and death, will return.

This dread of death from the air is increasing by
the hour.

At the recent Allied war conference in Tehran between Soviet dictator Stalin, President Roosevelt and Prime Minister Churchill, the Allied leaders had agreed that they would accept nothing less than Germany's unconditional surrender. The *Danville* editorial used this agreement to spell out an apocalyptic warning: '... although the Nazis don't say it, the alternative facing the German people is believed to be complete and utter destruction, much of which will come from the air'. Bloodthirsty rhetoric of this kind in mainstream media suggests that the Allied 'bomber barons' had been successful in engineering consent from independent opinion leaders, in support of their strategic bombing offensive.

And if senior editors in safe civilian jobs back home could think and write in such remorselessly belligerent tones, then the embedded war correspondents at the front could hardly be expected to offer a dispassionate analysis of the bombing and of its costs and effects. Of course, to do so would have quickly lost them their press accreditation, but the point stands. For example, Colin Bednall, another Australian war correspondent in London, who had flown in an earlier Berlin raid on the night of 30 January 1943, gave vent to similarly punitive and vengeful impulses as did the editor in Danville. In describing the release of his bomber's

4000-pound 'Cookie' that night, he wrote, 'I saw its great flash. Quite a nice chunk of Germany is now all the better for it.' Bednall's callous flippancy was seconded by the brutal editorial lines run by mainstream newspapers: the *Canberra Times* trumpeted for the edification of the Australian people that an 'Australian Squadron Helps Berlin to Burn'.

By now, the Allied media had identified itself wholeheartedly with the official bombing policy, and that policy was one of unflinching ruthlessness, as expressed by the RAF's commander, Air Chief Marshal Charles Portal, who in October 1942 outlined the projected impact of the Allied bombing campaign upon the German civilian population: he predicted that if the Anglo-American bomber forces were greatly expanded, by the end of 1943 they would have destroyed 6 million German dwellings, made 25 million Germans homeless, killed 900 000 German civilians, and injured another million. In the event the bomber fleet was not so strengthened, and only a fraction of this was achieved, but Portal was willing to state it unreservedly as an objective – and would have put it into effect if he could have done so. Before the 22 November 1943 Berlin raid, the head of Bomber Command, Air Marshal Harris, was similarly brutal in sentiment, urging his crews in the coming 'Battle of Berlin' to hit the enemy so hard as to 'burn his black heart out'.

Despite such rhetorical extremities, the Churchill government was too squeamish to candidly admit that inflicting this type of civilian carnage was the central purpose of the bombing, maintaining instead that the civilian death and destruction was just the 'unfortunate by-product of attacks on industrial areas'. Air Marshal Harris, however, suffered from no such moral scrupulousness, calling upon the government to publicly admit the purpose of the campaign, and spelling it out anew for the politicians just in case they had forgotten it:

> That aim is the destruction of German cities, the killing of German workers and the disruption of civilised community life throughout Germany.
>
> It should be emphasised that the destruction of houses, public utilities, transport and lives; the creation of a refugee problem on an unprecedented scale; and the breakdown of morale both at home and at the battle fronts by fear of extended and intensified bombing, are [the] accepted and intended aims of our bombing policy.

Judging by the tenor of much of the media commentary, it seems that the journalists and editors reporting on the bombing war had looked beyond the blander official version of the bombing policy offered by the government and understood the RAF's real intention only too well.

Perversely, among the population of Hitler's Germany, the pounding of Berlin was greeted with a certain amount of *Schadenfreude* by the inhabitants of other cities. This was because up to the onset of Harris's 'Battle for Berlin' in November 1943, far-flung Berlin had escaped serious bomb damage, whereas the cities of western Germany, all bombable by the RAF from 1940 onwards, had been repeatedly visited by British bombers. The citizens of cities like Düsseldorf, Duisburg, Krefeld and Köln in the much-

An RAF post-strike reconnaissance photo of the Tiergarten district in Berlin, taken at the end of the RAF's series of Berlin raids over the winter of 1943–44. The industrial premises at top centre (marked as 'C') appear untouched, but are surrounded by a ruined residential district, with most apartment buildings unroofed and burned out by incendiary bombs. At top left (just above 'B') is a demolished area, the building structures flattened by the detonation of a large 'blockbuster' high-explosive bomb.

AWM Negative SUK11925

bombed Rhine-Ruhr region had developed a 'sense of rage' towards Berlin, on account not only of the usual regional envy and distrust of the power-capital, but also of that capital having so far got off scot-free from the bombing, in stark contrast to themselves. For such people, RAF Bomber Command's resumption of Berlin raids on the night of 16 January 1943 was good news. As historian Jörg Friedrich puts it:

> In early January 1943, the main topic of conversation in Krefeld was the bombing of Berlin. Without exception, the Krefelders showed profound satisfaction. It was high time the big-mouthed Berliners got what was coming to them ... It was whispered that it would be fine 'if the British flew more frequently to Berlin so that the inhabitants there would get a taste of how we in the west are feeling ...'

It seems that the only groups lamenting the bombing of Berlin were the capital's population, whereas both the Allied publics and the citizens of non-Prussian Germany shared primitive retributive impulses against the *Reichshauptstadt*, albeit for widely different reasons.

Given the repetitiveness of the raids themselves and of the reportage on them, the loss of the three journalists was so novel that it proved as newsworthy as the raid itself. Indeed, befitting the sacrificial dedication to their craft shown by Stockton, Bennett and Grieg, newspapers throughout the Allied world reported extensively on the fate of the missing journalists. For readers in Nebraska, the loss of the correspondents was front-page news the next day in the *Lincoln Evening State Journal*, which led with the report by Lowell Bennett, which he had written before take-off. As we have seen, his report on the raid and on his participation in it was written in advance and submitted for distribution to Britain's Ministry of Information in the event that he did not return. Despite his piece's unavoidable vagueness of detail, it was nonetheless run on the front page as a tribute to its lost author. Editors added further detail to Bennett's incomplete story of the raid, identifying Murrow and King as the survivors, and Stockton and Bennett as the missing; whereas for now Grieg's identity remained suppressed. Of course, the missing men were far from the first Allied war correspondents to lose their lives in this war: Nebraskans were reminded that these losses brought to thirty-seven the total of Anglo-American correspondents killed or missing so far in the course of their duties reporting the war.

Baltimore's *Evening Sun* also ran Bennett's story, albeit not on the front page. The editors were keen to emphasise for their fellow Marylanders the human-interest story of Bennett's life and loss, recapping his family background in New Jersey, his wartime marriage to his British wife, his family presently living in safety in New Jersey, his earlier war service as an ambulance driver, and his previous field assignment as an INS correspondent to Tunisia. Bennett would not have been displeased to see that he had not only reported the news, he was now *becoming* the news.

Back in Australia, the loss of Stockton did not seem to make a similar impact upon his countrymen as Bennett's loss did upon Americans: after the release of the story of the raid by Australian Associated Press on 5 December, both the Melbourne *Argus* and the *Sydney Morning Herald* published a restrained and succinct four-paragraph obituary, placing the story among the other war news without any particular emphasis, on pages 12 and 6 respectively. The Norwegian Grieg was likewise no household name throughout the English-speaking world, but once his death was finally announced on 6 February 1944 (more than two months after the event) even in faraway Australia papers published a report from the Australian Associated Press, announcing his identity as the third of the missing journalists from the 2 December raid, and giving tribute to his status as a noted poet, author and patriotic icon for Free Norway.

Indeed, once the news of Grieg's death was released throughout the free world, he was acclaimed and lionised in heroic terms. For example, the German-language journal *Aufbau*, published in New York as a voice for anti-Nazi German speakers worldwide, published a eulogy penned by American poet Joseph Auslander, whose wartime work championed the cause of the anti-Nazi resistance in German-occupied countries. Auslander's piece hailed the fallen Grieg as the 'eagle of Norway', recapped his adventurous life, and portrayed his death as a heroic act which would inspire Norwegian resistance and rebuild Norway free of Nazi tyranny:

> Battle shall breathe of your name,
> Courage shall honor your art,
> Freedom come home to your Norway!

CHAPTER 11

PRISONERS OF WAR

While readers throughout the world were sitting down with Ed Murrow's and Alf King's news stories about the big raid, Lowell Bennett and his party of shot-down survivors were undergoing the Luftwaffe's interrogation process at the Dulag Luft POW processing camp at Oberursel. This was a big facility, built to handle the huge numbers of POWs reaped by Germany's formidable air defences: by the start of September 1943, in anticipation of the coming Berlin offensive, the Oberursel facility was gearing up to process the estimated 1200 Allied flyers who were expected to be shot down and captured in the next four weeks. Although this estimate proved somewhat inflated, by late 1943 the camp was indeed processing 1000 airmen a month, and this number rose to a monthly average of more than 2000 in 1944. Despite the expansion of the facility to cope with the numbers, this number of men had to be processed quickly to avoid overloading the cell accommodation. Set up with solitary confinement cells for interrogation purposes, the camp necessarily had a limited capacity, holding only 250 POWs on any given day, with each captive usually held for less than a week for questioning before onward consignment to a permanent POW camp.

As each prisoner was processed into and out of the camp, he was questioned by one of the camp's interrogation officers. Contrary to war movie clichés, the interrogators did not rely upon physical torture or beatings. Their techniques were usually more subtle than that, being devious, coercive and highly manipulative: 'no amount of calculated mental depression, privation and psychological blackmail was considered excessive'. For example, for members of a chain-smoking generation, it was a torment for a prisoner to be deprived of cigarettes for the duration of the four- to five-day period of softening-up in solitary confinement. They were also a generation who prized the civilising gloss of daily shaving and hair cream, so the deprivation of toilet articles was a calculated affront to personal dignity. Once the 'softened-up' victim was brought out of his cell, he was subjected to a robust 'good cop bad cop' interrogation routine which drew from a well-proven playbook. Interrogators could stoop to threats of physical violence, of 'indefinitely prolonged solitary confinement or starvation rations', and of executing the prisoner as a spy. Such roughhouse tactics were sometimes used, but in general the interrogators found that such intimidation 'yielded inferior results' and that the 'friendly approach' worked better.

The destabilising impact of the psychological method was borne out in Bennett's case. Upon arrival he and his fellow prisoners were placed in solitary confinement in the cellblock known as the 'Cooler'. This not only loosened them up for their individual interrogations but also deprived them of the opportunity to collude. Locked into a 'seven feet by four' cell for five days – much longer than his previous confinements in holding units around Berlin – the sociable Bennett again found solitary confinement a 'severe test'. Classing himself neither as a 'philosopher' nor 'imbecile', but rather as an 'ordinary human', this sociable, inquisitive, and communicative person seems to have been especially vulnerable to the psychic strains of social isolation and deprivation: 'I will not describe my emotions except to say that, for me, solitary confinement was a mental torture which no physical torment could exceed.' As he fought to keep a grip on himself, he rehearsed what he might say in the interrogation. Bennett decided to exploit his civilian status to try to get out of captivity, rehearsing the lines, 'What about repatriation as a non-combatant? Am I not eligible for exchange?'

Bennett's torment was ended by being taken from his cell and led 'down the hall of the low barracks, past the long rows of identical cages, out into another small building which was the interrogation center'. There he was taken into the room of one of the interrogating officers, to find himself face to face not with the 'ape' of Allied anti-German propaganda, but rather with 'a handsome man of about thirty-five, wearing the Iron Cross First and Second class on his immaculate uniform, quiet-spoken, and an affable host'. Bennett later related that his interrogator was Lieutenant 'Joseph Borner', reputedly a Luftwaffe Stuka pilot and a veteran of seventy-eight bombing missions. But the names given in Bennett's post-war published account are pseudonyms, and in fact this officer's name was Bönningshaus. He was one of forty interrogating officers employed at Oberursel, and was the man who had been assigned the role of inveigling himself into the captured American reporter's confidence. Bönningshaus had been very well chosen for his role in putting newly captured Allied airmen at their ease, not only because of his empathetic credibility as a fellow operational flyer, but also from having before the war been a 'salesman for several years in England and America'. As a result, not only did he speak good idiomatic English, but also knew the right cultural references for his audience. For example, during Bennett's introductory interview the two men discovered that both had made their homes in England within the same area, in the 'northwest corner of London', and that they had also shared the experience of making 'peacetime trips into the tourist corners of France and England'.

Bönningshaus's opening gambit was well calibrated, a disconcerting mix of affability and provocation: he greeted the nervous captive with, 'How do you do, Mr Bennett? We have been wondering when we would see you again.' This discomfited Bennett, for he had been captured in France by the Germans in 1940 but had escaped to England, and now he realised that the German authorities had connected him, the captured war correspondent, with the man who had joined De Gaulle's Free French army three years before. For Bennett, it was 'an awful moment' to realise how much the Germans knew about him: 'I suddenly felt very afraid and weak'. The essence of interrogation technique was to undermine the captive's self-confidence and his confidence in his own cause, by suggesting that his captors already had comprehensive knowledge both of the individual they were interrogating and of the military organisation with which he had been serving. This worked exactly as intended for Bennett, who found it unnerving to be ambushed in the opening exchange by Bönningshaus's superior knowledge. Round one to the interrogator. After this subtle opening move, the German officer tried to put Bennett off his guard, 'Do sit down. Here, have a cigarette.' So Bennett sat down, suspiciously accepted the cigarette and had his first smoke 'in a week'.

Now the interrogator got straight on to business: 'So you wanted to see the RAF bomb Berlin? What did you think of it?' As a civilian, Bennett had not received training about resisting interrogation after capture, but he knew enough to recognise that Bönningshaus was toying with him conversationally so that he would start talking. He also knew that he was supposed to say nothing, so steeled himself to avoid being tricked into blurting out anything. As Bennett listened to his interlocutor, he kept silently reminding himself, 'Got to keep from registering emotion; don't say anything; don't think anything.' Maintaining as deadpan a manner as he could muster in his disquieted state, Bennett deflected the open-ended question with the non-committal response: 'Interesting.' With his first attempt at seduction thus spurned, now the interrogator ambushed his prisoner with a revelation of the sort of information he already knew about Bennett's flight to Berlin:

> Well, let's see. You flew from Skellingthorpe in 'B' of number fifty squadron of Bomber Command. Bolton was your pilot. He's a good boy; we've been waiting a long time for him.

> You know, the B.B.C. said three of your correspondents were lost the other night. You are the fortunate one. The other two were killed. That Norwegian chap and Stockton, the Australian, neither of them got out of their bombers. They were both killed. Yes, you're the lucky one.

Bennett's account of his interrogator's words, written a year after the event, conflates events somewhat, as Grieg's death was not yet known to the Germans, nor yet announced by the BBC, as we have seen. Nonetheless, the gist of the German officer's remarks as afterwards related by Bennett was authentic, namely that the Germans knew that three of the journalists had been shot down, and that one of them was Stockton, and that Stockton had been killed. Of course, this was the first Bennett knew of his colleague's fate, so the revelation must have hit him hard: not only in the deadly import of the news, but also in the extent of Bönningshaus's knowledge. To change the subject, now Bennett resorted to presenting his rehearsed petition to be repatriated as a civilian. His interrogator deftly deflected the question in such a way as to maintain the tension: 'Perhaps, we'll have to look into that. But for the moment, how about having "tea" with me?'

The prisoner was of course famished and so put up no resistance to this renewed charm offensive. Both men sat down to a meal, while conversing freely about 'solely ... non-military' subjects, during which they discovered their mutual interest in and experience of particular tourist attractions in France and England. As they swapped travel stories, the hungry captive gorged himself on the 'bread, liverwurst and jams' that a Luftwaffe orderly brought in; Bennett also 'swallowed several cups of coffee' and 'smoked a dozen of his cigarettes'. Indeed, he was so ravenous that he wolfed it all down despite suspecting 'doped coffee, doped cigarettes', and 'microphones in the jam bowl'. His suspicions seemed to be confirmed when, after the soldier came back in and cleared the table, Bönningshaus got straight back to business:

You know, our job is to identify you, to make sure no spies nor saboteurs are dropped out of the bombers. Now if you will answer some of the questions I have here, you will identify yourself completely and we will start work on the repatriation question.

First of all, what do you know about the Path Finder technique?

He was referring to the leading bombers' role in identifying the target and dropping target indicator flares to guide the crews following behind them to the aiming point – a process we have seen described repeatedly. Bennett pleaded his ignorance as a civilian, but further military questions followed, which the reporter nervously deflected with 'negative shrugs', all the whole becoming more and more ill at ease. The reporter was unlikely to have much technical knowledge about Bomber Command's Pathfinder Force, certainly less than the Luftwaffe already knew from its detailed ground observations of RAF marker flares, its radar tracking of pathfinder bombers across Germany, and also from its interrogations of captured pathfinder aircrew. But the interrogator was simply trying to break his victim down.

Having allowed himself to show 'only a mild disappointment' over Bennett's stonewalling response to the questions about the pathfinders, Bönningshaus now went for the 'Big Reveal': 'Well then, I'll tell you a few things you probably don't know … Would you like to hear something about your air forces?' The discomfited American of course had no choice but to listen as Bönningshaus dug into a 'stack of files' in a 'large folder'. From these he read out a stream of statistics which, if true, would have been classified information on the Allied side of the English Channel. He told Bennett that the German defences were shooting down an average of 13 per cent of US bombers raiding Germany, as well as 7 per cent of RAF bombers per raid; that 72 per cent of the American crewmen had got out alive from their shot-down bombers, but that the figure was only 27 per cent for RAF bomber crewmen; and that of those men who managed to escape their aircraft alive, 60 per cent of the American survivors and 44 per cent of the British came to earth injured or wounded. Unsettlingly, all these figures were credible, and were broadly representative of the actual facts. Bönningshaus then went on to recite the strengths of the Allied bomber forces in England: 1250 bombers with the US 8th Air Force and 1750 with RAF Bomber Command, including the nice detail that of this latter total, 175 were twin-engine Mosquitos. Again, these figures were plausibly close to the mark.

Bennett was amazed at the interrogator's stream of facts and figures, exclaiming, 'Where do you get all this information? From the shot-down fliers?' The interrogator responded by adding to his prisoner's sense of disquiet, further undermining Bennett's confidence in the competence, integrity and credibility of the Allied cause:

> Oh, there are agents on both sides. Your 'most secret' and 'highly confidential' documents in England are in our hands a few hours after their publication. I have the blueprints of your new jet-propelled fighters. You know, more people in Germany know your secrets than people in England or America.

After delivering this bombshell, Bönningshaus then opened up a discussion about the impending Anglo-American invasion of German-occupied western Europe, in which he further exploited Bennett's uncertainty, claiming that 'a lot of men on Eisenhower's staff don't believe it will work'.

Then he got to the point, revealing what he wanted from Bennett: for the American reporter to use his writing to undermine the faith of the American public in the viability of the coming Allied invasion of Europe:

> We surely cannot stop you with information alone. But, by knowing the facts in advance, we can make it terribly expensive for you, and we can make the American people realize the cost of the war is more than the victory is worth.

By now the German officer's gallingly provocative display of his apparent omniscience had goaded Bennett into barely concealed consternation, confusion and anger, and both men knew it. Again, advantage to Bönningshaus.

The German interrogation officer's claim about a network of double agents reaching right to the top of the Allied command chain was unsettling because it sounded plausible, playing upon one of the standard tropes of wartime propaganda and reporting, namely the imputation that enemy spies were everywhere. Of course, Bennett could not know that such claims were in fact false, so he was left as much prey to doubt as his 'good cop' tormenter intended. Contrary to Bennett's spy-riddled imaginings, the prosaic reality was that when Britain imposed wartime border controls in September 1939, most of the German agents operating in the guise of business travellers had been prevented from re-entering Britain; and that upon the outbreak of war the British counter-intelligence organisation carried out 'a small number of arrests', sweeping up the 'resident agents' and thereby leaving German intelligence services with 'no significant agents operating in Britain'. The exceptions were four spies who were 'turned' by MI5, and thereafter controlled by the British to operate in the role of double agents.

In the absence of German spies in Britain, Bönningshaus's statistics can safely be attributed to the silent achiever in intelligence work, namely signals monitoring – rather than spying. His figures about casualty rates and survival rates were explainable by the fact that the Luftwaffe tracked each raid by radar surveillance as well as by tracking the individual bombers' radio callsigns, radio transmissions, and radar and transponder emissions. The composition of all this data produced an accurate tally of how many individual bombers participated in each raid. Moreover, as the shot-down bombers fell within German-occupied territory, accurate counts of deaths, survival rates and injury rates were merely arithmetical calculations from solid data. But Bennett could not know that, so was susceptible to the claim, and accordingly his confidence was severely shaken, as intended.

Similarly, Bönningshaus's unsettling familiarity with Bennett's pilot, Ian Bolton, could be explained without recourse to espionage or omniscience on the Germans' part: Bolton had flown his operational tour with No. 50 Squadron through May to December 1943, and in that period, before he was shot down on his final mission, thirty-five of No. 50's men had survived being shot down, and so had been taken prisoner. This meant that the Luftwaffe had interrogated each of these men as they passed through Oberursel en route to their prison camps, storing whatever information they divulged in a file marked '50 Squadron' – and some of these men had mentioned Bolton, the squadron's veteran captain. It was normal for dazed, disorientated, frightened and shocked men to divulge 'harmless' facts to placate their interrogators. 'Name, rank and number' was the theory, but it was hard to maintain in practice. Despite the formulaic injunction to remain silent, many captured men talked. Snippets divulged by Bolton's shot-down squadron comrades had been filed away by the interviewing officers; these pieces of information were added to and elaborated as further divulgences were forthcoming, to build up a composite picture of mentionable individuals like Bolton, and facts about them. Such facts were then casually and disarmingly deployed against each incoming batch of newly captured airmen: to dismay and disorder, to shake their confidence, erode their defences, and elicit the revelation of further 'harmless' little titbits of information. Bönningshaus's performance in the role of an omniscient fact-conjurer was highly polished through frequent practice and it was highly impactful. It certainly rattled Bennett and sowed the seeds of doubt in his mind. The journalist's recollection of the experience testifies to the psychological manipulation inflicted upon the thousands of captured Allied airmen passing into Luftwaffe hands and explains how the Luftwaffe was able to build up such a comprehensive store of human intelligence, on top of the already substantial picture of Allied strengths, organisation, deployment, and capability revealed by signals intelligence.

The experience at Dulag Luft of captured Australian wireless operator, Norm Ginn, from No. 460's J-Johnnie, within days of Bennett's interrogation there, bears out this pattern of cunning psychological warfare at Oberursel, although it also shows that the Luftwaffe was indeed prepared to stoop to roughhouse tactics with some military POWs – harsh treatment to which it did not dare to subject a captured civilian reporter like Bennett. During his period of solitary confinement, Ginn was deprived of sleep, half-starved, and plagued by bed bugs in a cell kept blindingly lit up at all hours by a glaring overhead light. When he was brought out of his cell for his first interrogation, already in a state of exhaustion, Ginn was interviewed by what he correctly took to be a German officer masquerading as an official from the International Committee of the Red Cross. Ginn saw through the pretence at once and held out against the 'Red Cross' official's cordial advances. After that little victory, he was mentally kept off balance by his Luftwaffe interrogating officer alternating 'friendly' behaviour followed by very 'harsh' treatment. This schizophrenic performance culminated in the officer having Ginn dragged out into the yard to be executed by firing squad if he did not talk. Ginn was manhandled outside to be shot, but it proved to be a mock execution, a form of psychological torture, for when he remained silent the officer directed the firing squad to lower their rifles and ordered Ginn to be taken back to his cell. The next morning the interrogation resumed, this time conducted by the camp commandant, who resorted to somewhat subtler methods. The commandant 'berated' his captive in an intimidatory harangue, belittling him by showing him how much information he already held about 460 Squadron, just as Bönningshaus did for Bennett regarding 50 Squadron. Ginn found that the German officer already knew all the information that he himself could ever have about his own squadron, admitting that the commandant already 'knew it all'. Despite the sustained psychological pressure, Ginn remained silent and was ultimately released to a holding facility pending transfer to a POW camp. Advantage to Ginn.

The fact that Lowell Bennett underwent a milder, subtler form of interrogation than the Australian airman endured was no coincidence. For ordinary airmen like Ginn, even if their interrogation featured psychological torture like his did, once the interrogation officers at Oberursel had finished with them, they were simply shipped off to their POW camps. For them, the interrogation phase was over, even if their captivity did drag on to the end of the war. By contrast, Lowell Bennett was no ordinary prisoner, a significant fact that his captives quickly realised and sought to exploit. The captured American war correspondent would get special treatment, for he was reserved for special purposes.

Bennett's interrogation at Dulag Luft ended on an ambiguous note, providing a delayed response to his original request to be released from captivity because of his civilian status:

> ... the interview was at an end. Borner [sic] glanced at his watch, remembered an appointment, and announced that I would come back in the morning. 'You correspondents don't really belong, here', he added. 'I shall have to telephone Berlin and see what is to be done with you.'

As it proved, the phone call seemed to have done the trick, for Bennett's ordeal of incarceration, deprivation and interrogation was almost over. From the very next morning, he found himself living within a strange new dispensation. It started when Bönningshaus took him out of the camp for a two-hour walk, strolling through what Bennett described as 'the beautiful forest in the Taunus mountains north of Frankfurt'. As they strolled, their conversation initially stayed in safe territory, as they compared notes about their respective experiences a year previously during the Tunisian campaign. Despite the sensory delight of walking freely amongst 'giant trees veiled with frost', Bennett felt exposed and conspicuous in his American uniform as he accompanied his minder along paths well-used by frolicking Germany children and strolling couples walking hand in hand.

Excursion over, Bönningshaus took Bennett back to the camp, where the conversation deteriorated into a one-sided political harangue by the German officer about building the 'unity' of Europe under German leadership. Bennett saw that his interrogator's rhetoric was 'skillfully prepared propaganda', but he held his tongue, stifling his objections that Bönningshaus's ideal of European 'unity' was 'rooted in fear, in the suppression of disagreement by concentration camps, in the ballyhooed fantasy of a super-race'. Despite his own firm ideological opposition to the notion of a Nazi imperium over Europe, he was impressed by his interlocutor's 'solemnity and apparent sincerity. This man knew what he was fighting for. He would not surrender easily.'

CHAPTER 12

A GRAND TOUR

After this interlude Bennett was left to his own thoughts, isolated in his cell until the afternoon, when he was called again to Bönningshaus's office. There, his interrogator cheerily announced some big news: 'We are going to Berlin. There are people there who want to see you. We will leave tonight by train.' This was certainly unexpected, suspicious even. What was the catch? Despite his suspicions of the German officer's ulterior motives, Bennett can only have been relieved to thus obtain a release pass from the solitary confinement and deprivation of his Dulag Luft cell, whatever might await him back in Berlin. For now, he would enjoy the special treatment, whatever the Germans' secret agenda. It started when Bönningshaus presented him with a pair of boots provided by the International Committee of the Red Cross for ill-shod POWs. He was finally able to ditch the poorly fitting slippers he had been wearing since the morning of 3 December, those lent by his original captor, the ill-used boatman by the lake. Enjoying the novel pleasure of warm, dry feet and a secure grip upon the earth, that evening Bennett followed his minder to the local tram stop and boarded for a return overnight journey back to Frankfurt.

Upon arrival in blacked-out Frankfurt, they stood in the darkness in front of the *Hauptbahnhof*, where Bönningshaus paused for effect:

'Take a good look around', he suggested. 'What you can see in the dark is Frankfurt. In a few days, or perhaps weeks, you may hear that it has been destroyed. For in a single night your bombers can sweep away all of this with their fire-bombs.'

Bönningshaus was being rhetorical in overstating the capability of Allied bombing, but he had picked his man well, for Bennett was sympathetic to the plight of the German people and susceptible to doubts about the morality and efficacy of the Allied bombing. With their train delayed by Allied air raids while en route from Paris, they had a boring and frigid hour-long wait at the station for Bennett to think things over. He was certainly too tired to finely adjudicate his interlocutor's relentless factual claims and moral appeals, but on finally boarding the carriage, he was delighted to discover that his host had laid on a sleeper compartment for his now-VIP prisoner. This trip would be a lot more comfortable than the previous one. Tired out from the accumulated fatigue of five days in solitary confinement followed by several days of emotionally draining, morally enervating and intellectually discombobulating interrogation, any residual notions of escape were neutered by remembering travelling 'cattle class' with the other POWs on his trip to Frankfurt more than a week before. Bennett laid his moral scruples about Bönningshaus's arguments aside, sank into his bed and surrendered to sleep, which engulfed him in 'a heavy, deadening wave'.

Refreshed while recumbent during the 'fast and smooth' train trip across northern Germany, he awoke in the steely light of dawn to see the 'flat country west of Berlin sweep past', viewed from the corridor window on the left-hand side of the carriage. By 11 am, the train was entering the capital's suburbs, and as it slowed down the by-now wide-awake prisoner was able to take in the view of the bomb-damaged city passing by the train's windows:

> Bomb damage was at first scattered, but it increased in concentration and in totality as we drew nearer the center of the city. Germans standing in the train corridor watched the passing destruction without visible emotion. For the last few minutes before we reached the station, damage along the left side of the track was stupendous. Almost everything was destroyed or burned out.

Bombed-out Hamburg, photographed in 1945. Lowell Bennett might have obtained this very view on his guided tour of the city in December 1943, after the devastating RAF raids in July that year. He was shocked to see the same sort of scene in Berlin from close up, after being shot down and taken prisoner.
AWM Negative P00687.338

But as the train made its slow way through the marshalling yards, he noted that the bombs had once again fallen in such a random distribution they barely affected the operation of the station complex itself: 'there seemed no shortage of rolling stock, nor serious damage to the warehouses and depots'. When he had departed Berlin only a week and a half before from Anhalter Station, Bennett had noted a similarly perverse pattern of widespread damage around the station, while the station itself remained fully functional. As the train now pulled into Potsdamer Station, he perceived a similar pattern, seeing that the station was 'roofless, and parts of its walls were missing, evidently from bomb blast, but it was crowded and busy'.

From there, Bennett and Bönningshaus were whisked off in a car to meet the unnamed people in Berlin whom Bönningshaus had said wanted to see him. When they were dropped off outside a building in the Wilhelmstrasse government sector of the inner city, Bennett could not help feeling a bit intimidated. He saw that the stately government buildings in Wilhelmstrasse had 'not yet suffered heavily from the bombing', and when he was taken inside, found that the interior office spaces were 'as modern and as well heated as any in America'. As he waited in this opulent setting to be called into the meeting with the unknown official, his memories of corny war movies led him to expect a clichéd 'Hollywood-type Gestapo grilling'. In the event he was 'almost disappointed' not to get it, instead being ushered into the office of a senior Foreign Office diplomat, where he was put at his ease: he and Bönningshaus were 'bade to make themselves comfortable', and Bennett was asked 'if there was anything I needed'. After days of dirt and deprivation, Bennett came back with a very direct and specific answer: 'A haircut, a meal, and some cigarettes'.

In Bennett's narrative, he identified the Foreign Office official as 'Dr. Steiner', but German official records show that it was Embassy Councillor von Strempel. As in the case of Captain 'Borner', Bennett chose to disguise the real identity of his German interlocutors in his published account. Strempel was as proficient in English as Bönningshaus was, having served as First Secretary of the German Embassy to the US from 1938 to 1941. As a designated expert on America, working on the American desk of Berlin's Foreign Office, he took a close interest in this captured American reporter.

The first thing Strempel did was grant the deprived young American his wish: Bennett was driven a few blocks away to the Esplanade Hotel, situated on Potsdamer Platz. There an Italian barber cut his hair, with Bennett feeling conspicuous because of the US insignia on his war correspondent's uniform jacket. As he sat in the barber's chair, he was watched impassively by the other customers sitting around the walls awaiting their turns, including several German military officers. An elderly general, who overheard Bennett's conversation with the barber conducted in mixed French and German, responded with ponderous but restrained curiosity, as described by Bennett:

> [He] ... put down the *Völkischer Beobachter* he was reading, walked over to my chair, squinted at me, at the uniform, then back at me, and turned away. Borner [sic] walked with him to an empty corner of the room and explained the situation.

For the general returned to his chair, picked up his newspaper, squinted at me again, and resumed reading.

Refreshed and rehumanised by haircut, lunch and smokes, Bennett was taken back to the Foreign Office to commence the interrogation, which Strempel and two of his colleagues conducted. They asked him a series of fairly general questions, mostly pertaining to the Allied public's attitude to the war, and public morale on the Allied side. Bennett recorded that he answered them either with non-committal shrugs or flippant, generalised answers. Indeed, he claims that he became so amused and self-confident by their inept questioning that he dared to interrupt proceedings with a renewal of the tactical ploy he had tried with Bönningshaus at his first interrogation back at Oberursel: 'Look here, am I going to a prison camp or will you repatriate me?' Strempel gave only a non-committal reply in the form of a 'whimsical shrug'. However, the mood suddenly changed for the better when Bennett expressed an interest in seeing more of the *Hauptstadt*; the diplomat offered to take him on a 'sightseeing tour around the capital'. This was certainly a good way of ending the interrogation (for now at least), and corresponded closely with Bennett's real wishes, so for the second time in twenty-four hours he jumped at his captives' generous offer.

A wide-ranging four-hour-long driving and walking tour ensued, with Strempel and Bönningshaus as his tour guides and minders. They gave Bennett full access to bomb-damaged districts as well as closely supervised observation of what passed for normal life in this heavily bombed city. The rapidity with which this privilege had been granted, almost immediately upon Bennett's arrival in Berlin and after only a mild discussion of unthreatening topics, suggests that there was an agenda at play, and indeed there was: having heard of Bönningshaus's promising young American civilian prisoner at Oberursel, a group of officials at the Foreign Office had decided they would try to 'exploit Bennett propagandistically'. Strempel had conceived a plan to cultivate Bennett whilst he was in Germany: he would turn the American towards a sympathetic view of the Third Reich, and then let him go free, so that he would return to the US and weaken the American public's support for Allied war strategy by writing pro-German articles. The fact that a supposed expert on America, one of the Foreign Office's senior diplomats, could seriously entertain such a naïve plan is testament to the self-delusive folly even of Germany's well-educated professional bureaucratic elite during the Third Reich. Strempel's plan reveals minimal understanding, if any, of the patriotic group-think with which the Allied press had clothed itself during the war, nor of the rapidity with which a correspondent would lose his accreditation and credibility if he peddled a pro-German line – in a context where the Allied public had been well conditioned by years of critical reportage to hate Hitler, to deride the Nazi leaders, and to condemn Nazi policies, war actions and atrocities. The fact that these prejudicial opinions were well justified is beside the present point. As the saying goes, any pro-German reporting in 1944 would have 'gone over like a lead balloon'.

Nonetheless, in execution of Strempel's plan to put Bennett through a re-education program, the captured reporter was taken on his guided tour of Berlin on the very afternoon of the day he arrived in the capital. No matter his benefactors' and minders' intentions, for a man like Bennett, possessed of a curious temperament, one moreover who plied the avocation of journalist, and whose artistic inclinations tended towards narrative writing, this tour was a gift. Bennett avidly grabbed his chance and absorbed everything he saw and heard. His guided tour of Berlin confirmed his previous impressions of devastating damage from the RAF bombing:

> The varied sights of destruction I had glimpsed on the first drive through Berlin were multiplied throughout its entire breadth. Whole sections were reduced to gutted, gaping skeletons and tangled masonry. Some streets were completely blocked with mountainous debris; others were walled only by shells of burned-out buildings.

However, despite the extensive material damage, he found that Berlin society still functioned, as did the city's key infrastructure and industry:

> ... streetcars and the subways still operated. Train stations had lost their glass roofs, but they still handled a massive freight. It was a picture of a population fighting hard with every means at hand to prevent desolation from overwhelming them.

Even in the heavily bombed districts, the streets and roads were traffic-ready, assiduously cleared of rubble and repaired after each raid by gangs of labourers, many of whom were

Soviet POWs or forced labourers from occupied Europe. Because of this army of labourers, the street system was still functional, but the roads were almost empty of car traffic, an impression underlined by the contrast he could draw from his recent experience of the traffic in bustling wartime London. The 'dearth of vehicles' in Berlin was explainable by 'the severe fuel-rationing system', leaving the roads clear for 'a large number of giant trucks ... towing two or more trailers'. Despite all the damage, the road transport network appeared to be effectively mobilised in support of the war effort, just as the damaged railway system was.

Emphasising this impression of the substantial militarisation of Germany's society and economy, Bennett also noted the 'profusion of military personnel' on the streets. London's public spaces at this time were not exactly free of uniformed foot traffic either, so Bennett's impression again emphasises how far things had gone in Germany by comparison. He found that Berlin was 'crowded with troops', with a 'phenomenal quantity of saluting and Heil Hitlering'. Besides members of the army, navy and air force, the uniforms included those of the Nazi paramilitary arms, the SS, SA, and *Hitler Jugend*. As well as all these smartly uniformed servants of the Nazi state, more shabbily uniformed armies of unhappy expatriates toiled as forced labourers for the German war machine: 'thousands of Russian prisoners were to be seen working in the debris', as well as 'veritable armies' of French, Italian, Polish, Serbian and even British POWs, all dressed in their native khaki uniforms. For the Poles who had been captured in Germany's conquest of that country back in 1939, or even the Russians and Serbs captured during Germany's *Blitzkrieg* campaigns of 1941, it was a long war and a long captivity, and so their khakis must by 1943 have become threadbare, torn and much patched.

Juxtaposed among these uniformed throngs were the civilian Berliners, or at least those who remained living in the half bombed-out city. The civilians seemingly formed only a minority of the remaining population. Strempel told Bennett that because of the air raids, nearly two million Berliners had already been evacuated from the urban area – about half the pre-war population. These included the children (those too young to be conscripted as Flak helpers), the elderly and 'nonessential women'. Bennett found that the resultant relative depopulation gave the city a 'deserted, sterile appearance', an impression heightened by 'the capital's complete barrenness of children', an unnatural feature that he found most 'startling'. Again, Bennett was implicitly making comparisons with wartime London.

Bennett took a good look at the civilian residents who were left. The city having so far received 'nearly fifteen thousand tons of bombs', he thought 'the people's mannerisms clearly showed their fatigue and nervousness'. But despite their ongoing ordeal they remained 'well-dressed', with everyone well protected against the winter by 'Heavy coats, well-lined and collared with fur'. However, beneath the veneer of civilised niceties, he saw that life had become increasingly dreary for the people of Berlin. Strempel told Bennett that all public dancing had been banned since the beginning of the war, and that the government had also closed down nightclubs, popular music venues and the inner-city bars. The gist of this was accurate: dance events had indeed been banned in January 1942, but inconsistent and contradictory policing within the Reich meant that some dance venues had continued to operate, so that it was only Goebbels' proclamation of 'total war' in February 1943 that closed down the remaining semi-illicit but inconsistently tolerated clubs and bars. Bennett saw that although Berliners could no longer let their hair down by dancing, they could readily seek the solace of alcohol, which was freely available in all hotels: not only various forms of the ubiquitous Schnapps, but French, German and Hungarian wines; indeed French champagne was 'obtainable in far greater quantities and far cheaper than in London or New York'. Of course, the blockade meant that 'American rye and Scottish whisky were ... in short stock'. As the bombing had so far left standing two opera houses and the Wintergarten music hall, there was still some evening entertainment available, but under the prevailing cultural and social austerity as well as the nocturnal disruption of air-raid alarms, Bennett thought that 'Afternoon coffee gatherings seemed almost the sole social medium'. Many cafes, restaurants and hotels still attempted to maintain a semblance of normality by retaining small orchestras 'to entertain nerve-frayed Berliners'. The musicians seemed to be the only ones the military draft had left behind, all of them too old to be conscripted even into the auxiliary services. They played dutifully to lighten the mood, but Bennett had heard too much good jazz and swing to appreciate either the repertoire or the old men's musicianship, characterising the resultant musical fare as 'interminable violin drivel, more depressing than it was diverting'.

Despite the ready availability of booze and the vestigial civilised ritual of *Kaffeeklatsch*, Bennett unsurprisingly found the Reich capital in December 1943 to be a depressing place:

Berlin was a sober, grim city whose populace was too occupied struggling with the necessities of life to indulge in the luxury of social entertainment which keynoted life in London. Germany's capital was now, in effect, the blitzed London of 1940 – but graver, more depressed, lugubrious, and far more heavily bombed.

Moreover, for Bennett, well-used to the multicultural districts of New York, London and Paris, the heavy atmosphere of the suffering city gained a yet more sinister colouring from the conspicuous absence of Jewish people from this formerly cosmopolitan metropolis: 'The very few I observed wore a large, yellow star of David prominently displayed on an outer garment ... In the S-Bahn subway, the escalators were clearly marked, "Use for Jews forbidden"'. Bennett could not have known it, but the Anhalter railway station he and his band of fellow POWs had passed through a couple of weeks before was the same station through which groups of German Jews were being transported to the Nazi concentration camp at Theresienstadt. The first fifty had boarded a train for that place in January 1942, and by the end of March 1945, 9600 elderly Jewish citizens of Berlin would be deported to the death camps. Many of the same civilian Berliners who sought to distract themselves from the war with coffee, Schnapps and dancing would have seen the regular groups of fifty or 100 yellow-starred elderly citizens at Anhalter Station boarding the two special carriages which had been added for their exclusive use to the 6.07 am inter-city express to Dresden and Prague. These special trains were escorted by soldiers of the 'Göring Battalion', and chillingly referred to by the mundane term

Alterstransporte (Transports of the Elderly). In total 116 such trains departed Anhalter Station, which was only one of the three railway stations in Berlin used to deport Berlin's elderly Jews to the camps.

Bennett was unaware of these details, but he needed no tuition in perceiving the showy fakery and moral seediness of Hitler's 'Thousand-year-Reich':

> ... there was a glut of swastikaed flags and drapery, of postered ballyhoo for the National Socialist Party, and of gaudy war propaganda. The sharp contrast of billboards with their shrieking colors set against the somber background of ashen rubble was somehow symbolic: it painted a prologue to the death of vaunted, hollow nationalism.

With his mind full of impressions and reflections, at the conclusion of the city tour Strempel and Bönningshaus took him back to the office. He had been given a lot to think about. Having taken his 'crash course' in the 'real story' of bombed Berlin, unbeknown to his two interlocutors he had drawn the opposite conclusions to those they'd intended. By now it was early evening, so his two solicitous minders walked him to the nearby hotel – Bennett's program of special treatment included a major accommodation upgrade as well.

However, before they arrived at the hotel the air-raid sirens 'one after the other, began their haunting, swelling quaver'. Knowing full well that the RAF was intent upon blitzing his host city, Bennett had already started to feel 'gnawing' anxiety about being caught in a raid. Now here it was: 'I trembled with a deeper fright than I had experienced a few nights [sic] earlier above the city'. With the sirens wailing overhead and his heart full of dread, Bennett was only too pleased to be ushered downstairs by his two official minders into a nearby bomb shelter, situated as most of them were in the basement of an apartment. Now he obtained the unplanned follow-up to his afternoon tour, an authentic experience of how a raid touched the ordinary people caught underneath the bombs. Having taken his seat, he looked around inside the shelter:

> Inside was a normal cellar, converted into an air raid bunker by crossbeams and heavy wooden timber supports for the ceiling. About twenty women sat in groups of two or three huddling together on benches and canvas stools. Three old men and a youthful fire warden, in addition to ourselves, were the only males in the shelter.
>
> On the walls hung axes, shovels, first-aid kits, buckets, and a variety of civilian gas masks. Two small candles provided the room's only light.

Almost as soon as the three new arrivals had got themselves settled inside the shelter, Bennett's disquiet was heightened by a sudden salvo from a nearby Flak battery, the muzzle blasts of which resounded 'echoing loudly through the cellar'. Unseen by him, the guns' flak shells were ascending to 20 000 feet to star the unseen sky with angry bursts of black smoke and tearing shell splinters. By now Bennett had acquired enough insider knowledge to know what such barrage fire meant: the first few pathfinders were almost overhead. And he knew that these would be followed within scant minutes by the arrival of the main bomber force, seeking the target-marking flares dropped by the pathfinders:

> Soon the gunfire became an almost solid thunder as batteries all over the city spread a carpet of death over Berlin.
>
> I felt perspiration running down my arms and face. I was breathing in short gasps; my eyes were half closed and my hands tightly clenched. I was terribly conscious of the 'U.S.' insignia on my uniform – these people will recognize me I thought, and if the bombs don't kill us all, they'll kill me for what my allies are doing to their city.

Anxiously he opened his eyes and looked around him to check on what these two dozen cutthroat Berliners were up to. With relief he realised that 'no one in the shelter was interested in anything but himself':

> The women sat hunched over, their heads on their knees, their hands over their ears, holding themselves together, waiting for the bombs. One woman clutched two tiny children to her breast; one baby squeaked annoyingly and incongruously.
>
> The men stood against the wall, hands at their sides or crossed on their chests, eyes staring straight ahead into the opposite wall. One old man, wearing a last-war

helmet, stood stiffly at attention, rigid with fear and anticipation. The young warden paced an open space on the floor, watching the women, listening, waiting.

Then the bombs started. The staccato thunder of the guns was suddenly overwhelmed by an ear-rending avalanche of sheer terror. It was an express train, a waterfall, a drum fire ... whistling, swishing, screaming ... pounding, erupting, thumping.

'My God, this is a nightmare', I thought frantically as my fingernails dug painlessly into my palms ...

No words can describe the next twenty minutes ...

Overwhelmed by it all, rather than provide a coherent, sequential description of what followed, all Bennett could do afterwards was recall a series of impressions:

> I remember the clattering of incendiaries on the roof, on the street outside, the gushing, shuddering explosion of a land mine [a 'blockbuster' or 'cookie'] across the road. I remember one woman screaming in a high-pitched shriek, and falling prostrate across the floor. I remember the candles going out, plaster falling in strips from the ceiling, the door crashing open, and lumber from the floor above blocking the entrance, the air rushing from the room as another bomb smashed into a building on the same block ...

> After a while the bombs and flak stopped. A deathly lull hung over the dark cellar. Then bells clanged in the street outside; fire trucks raced past and I looked up to see a red panel of flame through the shattered door.

Bennett snapped out of his nightmarish reverie when Strempel suddenly announced, 'We can go now. It is finished.' Once outside and standing in the street, Bennett and the other occupants of the shelter looked up to see their building 'afire, the top two floors blazing fiercely'.

Having spent four hours in the afternoon touring Berlin, Bennett had just spent an hour in an air-raid shelter right underneath the bombs; and now, after the raid all-clear sounded, Strempel and Bönningshaus took Bennett on an additional hour-long walking tour of the freshly bombed and still-burning centre of the city:

> Here was a conflagration such as I had never seen in London. Whole streets were alight; billowing flames and smoke gushed upward from department stores, buildings, homes. Occasional streets were impassably blocked where the high-explosives had fallen.
>
> Ambulances and fire engines chased through the open streets. Wounded were carted past on stretchers in every direction. Dead were lying in piles along the gutter ...
>
> Parts of airplanes were scattered through the roads, strips of wings, tails, fuselage. Here a whole engine had buried itself in the macadam and a few yards distant lay a wheel from some unlucky Lancaster.

Fire-bombs which had fallen uselessly in the open streets patterned out neatly in long rows, each issuing a white-hot flame from its wasted phosphorus.

Before one house, which was being quickly devoured by fire, an old woman sat on a chair, sobbing bitterly above the crackling flames. She had saved two chairs, a suitcase, and a meshed hamper – that remained; the rest was gone.

The young American had already been in a highly impressionable state before this tour, and by the time he was finally taken to his hotel his mind had been vividly imprinted with a series of powerful impressions of the bombing's impact. The hotel, they discovered upon check-in, had lost most of its windows, broken by the bombs' shockwaves, and had lost part of the top floor, burned out by incendiaries before the fires could be put out. Nonetheless Bönningshaus and Bennett were able to check in to their room, attended by a corporal whose job it was to guard the prisoner. After such a day and such a night, both of Bennett's two German roommates were too tired out to watch over him particularly vigilantly, but he was also too exhausted to attempt any escape.

Bennett's published account places this raid on or about 9 December, but there was no raid on Berlin around that time. Identifying the night upon which these events happened eludes any definite adjudication, but the events as he described them best suit the heavy RAF raid on the night of 16 December. Indeed, after the 2 December raid in which Bennett had been shot down, the RAF did not visit

Berlin for a fortnight because of the full moon and poor flying weather. But Air Marshal Harris resumed his force's attacks upon this target as soon as conditions permitted, and so on the night of 16 December he launched the first raid on Berlin since 2 December, flinging nearly 500 bombers at the capital, timed to pass over the aiming point in fourteen minutes. From the RAF's perspective, this raid went unusually well. A layer of cloud hung over the city and stopped the searchlights from illuminating the bombers as they passed over the top of the cloud and obliged the Flak batteries to fire blindly under radar control. Despite the cloud cover, the pathfinders arrived exactly on schedule, using H2S radar to drop blind-marking parachute flares on top of the blanket of cloud, right over the area of the aiming point in the centre of the city. After that, the main force bombers passed overhead, dumping their loads through the patches of the cloud cover that were lit up by the pathfinder flares. The resultant bombing fell in a line across the city, blasting a swathe across the aiming point, along a beaten path 6 kilometres long and half a kilometre wide, running just south of the city centre. Given Bennett's description of the harrowing trial he went through in his bomb shelter within a residential district close to the city centre, he was likely located within this centrally situated beaten path. Indeed, in this raid it was residential areas that were the hardest hit, with 720 people killed or missing, of whom 279 were foreigners being used as forced labourers, of which number 186 were women. This raid brought the number of destroyed residential apartments within Berlin to 175 000, with a further 70–80 000 'seriously damaged and unlikely to be repaired as long as the raids continued'. Although the

16 December raid did not raise any large-scale, district-wide firestorms as some previous Berlin raids had done, it had to be rated as a 'success' if judged according to the RAF's criteria. Certainly, Bennett's testimony of a terrifyingly severe Berlin raid, experienced from a shelter in the centre of that city, is entirely consistent with the facts of the case on the night of 16 December. In short, the narrative timeline presented and implied in Bennett's published account needs to be reinterpreted chronologically, and the details of his experience match the 16 December event perfectly.

Within Bennett's narrative, the morning after this raid he and Bönninghaus returned to Strempel's office in the Foreign Office's Wilhelmstrasse complex. Shaken by the severity of the raid the previous night, the three men must have felt at least a little bound together by comradely instincts, given their shared ordeal in the shelter, their joint survival, and their mutual first-hand experience afterwards of the fires, wreckage, carnage, and human resilience of Berlin. The experience must surely have been almost as striking and memorable for Bönninghaus as it was for Bennett, as the German officer was unlikely to have witnessed any of the preceding heavy attacks during November–December, because of his duty post in Oberursel, 400 kilometres away to the southwest. Thus, his shared experience with Bennett on the night of 16 December was likely to have been his first face-to-face exposure to the torment undergone by the population of the *Reichshauptstadt*. Whatever his own innermost responses, he and Strempel coolly subjected Bennett to a debrief the next morning, lasting 'several hours'. Bennett recalled that they discussed 'comparative cultures', specifically a comparison between Germany and the English-speaking world. By now, perhaps emboldened by the privileged treatment accorded to him latterly, and by the recent remembrance of the bonds of comradeship the previous night during the raid, Bennett abandoned his policy of guarded reticence sufficient to advance a blunt criticism of the Nazi state:

> You people are riding on your grandfathers' laurels ... Your music and literature has nothing to do with this new fantasy of Nazism. You've been too busy making guns during the past ten years to turn out anything enduring.

This reproach seems to have hit home, stinging Bönningshaus into a rebuttal, albeit a superficial one which implicitly conceded the point to Bennett, in which he limited the claimed scope of Nazi Germany's 'culture' to the mundane sphere of state-controlled social infrastructure: 'You haven't seen Germany. We have wonderful architecture, fine roads and schools – all built since 1933.' Evidently, Bönningshaus lamely thought that a bit of civil engineering could counterbalance gratuitously launching a disastrous war of aggression upon Europe and the systematic industrial-scale murder of European Jewry.

It was now that Bennett came to realise what role he was supposed to be playing, why he was being accorded such special treatment. His account of the discussion he had with Strempel and Bönningshaus is highly consistent with the German Foreign Office's objective in their special handling of the captured reporter: their aim, and the justification for all the trouble and expense they were going to in according him special treatment, was to turn him into a friend of Germany and send him back to the States as a sympathetic explainer of Hitler's Reich. A debate about the cultural worthiness or otherwise of the Nazi state was therefore right to the point.

Despite the criticisms of Nazism that Bennett offered during this discussion, he must have shown at least some sympathy for the German perspective presented by his two interlocutors, for at the end of this extensive interview, Bönninghaus made a further offer, the terms of which made the curious and opportunistic Bennett sit up and take notice. The Luftwaffe officer explained that they were now scheduled to return to Oberursel, where he would be obliged to give Bennett over to the regular authorities for onwards processing to his assigned POW camp. So far Bönninghaus seems to have deliberately left vague the question of Bennett's repeatedly mooted repatriation as a civilian, but as an artfully 'spontaneous' follow-up to their interesting discussion about the cultural tone of Germany under Hitler, he blurted out the idea of extending Bennett's tour:

> Now, I have an eight-day furlough due me, I might be able to keep you out of the camp for these eight days. I have some friends here and I could get a car and fuel. If you would promise me that you would not try to escape, perhaps we could take a look around Germany. And you may see that we are not so primitive a people as you think.

Bennett was stunned to thus be offered a 'trip around Germany' right in the middle of the war. Given the preceding discussion, he knew that he was being played upon by his interviewers: that it was intended as a 'propaganda tour', and that so far from being a spontaneous idea on Bönningshaus's part in the heat of the conversation, in reality the offer had been 'all carefully planned and arranged by the Nazis'. But on the other hand, such a tour would give him 'a first-hand picture of conditions inside Germany'. For an ambitious reporter, such 'legalised spying' was 'compensatingly exciting'. He knew that he would be ushered from location to location by Nazi officers according to a pre-planned, officially sanctioned itinerary, but this orchestration did not mean he would take leave of his senses and moral instincts in interpreting what he saw. While playing the appreciative protégé, Bennett resolved to remain 'an American reporter who tried to forget neither his allegiance nor his profession'. Strempel and the Foreign Office, aided and abetted by Bönningshaus, were seeking to exploit Bennett, but meanwhile, Bennett was setting out to exploit them: he would cheerfully take advantage of their good offices by taking the tour, and then report whatever he liked about it afterwards.

Having made his deal, both with Bönningshaus and his own conscience, Bennett was furnished with the cover necessary to take the trip: a false identity card, a civilian overcoat and a civilian felt hat. His assumed identity was as 'Robert Durand', a French journalist from Paris. This was plausible given his fluent Parisian French and his familiarity with that city. The fact that his ID was ready at once seems hardly consistent with Bönningshaus's pretence of a spontaneous offer; similarly, his newfound colleagues did not take literally his promise not to attempt escape. Bönningshaus kept hold of the ID card so that his captive could not use it. Both men were playing a subtle and wary game with each other, despite the affectation of mutual confidence.

With itinerary, identity card, civilian clothes, civilian cover, car, driver, fuel and permits organised, a long road trip lay ahead of them to reach the first tour destination, Hamburg. It was a long journey to fit into the short winter's day, so they set out early the next morning – presumably on or about 18 December. Bönningshaus and Bennett departed Berlin, driven through Berlin's outskirts and out into the flat countryside beyond. The weather was 'dismal' – rainy and misty – but Bennett used his observant reporter's eyes to take in everything he saw en route. Bönningshaus had earlier attempted to praise the roads the Third Reich had built under Hitler, but this Autobahn evidently was not one of them: despite connecting Germany's two most populous cities, the new motorway had barely been started before the war began, whereupon the country's civil engineering resources were reallocated away from civilian to military projects, leaving the Hamburg–Berlin Autobahn uncompleted. In this instance the journey of perhaps 250 kilometres took five hours, despite driving along 'good roads' under traffic conditions so 'exceptionally light' that they 'passed barely a dozen vehicles'. Similar to his impressions of Berlin's urban traffic, Bennett saw that private vehicles were absent from the highway, with movement largely confined to large trucks carrying military loads.

They entered Hamburg via the industrial district of Harburg, which lay on the outskirts of the city, on the southern bank of the Elbe River. It reminded Bennett of Pittsburgh, with 'factories everywhere, smoke jutting finger-like into fog-laden skies'. Significantly, he saw that this pulsating industrial centre was little damaged, despite the RAF's supposedly complete destruction of Hamburg in July that year. Continuing on to Hamburg itself and crossing on to the northern bank of the Elbe, the scene changed abruptly as they drove through what must have been the inner suburbs of Hammerbrook, Borgfelde and Hamm, residential districts lying immediately east of the old city centre, areas which had been consumed by the great firestorm raid on the night of 27 July 1943. As Bennett now saw from the windows of the car, it was in these districts that 'the desolation began':

> ... for at least three miles there was not one house standing on either side of the street. I had seen the badly damaged areas of Berlin and the spotted destruction in London, but this was a devastation unimaginable by previous experience.
>
> This was one hundred percent destruction. It was desolation such as no earthquake, no natural phenomenon could have caused. It was deeply perturbing to witness what a terrible weapon man had invented in the air force and the incendiary bomb.

Bönningshaus and Strempel were presumably perceptive enough to notice that Bennett's humanitarian instincts railed in horror at the indiscriminate brutality of the RAF bombing. But whether this very human reaction would ultimately give them the result they wanted was another matter altogether.

As they drove on, heading further into town, Bennett noticed the perversely arbitrary pattern of the bomb impacts, for he found that the city centre itself was 'not badly damaged'. Hamburg's *Hauptbahnhof* had lost its roof, but just as he had seen with the Anhalter and Potsdamer stations in Berlin, despite this the train schedule was still operating 'to all major cities in Europe'. His minders must have been keeping him on a short leash during his heavily choreographed tour, for there were other inner-city architectural monuments which had also been hit, but which he evidently did not see, such as the City Hall, St Nicholas Church, the main police station, and the main telephone exchange. After arrival in the city centre, Bönningshaus took Bennett to the police station, introducing him to a 'Lieutenant Freier' as 'a French journalist whom I am accompanying on a trip around Germany'. Freier took him on a tour of one of the burnt-out zones, areas which were now barricaded off from public access with 'Entry Strictly Forbidden' signs. Bennett described what he saw inside one such zone, which he later measured from a street map as encompassing an area of nearly 4 square miles:

> The totality of destruction was appalling. Street after street of dwelling houses was smashed and rubbled, levelled and pulverized into heaps of granulated greyness. Sometimes a broken radiator, a stove, or part of a bathtub poked out of the ruins. One thought of Pompeii, but surely this was worse.

As in Berlin, the ruined areas were being picked over by armies of forced labourers, 'French, Italian, and Russian war prisoners', as well as 'Political prisoners, in striped blue and grey uniforms'. These gangs of workers were employed in the hard labour of collecting 'rubble to be used in the port area', but also in digging for and collecting the bodies of the fire-raid victims, which were still being discovered and disinterred five months after the raids. Like in Berlin, the streets had been cleared for traffic, but there was no traffic save 'the prisoner columns with their picks and shovels and a few dump trucks with rubble'. Lieutenant Freier told him, quite truthfully, that the July raids had killed 40 000 and injured 65 000 people. Bennett was an imaginative, reflective, humane man, and the tour was having its effect upon his thinking:

> Such figures are cold, brutally indescriptive. They convey no impression of death in its myriad and terrible forms and the grotesque maiming of human beings through air bombardment. Happily, America has known nothing of air attack in this war. But because of this good fortune, our people have little conception of the tremendous horror of such raids.

Again, it is likely that Bönningshaus and Strempel had opportunity to observe Bennett's reaction close up, noting him down as someone only too amenable to harbouring humane thoughts about the enemy. To rub in the message, Freier took Bennett back to the police station and showed him gruesome photographs of the raids' victims, the bodies all 'charred, chipped, cremated with scorch, lying in impossible positions, with arms and legs stretched out at grotesque angles':

> These were not propaganda pictures. When I asked if they had been printed or circulated, Freier said, 'they are too terrible. Propaganda should not be carried that far.'
>
> But I cannot help feeling that they should be circulated to all of us ...
>
> I could not think, 'These are Germans ... it is all right because they are the enemy.' That was impossible. I could only think of London, Berlin, Warsaw, and Moscow. These pictures showed not only Germans. They represented humanity. They disclosed with a clarity and a horrible exactness just what we did to each other during the war.

Then Freier showed him a large-scale map of Hamburg marked with each area colour-coded to indicate the weight of bombs that had fallen within it. Bennett saw that although about 60 per cent of the city area had been affected by the bombing, 'no more than a dozen RAF bombs had fallen anywhere near the dock or shipbuilding areas on the outskirts of the city'. To corroborate the map with first-hand observation, Freier took him back across the Elbe to the Blohm & Voss shipbuilding yards. There he saw sixteen U-boats under construction on the slipways and six 'finished submarines' in the water. After an 'extensive tour' of the workshops and sheds within the shipyard complex, he estimated that 'less than five percent of the entire area had suffered from air bombing'. This exposé was the culmination of his guided tour of Hamburg.

By now the pattern of the accumulated impressions had aroused Bennett's indignation:

> It was incredible that the Allies had not yet inflicted more damage on such an important element of the German U-boat production ...
>
> I recalled the smug pride of RAF officials after the Hamburg attacks. 'Wiped out', they said ...
>
> 'Wiped out' was true. Most of the city was gone. And the cost to Britain was tremendous ...
>
> But the dockyards, U-boat slipways, and huge warehouse facilities ... were still operating all out for a Nazi victory.

No doubt Bönningshaus closely observed Bennett's reactions during the tour. He must have noticed the emotional impact it was having upon the young American. Almost certainly Bennett made some comment about his impressions and reactions afterwards with his minder, who could only have been encouraged by any signs of his protégé's disaffection with the Allied bombing campaign.

According to Bennett's narrative, the next morning they drove to Bremen, a major port city on the Weser River, and only a 100-kilometre drive from Hamburg. Bönningshaus had phoned ahead to tee up a local guide, a newspaper journalist. Upon their arrival this guide took them to a restaurant for 'a somewhat incongruous' lunch of smoked eel, herring and ice cream. Afterwards the German newspaperman took them on a walking tour of the inner city, and then for a drive to view the dockyard and shipbuilding districts. Bennett was told that so far in the war, Bremen's city authorities had tallied 122 air attacks upon their city, and that the locals claimed that they had sustained more air raids than any other city. Despite this weight of attack, after a 'comprehensive visit' to Bremen's central city and port area, Bennett estimated that the town had suffered 25 per cent damage, while the waterfront area had suffered only 7.5 per cent. In response to Bennett's questioning, the guide told him the official figures, which corroborated his rough estimate: 30 per cent of the town was destroyed but only 10 per cent of the dock area. He saw with his own eyes that the harbourside industrial district was so extensive that he estimated it occupied a space 'at least as great as the city itself'. Within this industrial zone he saw that most of the warehouses were still intact and noted with astonishment 'a veritable city of oil storage tanks' standing intact, safely hidden beneath a vast spiderweb of camouflage netting. The U-boat construction pens were similarly untouched within their cavernous reinforced concrete shelters, while the 'fields of loading cranes, dockyards' and 'railroad switching areas' were operating as normal, seemingly almost undamaged. Clearly, the pattern of bomb damage at Bremen was similar to what he had seen in Hamburg.

Bennett had been given further food for thought, but before he could digest his latest observations, he was interrupted by another British air raid. After completing the tour, he and Bönningshaus had checked in to the hotel and were waiting in the lobby for dinner, when soon after 6 pm the air-raid sirens 'opened their mournful chant'. The advantage of being in the hotel was the real-time raid updates which were broadcast over the public address system in the lobby. Large public facilities such as this were connected to the city's air-raid control centre, and so ordinary people could follow the raid's movement via a running commentary broadcast through the PA speakers by a young woman posted in the air defence operations room. After so many raids, the people of Bremen were old hands at this, and Bennett sat in the lobby listening and watching as the guests disappeared upstairs to their rooms, then reappeared carrying 'suitcases, hampers, and rucksacks', just in case. They did not descend into the cellar bomb shelter, but instead 'settled into chairs' in the lobby, following the running broadcast in comfort. Only when the danger was declared 'imminent' would they go below into the 'stuffy cellar'.

At 6.30 pm, 'the radio crackled back to life' with an announcement that the raid was now 120 kilometres to the southwest, heading east. This might have suggested that the bomber stream was skirting Bremen, heading inland towards Hanover or Berlin, but five minutes later came another transmission, announcing that enemy bombers were now only 50 kilometres southwest. Had they turned towards Bremen?

> The atmosphere in the lobby, crowded with a hundred men and women, fully dressed with coats and hats, each with a small pile of luggage beside his seat, was charged with tension.
>
> ...

There was no pretense here. In England, during the blitz, it had not been 'good form' to display emotion, fear, worry. But here, with a frankness approaching intimacy, no one attempted to cover the fact that he was waiting, watching, listening – would that terrible horror burst in a few moments over Bremen?

After another five minutes a steel-helmeted air raid warden hurried in to announce that Bremen's Flak batteries were opening fire and that everyone must now go down into the shelter. As the queue of people patiently filed down the stairs, the radio crackled into life again providing the same information, the message now emphasised further by the 'dull, erratic rhythm of anti-aircraft guns, pounding distantly, hollowly into the night sky'. Once seated down below, Bennett saw that the hotel was equipped with an excellent bomb shelter:

> We sat for a while ... in the low-ceilinged shelter, hearing nothing, for we were deep in the earth. Thick timbers supported the roof and the basement had been divided into a maze of interconnected rooms, separated by heavy steel doors which bolted on both sides.

Bennett and the others had barely had time to settle into their places when, just before 7 pm, through the speakers came another announcement from the control room: the raid was heading away from Bremen, going further inland, with the leading edge of the bomber stream already 250 kilometres southeast. Soon after that the sirens 'screeched a welcome but anticlimactic all-clear', and everyone was allowed back up to their rooms. Bennett and Bönningshaus were now able to enjoy a 'late supper'.

Bennett's account provides a vivid impression of his experiences of an air raid, although once again, the timeline in Bennett's published narrative has this event occurring earlier in the month where it cannot be matched with any RAF raid in that timeframe. After the 3 December Leipzig raid, the only major RAF raids into Germany were the 16 December raid to Berlin (which ordeal Bennett had suffered through in a bomb shelter with Bönningshaus, as we have seen); a 20 December raid to Frankfurt, which took a direct path from the coast and so went nowhere near Bremen; a 23 December raid to Berlin, which could not have been the event experienced by Bennett in Bremen as it was routed far to the south and would only have passed Bremen on the way home, much later in the night than 7 pm as reported by Bennett (indeed so late that the bombers returned to England in daylight); and a 29 December Berlin raid. Although the latter was much later in the month than his account puts it, it is the best candidate for the experience Bennett relates: this raid passed close by Bremen, just as Bennett described, and in the 7 pm timeframe. By contrast, the next raid in the RAF sequence, to Berlin on the night of 1–2 January 1944, although it also passed close by Bremen, it did so very late in the night, in the early hours of 2 January, and not at dinner time as Bennett describes. Thus the 29 December Berlin raid is by far the best match with Bennett's experience in a Bremen air-raid shelter, rather than 16 December as he states in his account.

Once again, the timeline presented in Bennett's post-war published account does not seem to be presented in a literal chronological sequence. Bennett's accounts of his observations in both these raids provide plausible, immediate and authentic testimony, but these experiences seem to have occurred on a different timeline from that presented in his book. As we will see, he was in Germany long enough to have experienced several such raids, and from the vantage point of either place. Given the inconsistencies between the chronological details presented in Bennett's narrative and those of RAF raids in actuality, it follows that he had evidently reshuffled his vividly remembered experiences to fit his chosen narrative structure. In short, his narrative appears to be chronologically compressed, with the real events strung out in a longer chronological sequence than he presents us with. This raises the question: if he was in Berlin during the best-candidate 16 December raid, and in Bremen during the best-candidate 29 December raid, then what had he been doing in the intervening period?

The answer must be that Bennett spent longer in Berlin undergoing Strempel's re-education program at the Foreign Office than he presents in his account, and also longer on his guided tour through Germany. Surviving German official correspondence strongly suggests more extended duration than Bennett describes: documents state that he had 'many conversations' with his handlers, who only 'gradually' succeeded in changing his views, after which further 'numerous conversations' took place; and in the course of his tours, he 'got to know a range of German facilities in many districts', on the basis of which experiences he 'finally' made some concessions towards the German viewpoint. The chronological facts strongly suggest that Bennett's guided tours of inspection, and the associated meetings and debriefs with Nazi officials, were more extensive and took place over a longer period than he represents. Nonetheless, whatever the actual timeline, Bennett's account of being repeatedly interrogated by his handlers is authentic in its essentials.

Peter Thurnhofer has suggested a convincing reason why Bennett was so loose with the chronological details of his account: given that Bennett's book, *Parachute to Berlin*, would be published in New York before the end of 1945, to meet this deadline he must have composed the text illicitly while still in German captivity; he must have smuggled the manuscript to safety during the chaotic days at the end of the war, and then subjected it to the quickest possible editing process before submission to his publisher with a view to attaining the earliest possible release date. Given his clandestine authoring in the POW camp, it follows that Bennett knew there was a fair chance of his authorial endeavour being discovered by the camp authorities, and of his text being confiscated and handed over to the secret police, who would exploit its intelligence. Therefore, not only was his account of his travels inside Germany written from memory without access to corroborated timelines, but he had also deliberately altered names, times and places to put any investigations and recriminations off track in the not-unlikely event of his manuscript being seized.

It follows that while we cannot be sure of the timeframe within which Bennett was taken on the next stage of his tour, to the city of Münster in Westphalia, we can use his account as an eyewitness testimony to the state of that city in the winter of 1943–44. According to Bennett's account, Bönningshaus organised a local historian to lead his protégé on a two-hour guided tour of the city. The guide presented Münster to Bennett as 'one of the most important Catholic centers in Germany', and indeed what Bennett saw bore this out. But here too the bombers had, as always, been undiscriminating: he saw that the imposing and 'magnificent' St Paul's Cathedral was 'at least three-quarters destroyed', and that the palatial official residence of Bishop Clemens von Galen, who had been 'one of the most vigorous and vociferous enemies of National Socialism in Germany', had been consumed by flames. The Nazi-minded historian 'gloated' to Bennett that although the Catholic population of the city had formerly made it a centre of anti-Nazi resistance under Galen's leadership, since the destruction of these holy places by the RAF, the bishop had 'not said one word against the Nazis'. The morally conscientious Bennett made an impressionable and receptive audience. He later summed up what he had learned about Catholic Münster:

> ... the city had been a weak link in the new Germany, for its population was too devout to be recruited into the ranks of Hitler's new religion.
>
> But the grumblings and the discontent were ended. Our bombs had done that. However much we might propagandize ourselves as twentieth-century crusaders, as defenders of religious and political freedom, our bombs had splintered the heart of Catholic Westphalia. Our bombs, in truth, had bridged the breach between the Church and Nazi Germany.

As Bennett had realised from the very outset of their interaction, Bönningshaus's objective was to convince this American of the worthiness of German *Kultur* under the Nazis, thereby rebutting the critical portrait of Hitler's new Germany which had for years been painted by the media in the western democracies. Now, as the two tired men drove out of Münster, both worn out by a busy day conversing and interpreting between two languages, Bennett was left in the ensuing exhausted silence to debrief his day in his own thoughts. Coming on top of what he had seen in Bremen, the visit to Münster had confused and unsettled his preconceptions, though not for the reason Bönningshaus might have hoped. As Bennett related:

> His efforts to acquaint me with Germany's *Kultur* were falling flat. I was witnessing, instead, something else, an aspect of the war which was providing disturbing reactions. The only consolation, and it was a dubious one, was that perhaps further along the line I would see evidences of success to balance the three clear failures so far.

Whereas Strempel and Bönningshaus intended to rehabilitate Nazi Germany's reputation, Bennett's response was heading in another direction: for him, the tour had become a search for the rehabilitation of the reputation of Allied strategic bombing. Nazism itself was beyond rehabilitation, so there was no arguable case there. But at least he might find one German city where the bombers had actually hit and destroyed military targets.

After the disillusioning visit to Münster, the tourists next made the short drive south to Germany's heavy industrial heartland, to the 'Ruhr', a concentration of industrial cities of which the most famous was Essen, home to the Krupp armament works. Located in western Germany within easy reach of the RAF, Essen and the other cities of the Ruhr had featured on Bomber Command's bombing program since the campaign's inception in 1940. Bennett had read enough newspaper reports about raids to 'the Ruhr' to understand the significance of what he was about to see: 'For here the entire region was the target. Here, cities were adjacent; factories, mines, mills, and homes were sewn in a concentration unequalled anywhere else in the world.' Surely here in the Ruhr industrial district, with such a concentration of foundries, smelters, factories, warehouses and railway yards, in the course of so very many raids, the RAF had hit the installations in the heart of Hitler's arms industry? For Bennett, this would be the test case, the clincher. He was driven to Essen via the adjoining industrial centres of Bochum and Gelsenkirchen. They stopped there long enough for Bennett to assess that 'At least fifty per cent of each city was in ruins', but that nonetheless 'the heavy iron and steel works in each were still operating', a fact shown by the columns of black smoke 'surging' from 'scores of looming chimneys on the outskirts of the towns'. It was clear to him that 'the center of both cities had obviously been the main target and only stray bombs had fallen in the war-plant areas on the fringes'.

After that, Bennett viewed an apocalyptic scene as he and Bönningshaus made their entry into nearby Essen:

The road into Essen was walled on both sides by the gutted skeletons of burned-out buildings. The destruction was complete, continuous, mile after mile. Utter lifelessness was the predominant impression; the streets were barren and the darkening sky was half-occluded by the stark, jagged structures which had once been buildings.

They spent the night in the Krupp-built Essenerhof Hotel, one of only three un-bombed hotels remaining in the city, and only a few hundred metres from the seemingly miraculously undamaged *Hauptbahnhof.* The next morning a chauffeur arrived from the *Gauleiting*, the local Nazi Party organisation, to act as a tour guide. He took them on an 'extensive walking tour' of the city centre. Even Bönningshaus was caught out by the scale and extent of the destruction. As in an earlier stop in Osnabrück, he had intended to show Bennett some of the local architectural glories as exhibits of German *Kultur*, but by now still-standing architecture had become even harder to find in Essen than in Osnabrück, for the same reason: the guide declared that twenty-two of the city's twenty-five major churches were 'gone', demolished by the bombs. A visit to Essen Cathedral proved the point. On the other side of a sign declaring it the 'oldest Christian structure in Germany' (founded in 845 AD), Bennett saw that 'there was little left of the building. Inside was a tangled jumble of iron and leaded glass and mortar, where most of the dome and walls had been exploded inward.' The damage had been done by the RAF raid on the night of 5 March 1943, which had destroyed 160 acres of the city, including the destruction of 3018 houses. Bennett viewed the results:

> The city's center had been obliterated by high-explosives. An area of six square miles in the heart of Essen was ninety to one hundred per cent destroyed. The city hall, museum, post office and almost every other building and store in the business area had all been hammered into nothingness ...

> We came to an old man who was staring at the rows of destroyed buildings, as if fascinated by the sight. He was eighty-seven years old, he told us, and had been in three wars, a camp helper in 1870, an infantryman in 1914, and he said, 'The first two were wars. This is not war. I do not understand this.'

In two hours, Bennett and his two minders criss-crossed the whole central city area on foot. Contrary to his quixotically optimistic expectation that here at last he might see a reversal of the previous pattern of bomb damage, Bennett instead found another deflating example of the same 'astounding' phenomenon: 'As badly damaged as was the center of the city, so its many factories were almost unanimously intact and working'. They passed a dozen large Krupp plants, and only one showed any evidence of damage. The guide told him that about 10 per cent of the city's industrial plants had been 'immediately affected' by the bombing, but that repairs were generally completed within a fortnight. Bennett saw that the city's railway yards looked 'completely undamaged and operating on what seemed a full schedule'. Then they toured the surface installations of the Zollverein coal mine complex, claimed to be the largest in the world: of a dozen mines they 'passed' en route, Bennett assessed the 'apparent damage' at no more than 1 per cent. He noted that surface installations had been 'bomb-proofed' by the provision of steel-reinforced concrete and brick protective structures.

After Essen came visits to Düsseldorf, where the pattern of the bomb destruction was similar to Essen, and then Cologne, where at last Bönningshaus found a still-standing architectural exemplar of German *Kultur* to show Bennett – the great cathedral. Bennett was duly impressed by the 'lofty serenity' and 'sublime aloofness' of the structure, damaged but still intact. But that same afternoon, Bönningshaus advised him that he had been recalled to Berlin and that they must return immediately. Bennett's tour of Germany was over. For an ambitious reporter and an aspiring author, it had all been a great opportunity, but he was glad the tour was over:

> My memory taxed with the details of what I had seen. I wanted to think about it and plan an escape from this desperate country.
>
> The most perplexing thoughts were those of the bombing. I had come to Berlin to witness one attack against one city, and now I had seen the results of hundreds of attacks against a dozen cities.

The experience, clearly, had been illuminating, but highly disillusioning.

CHAPTER 13

PERSONAL IMPACTS

While King and Murrow returned to their news offices in London, while Stockton and Grieg were being buried, and Bennett was being taken on his guided tours, the men who had hosted the journalists continued their war. Those airmen who had not been shot down the same night as Stockton and Grieg were left in that liminal zone between life and death, the all-too-finite interval between now and when they finished their tours – whether alive or dead. At Binbrook, a journalist colleague of the ill-fated Stockton and Grieg had been left waiting for them on the ground in shocked contemplation of the arresting finality of their non-return. As we have seen, the Air Ministry's initial offering of four bomber seats to selected journalists had been swollen to five by the inclusion of the tragically fated Nordahl Grieg, but one extra seat had been made available in addition to these. This sixth journalist who was granted a 'spot' to fly a mission was yet another Australian, Colin Bednall, who wrote for the London *Daily Mail*. Embedded with No. 460 Squadron at Binbrook at the same time as Grieg and Stockton but assigned to fly on the next big raid after the Berlin operation on the night of 2 December, he had firstly to endure the impatient tension of watching his two colleagues go off without him, and then the wait for them to show up once their aircraft became overdue. He was left hanging around Binbrook as the surviving crews started returning and being debriefed. And then he had to endure the tension of waiting for news once it became clear that neither Stockton's nor Grieg's aircraft had landed anywhere in Britain. Unlike the other journalists, he had already flown on a Berlin raid the previous January, so his imagination had plenty of material to work with as he nervously awaited his turn to fly.

Bednall was given a lot of time to take in the enormity of the Australian squadron's losses that night: of the twenty-five crews dispatched on the raid, five crews failed to return – thirty-seven men gone. Even for a battle-hardened outfit like No. 460, a unit which seemed to attract bad luck, and from which sixty-four seven-man crews failed to return during 1943 alone, such losses in one night were unprecedented: five crews was the squadron's average loss rate *per month*. Since commencing operations with the Lancaster a year previously, the squadron had often lost two crews in a single raid and had on five occasions lost three. But never before had it lost five. On the night of 2 December, no other squadron's losses came near this, with most losing the usual one or two, and with four unlucky squadrons losing three. We have already told the story of three of No. 460's losses – the crews of James English, with Stockton aboard; that of Alan Mitchell, carrying Grieg; and that of Tom Alford, from which Norm Ginn escaped. In addition, the squadron lost the crew of one of its most experienced pilots, Flight Lieutenant Edward Corser, a veteran airman on his second tour, as well as that of Flight Sergeant Colin Edwards, who was on his unlucky first op. Fate had showed no favouritism, reaping both the most and least qualified without discrimination. Out of the thirty-seven men who had taken off in the five lost aircraft, twenty-nine were killed, with only eight men surviving to go into captivity. This proportion of men who survived from No. 460's shot-down bombers that night – 21 per cent – was very close to the 20.6 per cent average survival rate from shot-down RAF bomber crews on that same raid, and provides a representative sample of crew survival rates in shot-down bombers.

Colin Bednall could not have known, and nor would he ever have been told, that No. 460's loss rate in the year since the unit commenced operations with the Lancaster was 3.7 per cent of the 1735 sorties launched by the squadron in this period. But Bednall could certainly take in the impact of No. 460's one-in-five loss rate on the 2 December op. This must have given rise to some sobering reflections on his part, as he waited on the ground to go himself on the following night. It must have seemed as if he too was running a 20 per cent chance of not returning, and it was hardly reassuring to think that two out of two of No. 460's journalist passengers had failed to return the previous night – an even worse loss rate of 100 per cent. The loss of Stockton and Grieg hit Bednall a lot harder than it did the squadron aircrew, not only because they were Bednall's colleagues, but also because the squadron had not even briefed the aircrew with any details about the journalists they carried; some airmen knew that some journalists were flying on the raid, but that was all. Because the journalists had been lodged in the officers' mess, the NCO aircrew in particular 'didn't know much about' it, as Norman Ginn admitted; he thought that the squadron officers had 'kept it secret'. But Bednall knew, and he was given plenty of time to think about it.

After a nervous day's waiting, it took considerable fortitude to proceed with his voluntary mission on the night of 3 December, but proceed Bednall did. Just as with the other journalists who flew, there were strong contextual reasons for going ahead: Bednall admitted that he enjoyed the privileged status that came with reporting from the sharp end of the war; he enjoyed the prestige his by-line brought him when attached to his first-hand raid reports, and the direct access this gave him to his newspaper's powerful and influential newspaper proprietor, Lord Rothermere. Or as Bednall put it: 'I kept on flying when invited to do so partly because it let me write of the air war with some semblance of authority but mainly because I lacked the courage to say no.'

The Australian station commander at Binbrook, Group Captain Hughie Edwards VC, perceptively sought to ease his fellow countryman's pre-flight nerves, for he lent the journalist his own good luck charm before take-off. The gesture was a noble one coming from a famous Australian airman with enormous prestige and moral credibility, who had survived critical injuries in a flying accident and then returned to operational flying, won Britain's highest award for valour while flying perilous low-level bombing missions, and survived two operational tours before being 'kicked upstairs' to a non-flying command job. Bednall might well have considered the good luck charm offered by such a prodigious survivor as being particularly auspicious. Nonetheless it was probably a highly strung Colin Bednall who got himself kitted up and clambered into his allocated Lancaster on the evening of 3 December. The target this time was Leipzig, and after the devastating losses of the previous night, No. 460 was only able to dispatch sixteen aircraft as its contribution to the large force of 527 bombers that Air Marshal Harris sent on this mission. Of this total, twenty-four were lost, but this time all of No. 460's aircraft returned, bringing with them a very relieved Australian journalist.

For Ed Murrow and Alf King, the lucky correspondents from the 2 December raid who landed back in England afterwards, they could go on to their next assignment, en route to their flourishing post-war careers as distinguished journalists. Unhappily, similar longevity would not apply either to the men who flew these two lucky reporters to Berlin, nor to the machines in which they flew. Murrow's admirable pilot, Wing Commander Jock Abercromby, 'the finest pilot in Bomber Command', left 619 Squadron straight after completing the raid and saying goodbye to his famous guest. As his swansong in command of No. 619, he delivered the briefing for the raid to Leipzig the following night; and in the brief interval given to them before going off to get kitted up for the mission, the squadron officers 'wished him luck' and said how sorry they were 'to lose him'. And that was that.

Having now completed two tours of operations, Abercromby was transferred to the highly prestigious Pathfinder Force, taking over command of No. 83 Squadron at Wyton. A squadron commanding officer on his third tour did not have to fly more than the occasional operation, but to start off on the right foot by setting a good example, Abercromby put his name on the ops board for a mission to Berlin on the night of 1 January 1944, taking along a crew of pathfinder freshers on their first or second trips.

Abercromby's Lancaster was one of the twenty-eight that did not return that night, with only a single man from his eight-strong crew surviving to be taken into captivity. Jock Abercromby had died on his forty-seventh operation. Now No. 83 would have to find another commanding officer.

The lucky Lancaster in which Abercromby had conveyed Murrow to Berlin and back on the night of 2 December, D-Dog, was reallocated to a succession of fresher crews within 619 Squadron, in whose hands it flew two more operations before the end of the year, both to Berlin. For another trip to the Big City on the night of 2 January, the aircraft was allocated to another fresher crew, led by Flying Officer JA Heffernan RCAF. That night D-Dog was shot down over Germany, exploding in mid-air; all seven crewmen died.

Just like Ed Murrow, Alf King chimed in with expressions of admiration not only for the men of his host crew, but like his American colleague also eulogised his hosts' aircraft, in this case No. 467's G-George:

> But one must not forget, in telling of this drama of the skies, one other actor – 'George', who carried us without hitch. Every crew which flies 'George' worships him. His engines for seven hours last night did not miss a beat. They gave unstintingly of their power, and the body protected us in a temperature of 70 deg. Fahr. below.

Upon G-George's safe return to Waddington with a relieved journalist aboard late in the night of 2 December, King's pilot, Bill Forbes, along with his crew, had now become tour-expired. 'George' was therefore allocated to another crew within 467 Squadron, captained by Flying Officer Colin Reynolds, for the squadron's next operation on the night of 4 December. Reynolds was no sprog, but a reasonably experienced pilot by Bomber Command standards, with 518 flying hours in his logbook, including 172 hours at night and 211 hours on Lancasters. On take-off that night he got the heavily loaded aircraft airborne, but immediately afterwards both port engines cut out. The fully fuelled-up and bombed-up bomber was now uncontrollable, for with full power coming from one side only, it swung violently to the left. To stop the aircraft rolling on to its back and cartwheeling into the ground, Reynolds reduced the power on the two good engines, held the wings level, warned his crew to prepare for a crash landing, and set up for a forced landing off the runway. The now barely controllable aircraft came down within the airfield boundaries, ploughed into a parked Lancaster from 61 Squadron and ran over two of the squadron groundcrew who could not run clear in time: one of them, Sergeant Laurie Parker, from G-George's own servicing party, was killed. He was the same man who had explained to Alf King about the beer mugs painted on the bomber's nose. The crash was so violent that the rear turret was severed from the fuselage and flung clear, landing away from the rest of the wreck; the 4000-pound 'Cookie' tore from its mountings and rolled away from the bomb bay – fortunately without going off – and the incendiaries scattered all over the ground, having broken loose from their bomb carriers. The six crewmen in the forward and centre fuselage were lucky to emerge from the wreck alive. Reynolds was last out, and with escaping petrol spreading upon the ground was concerned to find incendiaries lying around underfoot. He kicked them away from the wreck to reduce the fire hazard and then walked back along the debris path looking for his missing rear gunner, Flight Sergeant Cecil Frizzell. He found him 'some distance away', but Frizzell had suffered a fractured skull from violent head impacts against the turret structure. He died the next day from the resultant cerebral injury. Although Reynolds and the other five men survived the wreck of their aircraft that night, they were themselves lost soon afterwards, on the night of 5–6 January 1944 in a raid on Stettin. 'George' herself had survived 168 flight hours before her self-destructive crash landing. Even this limited longevity was longer than that of many aircraft, given the prevailing loss rate: in its first year of operations, to the end of January 1944, No. 467 lost forty-seven crews and forty-nine aircraft.

Bill Forbes and his crewmates survived longer than their own comparatively short-lived 'G-George'. The seven men had flown their tour together, and so finished it together, posted away to serve as instructors at a training unit. This was the customary way of giving tour-expired airmen a 'rest' between operational tours. After a half-year term serving as instructors, Forbes and three of his former crew comrades were posted together back to the second Australian Lancaster squadron at Waddington, No. 463. There they crewed up together for their second tour, with Forbes promoted to Wing Commander and appointed to command the squadron on 25 June 1944. In October that year he attended an investiture at Buckingham Palace, to be presented with his Distinguished Flying Cross, which was awarded for his 'devotion to duty' while flying his first tour

Lancaster H-Harry of the Australian 467 Squadron, a veteran aircraft with twelve missions recorded on its nose, in its parking bay at RAF Waddington, running up its engines before take-off, watched by the aircraft's groundcrew. Depending on the time of moonrise and season of year, the bombers often took off while it was still daylight in England, timed to penetrate enemy airspace after nightfall. All too often the nervously expectant groundcrew did not see their aircraft return: although H-Harry is a veteran of twelve missions he runs a one in twenty chance of not returning from each trip to Berlin.

AWM Negative UK0474

with No. 467. Forbes proved an active CO at the head of No. 463, leading the squadron in the air as well as on the ground. And so he failed to return from a raid on Mehringen on the night of 21 February 1945. Five of the eight men aboard the Lancaster survived to become captive, but neither Forbes nor two of his old comrades from Alf King's mission lived.

At Skellingthorpe on the night of 2 December 1943, the men of No. 50 Squadron had been spared having to cope with losses on the scale of No. 460's that night, but they were nonetheless left to contemplate the sad loss of Ian Bolton and his crew on the last trip of their tour. It was a demoralising thought. No-one was yet aware of the fates of any of the missing men from that night, so it was reasonable for everyone to suppose they were dead; it usually took months before the names of captured men filtered back to Britain via the International Committee of the Red Cross (ICRC), by which time their squadron comrades had either themselves failed to return or finished their tour and left the unit. Those airmen who had been on the squadron long enough to have followed such announcements from the ICRC knew that when Lancasters were shot down, most men died. Although No. 50's crews would at least have the consolation of seeing two crews finish their tours alive during December 1943, in that same month another five crews failed to return.

The fates of Grieg, Stockton and Bennett on the night of 2 December, the subsequent fates of Murrow's and King's crews, and the fates of the aircraft which took them to Berlin and back, speak eloquently not only of the brevity of the operational lives both of crews and aircraft, but also of the dangers the journalists had run in going on the raid. A similar impression of risk can be obtained by a statistic from the hard-flying No. 460 Squadron, which had so tragically conveyed Stockton and Grieg to their deaths on the night of 2 December 1943: of the twenty-five pilots who took off that night, only ten survived their tours alive. No. 467's figures are very similar: out of the twelve Australian pilots who captained Lancasters in the 2 December 'show', only five survived the war. These survival statistics provide a good impression of the risks and chances that the aircrew of Bomber Command assumed in plying their dangerous avocation.

By comparison, the journalists had only to fly one mission, not a full tour. But they too had taken a big risk, as the outcome proved. These reporters had taken their chances for mixed motives, as we have seen, including some combination both of professional ambition and of commitment to the Allied cause. On their part the aircrew were all volunteers, knowingly putting their lives on the line in service to 'King and Country' for a similar mix of motives: not only to achieve personal ambitions, such as the desire to fly, or to better themselves, but out of a sense of responsibility to save the world by fighting for others. Australian Flight Sergeant Norm Ginn, the wireless operator in Tom Alford's 460 Squadron crew, who had evaded capture for several days after getting shot down on the night of 2 December, was typical of many. He had led a hard life in a poor family in rural Victoria, leaving school early and doing manual labour to keep his family afloat. Like so many other air force recruits, he went to the trouble of attending night school to qualify for the academic standards required to be eligible for aircrew selection. He freely chose to join the RAAF at a time in the war when 'things looked bad for the Allies', because 'We had to fight the war to save England and France'. It was for decent-minded ideals like this that so many airmen placed themselves in the blind hands of fate and participated in one of the most ruthless and costly military campaigns in human history.

Ginn's family, like hundreds of others throughout Britain and the Commonwealth, were within days of the raid confronted with the shocking realisation of what they had feared all along once their men joined the air force and been posted on to bombers – Norm was missing in action. At about the same time as Bennett and his party were entering Oberursel, the RAF casualty notification process was underway. Over the next few days, families of the airmen shot down in the 2 December raid received their dreaded casualty notification telegrams. An example was that announcing the loss of the doomed rear gunner in Stockton's aircraft, Flight Sergeant Alex Kan, who in our narrative was left wounded by night fighter gunfire and then trapped in his turret when the aircraft disintegrated in mid-air. It was on 4 December that the Air Ministry in London advised RAAF HQ in Melbourne that all seven men in Kan's crew were missing. His father, Mr Hartog Kan, living in the Melbourne suburb of Elwood as part of that city's populous and well-established Jewish community, received the 'Deeply regret to inform you ...' telegram at 2.55 pm on 7 December, in which Australia's Minister of Air, Arthur Drakeford, expressed his 'sincere sympathy in your anxiety'. Back at Binbrook, 460 Squadron CO, Wing Commander Frank Arthur, spent much of 3 December writing condolence letters to the next of kin of the thirty-five squadron members who had failed to return from the raid on the night of 2 December. His letter to Hartog Kan, posted on 4 December, offered some hope that his son might have survived, and an assurance that he was a valued member of the squadron:

> Your son's personal effects have been collected and placed in safe keeping with the RAF Central Depository, Colnbrook, Slough, Bucks.
>
> Your son carried out his duties in a very keen and conscientious manner and his loss will all the more deeply be felt in the Squadron.
>
> It is of some consolation that quite a number of airmen reported missing are eventually found to be prisoners of war, and I sincerely hope that it will be my pleasure to let you have such good news of your son and the other crew members before long. In the meantime, on behalf of all members of the squadron may I offer you my deepest sympathy in your anxiety for his safety.

The letter was certainly decently expressed and appropriate. It was also worded in very similar terms to the other thirty-four letters he wrote that day. This was of course a practical necessity, given the scale of the letter writing that devolved upon the commanding officer in such times. As a new CO, Arthur was inexperienced in the role, but the squadron orderly room staff had hundreds of such letters already on file to serve as templates for what became, in effect, a CO's condolence form letter. In this respect, we can note that in the course of the war, No. 460's orderly room must have produced well over 1000 such condolence letters, for the squadron's dead alone came to 1018 men, as well as the smaller total of POWs whose families initially received the same formulaic correspondence over the CO's signature. By the end of the Battle of Berlin, two months after Kan and his crew disappeared, the squadron orderly room would type up another seventy condolence letters, for the members of the ten crews lost in that interval.

As was customary – and probably necessary – in such cases, Alex Kan's CO had tried to console the grieving father with polite fictions, in this case about Alex's loss being felt 'deeply' by his surviving squadron comrades. Disabusing this sentimental albeit comforting notion is the brutal fact that nineteen crews from No. 460 would 'go west' in the course of Air Marshal Harris's Battle of Berlin, all within the three-month period November 1943 to January 1944. That meant 133 men suddenly disappeared from the unit; that number of faces had come and gone in the mess; that many beds suddenly left vacant; that many sets of lockers and drawers emptied and belongings collected by the 'Adjustment Committee'; that many replacement aircrew arrived on the squadron, to be allocated billets in the missing men's former huts and messes; that many names now only partly remembered by the few surviving men who had known them when they were still there. In such a context, it is hardly likely that the survivors could feel every loss 'deeply' – for if they had, how could they themselves possibly have gone on?

After receipt of Frank Arthur's kindly expressed letter, Mr Hartog Kan may well have quietly held on to hope that his son had survived to become a POW, but on 20 January 1944 RAAF HQ in London advised Melbourne that the ICRC had determined that from the members of Kan's crew, Anderson, Catty and Miller were alive as POWs, but that the others were 'all dead'. That same day, the RAAF Casualty Section in South Yarra responded by dispatching a letter to Mr Kan, advising the anxious father of the Air Board's 'deep regret' that his son was now 'believed to have lost his life'. Over the signature of Mr MC Langslow, the Secretary of the Department of Air, the letter assured Mr Kan that his son's personal effects would be returned to him in due course, and that he could assure himself of the 'sincere sympathy of the Department'.

The signature of Melville Langslow, a senior Commonwealth public servant and member of the Air Board, appeared on thousands of letters sent to the next of kin of missing, dead, wounded and injured RAAF airmen. For example, when Mr Kan received a letter dated 7 June 1944, officially advising that his son was now assumed for administrative purposes to have died on 2 December 1943, another thirteen such 'presumed killed' letters went out over Langslow's signature to other families that day in the same round of notifications, with the relevant airmen's deaths dating from 18 November to 29 December 1943. It had taken about half a year to catch up and clarify their status. The RAAF suffered 13 754 casualties during the war, each of which was subject to the same punctilious round of notification telegrams and letters as received by Mr Kan. Under the deadly odds of the air war, from the above total, 10 562 were ultimately confirmed killed or presumed dead, each triggering the drafting and dispatch of the same sort of piously worded condolence letters as received by Mr Kan. With an average RAAF casualty rate through 1942–1944 of 307 men lost per month, that meant Mr Langslow was signing at least fifteen casualty letters per working day. Under the press of such a work rate, it is hard to believe that either he or his clerks could actually feel the 'profound sympathy' that their letters expressed, if they were to continue to function by efficiently discharging their important and decently intended duty. It was the decent thing to do nonetheless, expressed in compassionate terms in order to humanely soften the blow upon families who had given their sons to the government to use in the war.

For his part, Mr Kan accepted these terms of engagement with the air force bureaucracy, reciprocating in formulaic fashion his thanks for the department's expression of sympathy. But by June 1944, six months after learning that Alex had gone missing, Mr Kan's concerns had become pragmatic as well as sentimental: he sought recovery of the £15 which he had forwarded to his son via the RAAF financial branch on 30 November 1943, but which Alex could not have received before his death two days later; Mr Kan also expressed his concern that his son's weekly allotment from his pay of £2 and 10 shillings to his mother, Mrs Rachel Kan, had ended in March 1944, so now Mr Kan 'laid claim' on his wife's behalf to a pension of £1 per week in lieu of the discontinued allotment. In October 1944, the Kans received a certificate from the Air Board, announcing that Alex had been 'Mentioned in Despatches'. Mr Kan responded again with dignified correctness, assuring the department that, 'We have the consolation of knowing that he died doing his duty.' More practically, however, Mr Kan was successful in obtaining the pension for Mrs Kan. In February 1945, the Kan family underwent the final official rite of bereavement, at last receiving the shipment of Alex's 'personal effects' collected from his room at Binbrook, the items of which included:

- a photo album and a photo wallet, with 286 photographs
- a camera in a leather case, with five rolls of negatives
- a leather writing case, with an address book, a Waterman fountain pen, three pencils, ten greeting cards, three airgraphs and a portrait
- an engraved waterproof wristwatch and a silver ring
- fifty-six books
- four souvenir coins, three carved ivory ornaments, and a souvenir of Cape Town
- two pipes
- a pair of swimming trunks and an athletic support.

Whatever 'closure' the receipt of these items gave the bereaved parents in relation to their son's death, it was disturbed in November 1946 when the RAAF's Central Repository advised his mother that a gold ring bearing the RAAF crest had been recovered from German authorities, collected by them from the remains of Kan's crew. Was it Alex's? In her reply, Mrs Kan advised that the item had been presented to her son by Miss Joan Rubens before his embarkation for overseas. The relationship had clearly meant a lot to Alex, as he had worn the ring on operations, whether as a memento of love or as a good luck charm, and so now the sentimental object was duly sent home to his mother. In January 1947 came further advice, to the effect that the material remains of Alex Kan had been reinterred in the British Military Cemetery in Berlin. Alex Kan now lay two graves away from Norman Stockton, and three graves away from his old captain, James English. The Kans were assured that their son's grave would be 'cared for in perpetuity by the Imperial War Graves Commission'.

The service career of Alex Kan, aged 24 when he died, can be taken as representative of so many of his comrades in Bomber Command, and those men who failed to return from the raid on the night of 2 December 1943. He had enlisted on 10 October 1941, age 22, specifically volunteering for service as aircrew, and after initial training commenced his instruction as an air gunner on 11 December, at No. 3 Wireless Air Gunners School at Maryborough in Queensland. Training complete and promoted to sergeant, after some pre-embarkation leave to see his loved ones in Melbourne, he left for overseas service from Sydney on 24 August 1942, disembarking in Britain on 18 November. After kicking his heels in the aircrew pool at Bournemouth, he recommenced his training at No. 7 Air Gunnery School on 16 January 1943, followed by crew training at No. 20 Operational Training Unit from 2 March, and then the crew finishing school at No. 1656 Conversion Unit from 20 May. Training complete, he and his crew joined 460 Squadron on 25 June. Less than six months later he was dead, having flown twenty-eight operations, within a whisker of surviving his tour alive.

Before taking off for Berlin in the late afternoon of 2 December, Kan's survival thus far had given him some status on the squadron as a veteran airman on the verge of completing his tour. Of course, an individual's enjoyment of superior status within the squadron was no guarantee of survival, as the fates of several airmen we have so far seen attest. An example of fickle fate triumphing over experience and proficiency was that of 460 Squadron's Flight Lieutenant Ed Corser, a man imbued with a fivefold status advantage over the humble Flight Sergeant Kan: Corser had not only completed his first tour, but had recently joined No. 460 to undertake his *second* tour; he was moreover a pilot, and hence clothed in the high-status role of aircraft captain; he was an officer, not an NCO like Kan; he was on the verge of being promoted to squadron leader, groomed to ascend the command ladder by being appointed as one of the squadron's flight commanders; and last but by no means least he wore the much-coveted and highly prestigious ribbon of the Distinguished Flying Cross above the breast pocket of his tunic. Within the galaxy of Bomber Command's middle-ranking leaders, Corser was a rising star destined for command, likely to win a bar to his Distinguished Flying Cross, and maybe even a Distinguished Service Order – if he managed to survive.

But Corser's aircraft too had failed to return on the night of 2 December, just like Kan's. Whereas three men in Kan's crew survived to be taken prisoner, there were no survivors from Corser's aircraft, which crashed near Grossbeeren, another village southwest of Potsdam, only about 13 kilometres from Nordahl Grieg's crash site near Kleinmachnow. He was on only the fourth op of his second tour when he died, having been on the squadron for a fortnight. Unluckily, all four of his missions since joining his new squadron had been to Berlin, the most dangerous target of the lot.

CHAPTER 14

AFTERMATHS

After his official tour of western Germany's bombed-out cities, Lowell Bennett's story took a remarkable turn, but one which must fall outside the scope of this book; indeed, it deserves a book of its own. Having groomed him (or so they thought) to adopt a pro-Germany viewpoint for his US audience, his captors staged his 'escape' from captivity, and while 'on the run' he wrote a news article entitled, 'Inside Nazi Germany', which was smuggled out of occupied Europe to neutral Spain by business travellers – just as his handlers intended. The story itself dealt only with the story of his shoot-down and initial capture, entirely avoided any reference to his special treatment or special tours; and was complimentary of the good treatment he had received in Germany – again, all just as Strempel must have intended. Bennett no doubt meant to tell the whole story in his forthcoming book. His deliberately evasive article was published in the States on 24 January 1944, to considerable acclaim because of the sheer novelty value of a war correspondent using a dateline inside Nazi Germany. But he was 'recaptured' soon afterwards in Prague and was returned to the normal POW system: other agencies within the Nazi power apparatus such as the SS, the Gestapo, and the Abwehr (intelligence agency) had in effect vetoed the Foreign Office's 'release action' of their cultivated client, so the special treatment was brought to an abrupt stop. Bennett sat out the rest of the war in the Stalag Luft I POW camp, near Barth on the Baltic coast of Pomerania in northern Germany, where he was again happily reunited with his pilot, Ian Bolton.

While Bennett was languishing in captivity, mulling over his disillusioning experiences in the bombed cities, the colleagues who had flown that fateful night and survived continued their journalistic careers, although on different trajectories. Ed Murrow kept working in London and went on to report the next big story, D-Day, he and his CBS colleagues continuing to develop the live radio broadcast as a news medium. On 12 April 1945 it was to Murrow that fell the heavy task of visiting the Buchenwald concentration camp, making a broadcast three days later in which he confronted his fellow Americans with one of the first publicly available revelations of Hitler's industrial-scale Holocaust against the Jews. Describing a pile of an estimated 500 emaciated corpses in the camp, he declared that 'Murder has been done at Buchenwald'. Of what he had witnessed, he said, 'for most of it I have no words'.

Lowell Bennett was confronted with similar scenes when he visited the concentration camp at Barth after liberation from his nearby POW camp. There too he found 'scenes that no camera could picture', declaring that the 'stupifying [sic], unbelievable horror' of the place 'was no subject for photography or words, but one for bitter personal experience'. Both men would be touched forever by receiving their own personal revelations of these Nazi atrocities, which Bennett characterised as 'the most frightful corollary to Hitler's New Order'. In that sense, his observations at Barth concentration camp resolved for all time the arguments he had had with Bönningshaus about the worth of German cultural achievement under the Third Reich: Bennett's critique of Nazi authoritarianism had been confirmed in nauseating detail, and the German officer's high-sounding arguments exposed as hollow obfuscation and complicit misdirection.

Murrow would continue to work in his 'preferred medium' of radio after the war, headlining the innovative *Hear It Now* program before launching his television career with the *See It Now* program, which started in 1951. After innovatively pioneering radio reporting as a serious medium, he went on to do the same with the new medium of TV, which in 1954 he used to air an influential documentary-style exposé of the notorious Senator Joe McCarthy. In 1961 he was appointed to the prestigious role of head of the US Information Agency, the propaganda arm of the State Department tasked with spreading positive stories worldwide about US culture and society. Sadly, Murrow's chain-smoking life was cut short in 1965, when he died of lung cancer aged 57.

In contrast to Bennett's disillusionment with the RAF bombing campaign, Alf King's first-hand experience of the raid on the night of 2 December 1943 seems to have enhanced his enthusiasm for bombing, for in February 1944 he was reporting in laudatory terms about Air Marshal Harris's embrace of scientific methodology to revolutionise the bombing results of his 'coldly calculated and ruthless plan of battle', which he had built up into a 'devastating air offensive against Germany'. However, by then King's reporting days were almost over, for by April 1944 he was back in Sydney for 'consultation' prior to returning to London to take over a new job: his stint as the London correspondent for the *Sydney Morning Herald* had done his career no harm, for he was now appointed editor of Australian Associated Press, the syndicated wire service providing worldwide news stories for the Australian print media. King's time as a war correspondent was over, for in his new role he no longer had a by-line. But he had survived. King finished the war as a senior newsman, later becoming editor for Reuters in New York. He died in 1957, aged 60.

Bennett resumed his career as soon as he returned from captivity, rejoining INS as its Paris correspondent, before moving to Germany to cover the Nuremberg Trials. He was also briefly reunited with his wife, Elisabeth, and his two boys, Alan and David. The younger son, David, had been born in the US while the couple were apart, so this was Bennett's first contact with his second son. Unhappily, Bennett's commitment to his career meant that the couple continued to live apart while he worked in France and Germany. On top of his obligations as INS reporter, additional work pressure came from the production of his second book, *Parachute to Berlin*, which he wrote so intensively and rapidly that it was published in New York before the end of 1945. Under this work pressure, it may not have been incidental that the couple divorced in 1948, with Elisabeth later remarrying and living in Paris with the children. Bennett then covered the 1948–49 Berlin blockade, and turned this too into a book, *Berlin Bastion*, published in 1951. Bennett's next career move was into the US State Department, where he used his journalistic skills in the service of the US Information Agency, the same body which Ed Murrow would later lead. Happily, his career in the State Department brought him back within the orbit of his children, when he enjoyed a posting to the Paris Embassy from 1954 to 1960, allowing him to regain personal contact with his sons. After retirement, still as Francophile as ever, Bennett settled down in France, living with his second wife on her property. He died in 1997 after a full, diverse, and at times very eventful and colourful life.

Meanwhile Norm Stockton and Nordahl Grieg slept the sleep of so many of the 'bomber boys' whose experiences they had sought to report on. They lay at first beneath the sandy soil of Döberitz in cheap pine coffins. But then along with all the other dead airmen they were disinterred for identification by specially created post-war research and burial units, and then reinterred in the big Commonwealth War Grave at Berlin-Charlottenburg. There Norman Stockton's headstone stands to this day, as a lone 'Australian War Correspondent' buried amongst the thousands of Commonwealth airmen. His epigraph was 'The Rest Is Silence', and his gravestone is inscribed as 'remembered always' by his wife, Maree Patience Stockton, and by Anne.

For Nordahl Grieg and his loved ones, admirers and followers, there would be no such 'closure', for in December 1943 the Luftwaffe clerks and their co-opted grave diggers had buried him by mistake as another unidentified British airman. Nothing changed when the British graves units disinterred the airmen's bodies from Döberitz and then reinterred them at Berlin-Charlottenburg. The disinterment and reinterment process served the symbolic objective of concentrating the RAF bodies buried in German soil in one place, but it also served the pressing administrative purpose of positively re-identifying the bodies. If identities could be established by this re-examination of the remains, then casualties could be re-categorised from 'missing and believed killed' to 'killed in action', and as many headstones as possible upgraded from 'unknown airman' to an inscribed name, rank, and serial number. Not least among the considerations was the humanitarian impulse to provide the grieving families with certainty about the fate of their loved one. Through this unpleasant but necessary process, many bodies were reunited with their correct names, as the tangled ends of late-war German administrative confusion were unknotted and retied. Many 'unknowns' thus became known, but many others remained unidentifiable, with the remains perhaps too damaged, too incomplete for dental identification, and with any corroborative inscriptions burned away, destroyed, detached or lost.

In this manner Nordahl Grieg's body too remained anonymous, one of many dead flyers whose remains could not be re-identified upon disinterment. This was ironic, because the poet's death in 1943 had done wonders for his reputation in Norway. Posthumously he become a national hero, with his poetry enshrined in the national canon. By 2003, upon the dedication of the first memorial to the fallen poet near the crash site at Kleinmachnow, Peter Ölberg, envoy from the Norwegian Embassy in Berlin, explained Grieg's status thus: 'Nordahl Grieg is important for us Norwegians because he gave his life for the fight against fascism. We would have liked to have had in our country many more people such as him.' His status in modern Norway is shown by the fact that when the depraved fascist Anders Breivik murdered seventy-seven people in Oslo and

Utøya in 2011, the dead were remembered by mass public recitals of Grieg's poem, 'To the Youth'.

The Lancaster crash at Kleinmachnow had been a rare enough occurrence to be remembered by locals who were there that night. The dismembered fuselage had crashed to earth beside the canal, burning so fiercely that the .303-inch ammunition continued to 'cook off' for some time, in warning to the local sightseers who started gathering around. Most kept well clear of the still-hazardous wreck, but despite the dangers, some enterprising youths would creep close enough in their souvenir hunting to suffer burns from the fire. Bits and pieces were left scattered across the woodland north of the lake, within the grounds of the Hakeburg park. From the day after the crash the locals started collecting relics of the crashed Lancaster and its crew; some items were as small as pieces of a torn oxygen mask, and some as large as a sheet of Plexiglas from the bomber's cockpit canopy. The biggest relic was a section of wing from Grieg's Lancaster, which had been recovered in 1944 from Lake Teltow, and this was ultimately tracked down by researchers to become the sole tangible link between modern-day Norwegians and their fallen and vanished national hero. Only months after its discovery, on 4 September 2002 the cleaned-up wing panel was hung on the wall in the garden of the Norwegian Embassy in Berlin, in an official ceremony commemorating Nordahl Grieg, led by Norway's Minister of Culture. It hangs there to this day as a tribute to 'a Norwegian poet and playwright of quite some magnitude'. After this positive identification of his crash site a stone monument was prepared for placement by the shore of Lake Teltow and ceremonially unveiled there on 29 November 2003.

In attendance was Günter Käbelmann, the nephew of volunteer firefighter Franz Marz who had attended the crash scene of Grieg's Lancaster, and who had experienced the raid as a 7-year-old boy. Acting in the role of local historian, he had been instrumental in assisting the Norwegian diplomats in recovering the wing relic, but during the ceremony the embassy's exclusive focus upon the Norwegian national hero left him wondering, 'Why weren't his crew comrades mentioned?' It could be observed that 'Bomber' Harris's bloody campaign left so many thousands of dead airmen interred in war graves within Germany that there was nothing remarkable to mention about those particular seven flyers who had died with Grieg, nor indeed of those who had died with Norm Stockton. Aside from their connection to still-living relatives and ancestors, it was only the status of their doomed passengers which might qualify the members of either crew for any more attention than that given to any other of the 55 573 Bomber Command aircrewmen who died.

The relic in the embassy, and the Nordahl Grieg memorial by the lake, remain the only tangible commemorations of the forty bomber crashes on that fated night. And that was only one raid, in only one campaign. By December 1943, bomber crashes and aircrew burials were so common as to be almost banal. The same impression of the mundanity of death might be given by the seemingly endless listings of the dead and missing in present-day publications like the multi-volume chronicle, *Bomber Command Losses*. It was only Nordahl Grieg's posthumous fame in his own country that bestowed upon just one of these crews the reflected dignity of an official commemoration. And with that, Alan Mitchell and his crewmates have received better commemoration than had the majority of Bomber Command's dead airmen.

AUTHOR'S NOTE

This book is the brainchild of my colleague, Thorsten Perl, who has been working on this story for a long time. For years he has been researching, corresponding, and amassing the considerable personal archive of source material upon which this narrative is based. Thorsten developed a particular interest in the real-life characters of two of our protagonists: Nordahl Grieg, the unlucky Norwegian national poet; and Lowell Bennett, the lucky young American. In writing the book, I have sought to remain faithful to this emphasis by laying some stress upon these two people, while balancing the story with the perspectives of the other three journalists who flew to Berlin in Lancaster bombers on that fateful night of 2 December 1943 – the famous American broadcast journalist, Ed Murrow, and the two Australian newspaper journalists, Alf King and Norm Stockton.

I naturally developed my own author's perspective about the shape of this narrative and its main events and themes. It follows that in patching so many viewpoints and episodes together into a coherent story readable by a layperson, I have unavoidably produced a book which is different in significant ways from that Thorsten originally intended and hoped for. But hopefully it nonetheless does justice to the original story concept, and hopefully too it brings our main characters to a new audience. Nordahl Grieg needs no introduction to Norwegians, but this book will provide an introduction to this intriguing man for Anglophone readers. Ed Murrow was a household name to

American radio listeners and TV viewers in the 1940s and 1950s, but contemporary readers could probably do with a little brushing-up on how the war made his reputation as a very famous American. By contrast, while Lowell Bennett made a bid for prominence by writing two substantial books about his wartime experiences, he never came close to matching Murrow's public profile, while his post-war career took him away from the public spotlight. Therefore, it is likely that this book will be most readers' introduction to this vivid storyteller and born survivor.

The two Australian protagonists, Alf King and Norm Stockton, although evidently less glamorous than Grieg, Murrow and Bennett, were doughty professionals, dedicated to getting their story, and to getting it out to a wide public. I have sought to give both these modest men as much of the limelight as I could, alongside their more famous international colleagues.

Besides the documents in Thorsten's archive, a key source for this book is Lowell Bennett's published account of his experiences, *Parachute to Berlin*, published in 1945. It is with thanks that Thorsten and I acknowledge the kindness of the Bennett family for giving us permission to quote from his book.

My thanks to Harriet McInerney for believing in this book and for her valuable tactical advice on reshaping the narrative.

SELECT BIBLIOGRAPHY

Bartlett, Les; with Peter Jacobs, *Bomb Aimer over Berlin*, Pen & Sword, Barnsley, 2008.
Bennett, Lowell, *Assignment to Nowhere: The battle for Tunisia*, Vanguard Press, New York, 1943.
Bennett, Lowell, *Parachute to Berlin*, Vanguard Press, New York, 1945.
Boiten, Theo EW, *Nachtjagd War Diaries: An operational history of the German Night Fighter force in the West*, Volume One, Red Kite, Walton on Thames, 2011.
Boiten, Theo, *Nachtjagd Combat Archive 1943 Part 3: Freelance Nachtjagd and the road to Berlin*, Red Kite, Walton on Thames, 2018.
Boiten, Theo WW & Martin W Bowman, *Battles with the Nachtjagd: The Night Fighter air war over Europe 1939–1945*, Schiffer Military History, Atglen, 2006.
Chorley, WR, *Royal Air Force Bomber Command Losses of the Second World War, Volume 4: Aircraft and crew losses, 1943*, Midland Counties Publications, Leicester, 1996.
Cloud, Stanley & Lynne Olson, *The Murrow Boys: Pioneers on the front lines of broadcast journalism*, Houghton Mifflin Company, New York, 1996.
Cotter, Jarrod & Paul Blackah, *Avro Lancaster 1941 Onwards (All Marks): Owners' workshop manual*, Yeovil, Haynes, 2015.
Cronkite, Walter & Maurice Isserman, *Cronkite's War: His World War II letters home*, National Geographic, 2013.
Falconer, Jonathan, *The Bomber Command Handbook 1939–1945*, Sutton Publishing, Stroud, 1998.
Firkins, Peter, *Strike and Return: The unit history of No. 460 RAAF Heavy Bomber Squadron RAF Bomber Command in World War Two*, Australian Military History Publications, Sydney, 2000.
Friedrich, Jörg; trans. Allison Brown, *The Fire: The bombing of Germany 1940–1945*, Columbia University Press, New York, 2006.
Grayling, AC, *Among the Dead Cities: Is the targeting of civilians in war ever justified?*, Bloomsbury, London, 2007.
Greenhous, Brereton, Stephen J Harris, William C Johnston & William GP Rawling, *The Crucible of War 1939–1945: The official history of the Royal Canadian Air Force volume III*, University of Toronto Press, Toronto, 1994.
Grieg, Nordahl (ed.), Horst Bien, trans. Rosemarie Paulsen & Lutz Volke, *Im Konvoi über den Atlantik: Reportagen und Publizistik*, Verlag Volk und Welt, Berlin, 1972.
Grieg, Nordahl (ed.), GM Gathorne-Hardy, *All That Is Mine Demand: War poems of Nordahl Grieg*, Hodder & Stoughton, London, 1944.
Hamilton, Jim, *The Writing 69th: Civilian war correspondents accompany a US bombing raid on Germany During World War II*, Green Harbor Publications, Marshfield, MA, 1999.

Herington, John, *Air Power over Europe 1944–1945: Australia in the war of 1939–1945, Series 3 (Air)*, Volume IV, Australian War Memorial, Canberra, 1963.

Johnen, Wilhelm, *Duell unter den Sternen: Tatsachenbericht eines deutschen Nachtjägers 1941–1945*, Flechsig Verlag, Würzburg, 2012.

Longmate, Norman, *The Bombers: The RAF offensive against Germany 1939–1945*, Arrow Books, London, 1988.

Mackenzie, SP, *Flying Against Fate: Superstition and Allied aircrews in World War II*, University Press of Kansas, KS, 2017.

Magenheimer, Heinz, *Hitler's War: Germany's key strategic decisions 1940–1945*, Cassell, London, 1999.

Messenger, Charles, *'Bomber' Harris and the Strategic Bombing Offensive, 1939–1945*, Arms and Armour Press, London, 1984.

Middlebrook, Martin, *The Battle of Hamburg: The firestorm raid*, Penguin, London, 1984.

Middlebrook, Martin, *The Berlin Raids: RAF Bomber Command winter 1943–44*, Cassell, London, 1988.

Middlebrook, Martin & Chris Everitt, *The Bomber Command War Diaries: An operational reference book 1939–1945*, Midland Publishing, Hersham, 2011.

Moseley, Ray, *Reporting War: How foreign correspondents risked capture, torture and death to Cover World War II*, Yale University Press, NH, 2017.

Neillands, Robin, *The Bomber War: The Allied air offensive against Nazi Germany*, Overlook Press, New York, 2001.

Nelmes, Michael V & Ian Jenkins, *G For George: A memorial to RAAF Bomber Command crews 1939–1945*, Australian War Memorial, Canberra, 2010.

Overy, Richard, *The Bombers and the Bombed: Allied air war over Europe, 1940–1945*, Viking, New York, 2013.

Robson, Martin (ed.), *The Lancaster Bomber Pocket Manual 1941–1945*, Osprey Publishing, Oxford, 2017.

Röll, Hans-Joachim, *Im Strom feindlicher Bomber: Der Eichenlaubträger Heinz Strüning und die deutsche Nachtjagd 1940–1945*, Flechsig Verlag, Würzburg, 2014.

Rooney, Andy, *My War*, PublicAffairs, New York, 2000.

Smith, Stephen C, *From St. Vith to Victory: 218 (Gold Coast) Squadron and the war against Nazi Germany*, Pen & Sword, Barnsley, 2015.

Thorburn, Gordon, *Luck of a Lancaster: 107 operations, 244 crew, 103 killed in action*, Pen & Sword, Barnsley, 2015.

Wells, Mark K, *Courage and Air Warfare: The Allied aircrew experience in the Second World War*, Frank Cass, London, 2000.

Westermann, Edward B, *Flak: German Anti-Aircraft Defences, 1914–1945*, University Press of Kansas, KA, 2001.

Wilson, Kevin, *Bomber Boys: The Ruhr, the Dambusters and bloody Berlin*, Cassell, London, 2006.

Zorner, Paul & Kurt Braatz (ed.), *Nächte im Bomberstrom: Erinnerungen 1920–1950*, NeunundzwanzigSechs Verlag, Moosburg, 2007.

NOTES

1 - A big opportunity

p. 1   Bennett's summons: an account by Ernest O Hauser entitled 'Parachute to Berlin', in Thorsten Perl's files.

p. 5   Harris's strategy: Robin Neillands, *The Bomber War: The Allied air offensive against Nazi Germany* (New York: Overlook Press, 2001), p. 250; Greg Baughen, *The Rise of the Bomber: RAF-Army planning 1919 to Munich 1938* (London: Fonthill, 2016); Brereton Greenhous, Stephen J Harris, William C Johnston & William GP Rawling, *The Crucible of War 1939–1945: The official history of the Royal Canadian Air Force volume III* (Toronto: University of Toronto Press, 1994), p. 730.

p. 5   Harris's Berlin raids: Neillands, *Bomber War*, p. 242; Charles Messenger, *'Bomber' Harris and the Strategic Bombing Offensive, 1939–1945* (London: Arms and Armour Press, 1984), p. 142; Martin Middlebrook, *The Berlin Raids: RAF Bomber Command winter 1943–44* (London: Cassell, 1988), p. 376.

p. 6   Effects of the November 1943 Berlin raids: Martin Middlebrook & Chris Everitt, *Bomber Command War Diaries* (Midland Publishing, Hersham, 2011), pp. 452–455; Middlebrook, *The Berlin raids*, pp. 129, 140; Report by Luftwaffe 1. Flak Division, dated 13.12.1943, in Perl files.

p. 7   Bennett's statement: Lowell Bennett, *Parachute to Berlin* (New York: Vanguard Press, 1945), p. 4.

p. 8   Hitler's rhetoric: Jörg Friedrich; trans. Allison Brown, *The Fire: The bombing of Germany 1940–1945* (New York: Columbia University Press, 2006), pp. 426–427.

p. 9   The 'American Pool' and the paper in the cap: '3 Newsmen lost in raid', the *Minneapolis Star*, 3.12.1943, <www.newspapers.com>; 'Writer pulls raid assignment from army cap; fails to return', the *Tennessean*, 4.12.1943, <www.newspapers.com>.

p. 10 Bennett's inclusion: *Lincoln Evening State Journal*, 3.12.1943, <www.newspapers.com>; Bennett, *Parachute to Berlin*, pp. 5–6.

p. 14 Harris's 'permission': 460 Sqn unit diary, National Archives of Australia: A9186, 146.

2 - The lucky five

p. 17 King's impressions at Waddington: King, 'Terrible picture of devastation', *Sydney Morning Herald*, 4.12.1943, in Perl files.

p. 17 King's career: Letter, Alf King to 'Lal', 19.2.1942, in Perl files; various newspaper reports, in Perl files, including 'Empire press disabilities', *Sydney Morning Herald*, 9.11.1942, <trove.nla.gov.au>; 'Huge bombers inspected', *Sydney Morning Herald*, 13.8.1942, <trove.nla.gov.au>.

p. 20 Murrow's career: Murrow Collection, 'The life and work of Edward R Murrow', <dca.lib.tufts.edu>; Stanley Cloud & Lynne Olson, *The Murrow*

Boys: Pioneers on the front lines of broadcast journalism (New York: Houghton Mifflin Company, 1996), p. 122.

p. 23 Murrow's character and motivation: Murrow Collection, 'The life and work of Edward R Murrow', <dca.lib.tufts.edu>; Stanley Cloud & Lynne Olson, *The Murrow Boys* (Houghton Mifflin Company, New York, 1996), pp. 97, 120, 202.

p. 26 Cronkite's statement: Jim Hamilton, *The Writing 69th* (Green Harbor Publications, Marshfield, MA, 1999), p. 25.

p. 26 'Cub reporter': an account by Ernest O Hauser entitled 'Parachute to Berlin', in Perl files.

p. 26 Bennett's impressions at Skellingthorpe: Bennett, *Parachute to Berlin*, p. 9.

p. 26 Bolton: Ian Bolton, 'D-Day viewed from inside a POW camp in Germany', unknown newspaper, in Perl files; Les Bartlett, *Bomb Aimer* (Pen & Sword, Barnsley, 2008), p. 95.

p. 28 Bennett in Tunisia: Lowell Bennett, *Assignment to Nowhere: The battle for Tunisia* (New York: Vanguard Press, 1943); 'Lowell Bennett tells how the Allies took North Africa', *New York Times*, 20.6.1943, <www.nytimes.com/1943/06/20/archives/lowell-bennett-tells-how-the-allies-took-north-africa-assignment-to.html>.

p. 29 Bennett's previous career: Samantha Bennett, 'My grandfather – Lowell Bennett', in Perl files; Ernest O Hauser, 'Parachute to Berlin', in Perl files; 'Ambulance drivers released in France', *Pampa Daily News*, 23.7.1940, in Perl files.

p. 30 Bennett's impatience: Bennett, *Assignment to Nowhere*, p. 316.

p. 33 Wade's previous flight: Hamilton, *The Writing 69th*, p. 49.

p. 33 Bednall's permission: 460 Sqn unit diary.

p. 35 James English: '02/03.12.1943 No. 460 Squadron (RAAF) Lancaster I W4881 AR-K P/O. James Herbert John English D.F.C.', <www.aircrewremembered.com>.

p. 35 Norm Ginn recollections: Norm Ginn interview by Thorsten Perl, in Perl files.

p. 36 Stockton's marriage: Memorial notice dated about 2.12.1944, <archiver.rootsweb.ancestry.com/th/read/GENANZ/1997-04/0860129243>, in Perl files.

p. 37 Marie's return: 'Woman journalist who saw six-day bombing of Canton tells story of two years in China', the *Telegraph*, 20.9.1939, in Perl files.

p. 37 Stockton's reporting: 'Pat and John are square', *Barrier Miner*, Broken Hill, 17.6.1942; 'Smashed Japs' Armada', the *Sun*, Sydney, 19.6.1942; 'U.S. correspondent on raid on Rabaul', *Barrier Miner*, 28.4.1942; 'Sydney journalist missing in Berlin raid', all newspaper articles in Perl files.

p. 40 Stockton's memoir: National Library of Australia: MS 10069, Folder 1 & 2.

p. 40 Grieg's life and work: Nordahl Grieg (ed.), Horst Bien, trans. Rosemarie Paulsen & Lutz Volke, *Im Konvoi über den Atlantik: Reportagen und Publizistik* (Verlag Volk und Welt, Berlin, 1972).

p. 43 Grieg's escape from Norway: Grieg, 'Der Goldtransport' (1940), *Im Konvoi*, pp. 234–239.

p. 44 Grieg's statement, 'I knew ... ': Grieg, 'Der Goldtransport' (1940), *Im Konvoi*, p. 259.

p. 44 Grieg's verse, 'Never, save ... ': Grieg, 'The Ninth of April', in GM Gathorne-Hardy (ed.), *All That Is Mine Demand: War poems of Nordahl Grieg* (London: Hodder & Stoughton, 1944), p. 21.

p. 44 Grieg's statement, 'on board ...': Grieg, 'Der Goldtransport' (1940), *Im Konvoi*, p. 254.

p. 45 Grieg's verse, 'a Norway ...': Grieg, 'Song for the Norwegian Legion', in Gathorne-Hardy (trans.), *All That Is Mine Demand*, p. 26.

p. 45 Grieg's verse, 'For home': Grieg, '"Eidsvoll" and "Norge"', in Gathorne-Hardy (trans.), *All That Is Mine Demand*, p. 25.

p. 46 Winsnes's statement: 'Poet killed in RAF raid', *Sydney Morning Herald*, 7.2.1944, in Perl files.

p. 46 Grieg's war reporting: 'Der Überlebende' (1941), 'Im Konvoi über den Atlantik' (1941), 'Die Flagge' (1942), in *Im Konvoi über den Atlantik*, pp. 268–270, 271–284, 285–290.

p. 47 Grieg's statements to Rytter: Olav Rytter's recollections, *Nordahl Grieg During The War*, in Perl files.

p. 47 'Closet of death': 'Den menneskelige natur' (Human nature), trans. Lars Ulrik Thomsen, in 'Nordahl Grieg's commitment to peace' (2018), <www.cpa.org.au/amr/67/amr-67-05-nordahl-griegs.html#footnote-40125-12>.

p. 47 Grieg's verse, 'The strong ...': Gathorne-Hardy (trans.), *All That Is Mine Demand*, p. 45.

p. 48 Grieg's statement, 'The difference ...': Olav Rytter's recollections, *Nordahl Grieg during the war*, in Perl files.

p. 49 Grieg's pendant: Rolf Brockschmidt, 'Tragfläche mit Tragweite', *Tagesspiegel*, 9.4.2018.

p. 49 Alan Mitchell's crew: John Watson, '460 Squadron pilots and crews', <www.ozatwar.com/460sqdn/crewm.htm>.

3 - Forerunners

p. 50 Thornton-Smith: Stephen C Smith, *From St. Vith to Victory* (Pen & Sword, Barnsley, 2015), p. 84; 'Oil painting – RAF Marham 1941', <218squadron.wordpress.com>.

p. 50 Vaughan-Thomas's flight: Stephen Evans, 'Bombing Berlin', <www.bbc.co.uk/programmes/b039lmkg>; 'RAF Bomber Command at war 1939–45 (Vol. 2)', <www.1940.co.uk>; Jeff Parsons, 'Horrors of WW2 bombing mission revealed as VR experience puts you in the cockpit of a Lancaster over Berlin', 4.9.2018, <metro.co.uk/2018/09/04/horrors-of-ww2-bombing-mission-revealed-as-vr-experience-puts-you-in-the-cockpit-of-a-lancaster-over-berlin-7911046/>.

p. 50 RAF loss rates: Middlebrook & Everitt, *Bomber Command War Diaries*, pp. 417, 428.

p. 51 Journalists on 16 January 1943 Berlin raid: Hamilton, *The Writing 69th*, pp. 34–35; Middlebrook & Everitt, *Bomber Command War Diaries*, pp. 218, 344; 'Australian squadron helps Berlin to burn', *Canberra Times*, 19.1.1943, <nla.gov.au/nla.news-article2617850>.

p. 51 Bomber Command publicity: Stephen Evans, 'Bombing Berlin', <www.bbc.co.uk/programmes/b039lmkg>.

p. 53 USAAF publicity: Hamilton, *The Writing 69th*, p. 25.
p. 53 *Memphis Belle* film: 'Memphis Belle: A story of a Flying Fortress', <en.wikipedia.org/wiki/Memphis_Belle:_A_Story_of_a_Flying_Fortress>; 'Complete reality: the war documentaries of William Wyler', <themovieprojector.blogspot.com/2012/06/complete-reality-war-documentaries-of.html>; 'Harold J Tannenbaum', <www.americanairmuseum.com/person/86826>.
p. 54 Cronkite 'most trusted ... ': 'Walter Cronkite dies', <www.cbsnews.com/news/walter-cronkite-dies/>; 'Walter Cronkite', <www.biography.com/people/walter-cronkite-9262057>.
p. 54 Journalists on the 26 February 1943 raid: Roger A Freeman, *The Mighty Eighth* (Orion Publishing, London, 2000), p. 36; Eighth Air Force Historical Society, 'WWII 8th AAF combat chronology', <www.8thafhs.org/combat1943.htm>; Hamilton, *The Writing 69th*, pp. 51, 72–77, 80–81, 114; Walter Cronkite IV & Maurice Isserman, *Cronkite's War: His World War II letters home* (National Geographic, 2013), pp. 54–55; 'Robert Post (journalist)', <en.wikipedia.org/wiki/Robert_Post_(journalist)>.
p. 55 Rooney's statement: Andy Rooney, *My War* (PublicAffairs, New York, 2000), pp. 125–126.
p. 55 Journalists' motivations: Hamilton, *The Writing 69th*, pp. 22–23; Rooney, *My War*, p. 121.

4 - Bomber boys

p. 57 Bennett as 'lanky, boyish': an account by Ernest O Hauser entitled 'Parachute to Berlin', in Perl files.
p. 57 Bennett's account: Bennett, *Parachute to Berlin*, pp. 6–15.
p. 60 50 Squadron losses: 'No. 50 Squadron Royal Air Force in World War Two', p. 78, <www.no-50-and-no-61-squadrons-association.co.uk>.
p. 60 Bartlett's recollections: Bartlett, *Bomb Aimer*, pp. 76, 78–79, 94, 99.
p. 62 Ginn's recollections, 'nerve wracking': Norm Ginn interview, in Perl files.
p. 63 Wells's recollections: Gordon Thorburn, *Luck of a Lancaster* (Barnsley: Pen & Sword, 2013), excerpt in Gordon Thorburn, *Luck of a Lancaster: 107 Operations, 244 Crew, 103 Killed in Action*, in <books.google.com.au>.
p. 64 Stockton's crew: John Watson, '460 Squadron Pilots and Crews', <www.ozatwar.com/460sqdn>.
p. 65 Murrow's account: Murrow, 'Orchestrated hell', <www.americanrhetoric.com>.
p. 72 Bennett's prepared report: 'Three correspondents fail to return from a raid on Germany', *Lincoln Evening State Journal*, 3.12.1943, in Perl files.
p. 72 'Saint Cecilia' song: Lyrics at 'The shrine of Saint Cecilia: The Andrews Sisters', <genius.com>; soundtrack at <www.youtube.com/watch?v=WlhdT5PbW8c>.
p. 72 Superstitious rituals: MacKenzie, *Flying against Fate*, pp. 45, 49.
p. 72 50 Squadron rituals: Bartlett, *Bomb Aimer*, p. 99.
p. 73 50 Squadron losses: WR Chorley, *Royal Air Force Bomber Command Losses of the Second World War, Volume 4* (Midland Counties Publications, Leicester, 1996), pp. 413–414.

p. 76 King's account: King, 'Terrible picture of devastation', *Sydney Morning Herald*, 4.12.1943, in Perl files.

5 - A gathering storm

p. 83 King's account: King, 'RAF Raid on Berlin', in Perl files.
p. 84 Sequence of 460 Squadron take-offs: 460 Squadron unit diary.
p. 85 Bartlett's recollections: Bartlett, *Bomb Aimer*, pp. 79–80.
p. 85 Bennett's account: Bennett, *Parachute to Berlin*, pp. 16–21.
p. 86 Bennett's statement, 'I breathed easily': Bennett, 'Inside Nazi Europe', the *Despatch* (Moline, Illinois), 24.1.1944, <Newspapers.com>.
p. 87 Murrow's account: Murrow, 'Orchestrated hell'.
p. 93 German air defence system: Boiten, *Nachtjagd combat archive 1943 part 3*, p. 90; report by 1. Flak Division, 13.12.1943, in Perl files; Middlebrook, *The Berlin Raids*, p. 133.
p. 94 German civil defence measures: Richard Overy, *Bombers and the Bombed* (Viking, New York, 2013), pp. 228, 233, 235–236, 239–240, 247, 249–250, 263, 264; 'Berlin Bunkers', <fotostrasse.com/berlin-bunkers>; Richard Braun, quoted in Neillands, *The Bomber War*, pp. 136–137.
p. 95 German civilian accounts: Peter Kamber, 'Erst jetzt entdeckte Augenzeugenberichte erzählen, wie die Menschen in Berlin die Bombennächte von 1943/44 erleben haben', *Berliner Zeitung*, <berliner-zeitung.de>.
p. 98 Boy Flak-helpers, Neillands, in *Bomber War*, p. 139; Karl Heinz Schlesier, *Flakhelfer to Grenadier: memoir of a boy soldier, 1943–1945* (Warwick UK: Helion & Company, 2014), quoted in <www.amazon.de/Flakhelfer-Grenadier-Memoir-Soldier-1943-1945>; Jochen Mahncke, 'School boy crew for 88mm Flak gun in Berlin: Interview with ww2 veteran Jochen Mahncke', 18.12.2011, shared on YouTube by Tinus le Roux.

6 - The raid

p. 104 2 December raid: Middlebrook & Everitt, *Bomber Command War Diaries*, p. 456; Boiten, Nachtjagd combat archive 1943 Part 3, pp. 90–95; Boiten draft, '2–3 December 1943', in Perl files.
p. 105 Zorner's story: Paul Zorner, ed. Kurt Braatz, *Nächte im Bomberstrom: Errinnerungen 1920–1950* (Moosburg: NeunundzwanzigSechs Verlag, 2007), pp. 217–219.
p. 107 V-Victor/97 shootdown: 'Garlick crew, December 1943, 97 Squadron', in <www.firebynight.co.uk>.
p. 112 Spotting fighters at night: F.I.U. Report No. 201, 'Night combat trials with a Lancaster', 9 May 1943, in Martin Robson, ed., *The Lancaster Bomber Pocket Manual* (Oxford: Osprey, 2014), pp. 51–54.
p. 112 J-Johnnie/514 shootdown: POW debrief statement by John Alford, in Perl files; Simon Hepworth & Andrew Porrelli, *Nothing Can Stop Us* (Mention the War Ltd., Merthyr Tydfil, Wales, 2015), p. 51.
p. 112 Bail-out chances: Greenhous et al, *The Crucible of War*, p. 755.
p. 114 Bartlett's 'scarecrow': Bartlett, *Bomb Aimer*, p. 82.

p. 115 Murrow's story: Murrow, 'Orchestrated hell'.
p. 117 'within a house' statement: Norm Ginn interview, in Perl files.
p. 117 H2S inaccuracy: Greenhous et al, *Crucible of War*, pp. 658–659, 667.
p. 119 K-King/460 shootdown: Dave George, 'Blown out, bailed out', *Medal News*, December 2000/January 2001, p. 24, in Perl files; '02/03.12.1943 No. 460 Squadron (RAAF) Lancaster I W4881 AR-K P/O. James Herbert John English D.F.C.', <aircrewremembered.com>; statement made by Anderson at 11 PRDC, Brighton, in Perl files.
p. 122 Butticaz's recollection: Middlebrook, *The Berlin Raids*, p. 155.
p. 122 German civilian stories: Kamber, 'Erst jetzt entdeckte Augenzeugenberichte erzählen, wie die Menschen in Berlin die Bombennächte von 1943/44 erleben haben', *Berliner Zeitung*.
p. 127 B-Bolty/50 shootdown: Bennett, *Parachute to Berlin*, pp. 21–27, 40.

7 - 'Orchestrated hell'

p. 132 King's story: King, 'RAF raid on Berlin' & 'Terrible picture of devastation', in Perl files.
p. 137 Bombload: 467 Squadron unit diary, National Archives of Australia: A9186, 153.
p. 139 Wells's recollection: Thorburn, 'Luck of a Lancaster', excerpt in Gordon Thorburn, *Luck of a Lancaster: 107 Operations, 244 Crew, 103 Killed in Action*, in <books.google.com.au>.
p. 139 Johnen's recollections: Wilhelm Johnen, *Duell unter den Sternen* (Flechsig Verlag, Würzburg, 2012), pp. 113–114.
p. 140 Murrow's story: Murrow, 'Orchestrated hell'.
p. 145 Bennett's story: Bennett, *Parachute to Berlin*, pp. 28–31.
p. 147 Germans' experiences on the ground: Middlebrook, *The Berlin raids*, pp. 151, 153–154, 156–157; 'Feuerwehrscharen im HJ-Streifendienst', <www.feuerloeschpolizei.de>; Forum discussion, 'Flugzeugabsturz nahe Caputh', <www.schatzsucher.de>, in Perl files.
p. 149 B-Bolty's crash location: email from Perl, 28.9.2019.
p. 150 Bolton's story: Bennett, *Parachute to Berlin*, p. 40.
p. 151 Kleinmachnow events: 'Fliegerangriff am 2. Dezember 1943', Bericht des Bürgermeisters Engelbrecht, in Perl files; Letter, Royal Air Force Museum to Günter Käbelmann, 11.9.2003, in Perl files.
p. 151 Sequence of shootdowns: Boiten, *Nachtjagd Combat Archive*, 1943 Part 3, p. 93.
p. 152 Berlin flak statistics: '1. Flak-Division', <www.lexikon-der-wehrmacht.de>; Report by 1. Flak Division, 13.12.1943, in Perl files; Boiten, *Nachtjagd Combat Archive 1943*, part 3, p. 93; Report by 1. Flak Division, 13.12.1943, in Perl files.
p. 156 Bomber stream off track: Middlebrook, *The Berlin Raids*, pp. 133–134.
p. 156 Bennett's bail-out location: Peter Thurnhofer, 'Process from my point of view (Peter, son of Mrs Thurnhofer)', <thurnhofer-istrien.com/3-bennet>.
p. 156 Dummy fires: Report by I. Flak Division, 13.12.1943, in Perl files.
p. 159 Ginn's story: Norman Ginn interview, in Perl files.

p. 160　J-Johnnie/460 shoot-down location: Boiten, *Nachtjagd Combat Archive 1943* Part 3, p. 94.
p. 160　Alford's fate: Investigation Report by No. 4 MREU, RAF Germany, 21.10.1948, in Perl files.
p. 161　Bail-out chances: Greenhous et al, *Crucible of War*, p. 755.

8 - Survivors

p. 162　Bennett's story: Bennett, *Parachute to Berlin*, pp. 31–56.
p. 163　King's story: King, 'Over Berlin in a Lancaster', the *Age*, 6.12.1943, in Perl files.
p. 164　Murrow's story: Murrow, 'Orchestrated hell'.
p. 164　619 Squadron account: 619 Sqn unit diary, in Perl files.
p. 166　Bolton's story: Bennett, *Parachute to Berlin*, p. 41.
p. 167　Ginn's story: Norm Ginn interview, in Perl files.
p. 172　Frau Thurnhofer's story: Peter Thurnhofer, 'Process from my point of view (Peter, son of Mrs. Thurnhofer)', <thurnhofer-istrien.com/3-bennet>.
p. 173　Anderson's story: Anderson's statement at No. 11 PRDC, Brighton, in Perl files.
p. 173　Anderson's capture location: NAA: A705, 166/22/154, p. 19; email from Perl, 1.10.2019.
p. 174　Care of graves: Investigation Report by No. 4 MR & E Unit, 13.1.1947, in Perl files.
p. 177　Crew survival: computed from data in Chorley, *RAF Bomber Command Losses, Volume 4*, pp. 408–414.
p. 179　German civilian stories: Kamber, 'Erst jetzt entdeckte Augenzeugenberichte erzählen, wie die Menschen in Berlin die Bombennächte von 1943/44 erleben haben', *Berliner Zeitung*; Kevin Prenger, *War Zone Zoo: The Berlin Zoo and World War 2*, quoted in 'War Zone Zoo: Remarkable Story of the Berlin Zoo in WW2', <www.warhistoryonline.com/instant-articles/war-zone-zoo-berlin-zoo.html>.
p. 187　Berlin raid damage: report by 1. Flak Division, 13.12.1943, in Perl files; 'Luftverteidingskommando Berlin, Luftverteidigungskommando 1, 1. Flak-Division', <www.lexikon-der-wehrmacht.de>.
p. 193　3 December Leipzig raid: Middlebrook & Everitt, *Bomber Command War Diaries*, p. 457.
p. 194　Anhalter Station: 'Der Anhalter Bahnhof', <www.monumente-online.de>.

9 - The dead

p. 201　Potsdam raid alarms: Günter Käbelmann, 'Wie kam es zum Denkmal "Nordahl Grieg" in der norwegischen Botschaft in Berlin?', 26.8.2002, in Perl files.
p. 201　German civilian stories: Antonie Josch (née Sander) testimony, in report by Günter Käbelmann, 28.6.2005, in Perl files; Peter Thurnhofer, 'Process from my point of view (Peter, son of Mrs Thurnhofer)', <thurnhofer-istrien.com/3-bennet>.

p. 203 Lancaster crash in Kleinmachnow: Günter Käbelmann, 'Wie kam es zum Denkmal "Nordahl Grieg" in der norwegischen Botschaft in Berlin?', 26.8.2002, in Perl files; Günter Käbelmann, 'Gedenkenstätten für Nordahl Grieg (norwegische Literat) und seiner mit ihm verunglückten Flieger-Kameraden aus Grossbritannien und Australien', 26.11.2003, in Perl files; 'Sverre Jervells Einsatz', in Perl files; 'Fliegerangriff am 2. Dezember 1943', Bericht des Bürgermeisters Engelbrecht, in Perl files; 'Gedenken an Nordahl Grieg', *Märkische Allgemeine Zeitung*, 3.12.2013; Konstanze Wild, 'Absturz am Machnower See', *Märkische Allgemeine Zeitung*, 11.1.2006; Peter Könnicke, 'Flügel der Geschichte', *Potsdamer Neuesten Nachrichten*, 7.9.2002; Solveig Schuster, 'Das letzte Rätsel um den toten Dichter', *Potsdamer Neuesten Nachrichten*, 2.10.2018; 'Erinnerung an einen mutigen Norweger', *Märkische Allgemeine Zeitung*, 1.12.2003; conversation with Heinz Ortleb, reported by Dag Solstad, translated from Norwegian into German by Ingeborg Sperling, 22.11.2004, in Perl files.

p. 207 Bodies of the airmen: Günter Käbelmann, 'Zum Gedenkstein von Nordahl Grieg', December 2004, in Perl files; letter, Günter Käbelmann to British Embassy Berlin, 2.6.2002, in Perl files; 'Files of the Kleinmachnow Historian', in Perl files; Günter Käbelmann, 'Gedenkenstätten für Nordahl Grieg (norwegische Literat) und seiner mit ihm verunglückten Flieger-Kameraden aus Grossbritannien und Australien', 26.11.2003, in Perl files; Günter Käbelmann, 'Wie kam es zum Denkmal "Nordahl Grieg" in der norwegischen Botschaft in Berlin?', 26.8.2002, in Perl files.

p. 210 Distribution of RAF bodies in and around Berlin: Döberitz was the major collection, processing and burial point for all RAF airmen whose bodies were recovered in the greater Berlin area. 230 RAF airmen were killed on the night of 2 December 1943 (Chorley, BCL, 1943, pp. 408–414), most fell within Berlin's flak ring, and of the three cemeteries lying within the Berliner Ring, Döberitz would ultimately hold 73 per cent of the total bodies (Attachment 3A to 11.12.2013 letter from Norwegian Embassy Berlin to British Embassy Berlin).

p. 211 RAF identity tags: 4MREU unit diary, in Perl files.

p. 212 Burial of crew bodies: Original documentation appended to 11.12.2013 letter from Norwegian Embassy Berlin to British Embassy Berlin, in Perl files; report by Herr P Friedrich, *Amt für die Erfassung der Kriegsopfer*, dated 15.11.1949, appended to 11.12.2013 letter from Norwegian Embassy Berlin to British Embassy Berlin, in Perl files; Dr Manfred Kruger, recorded by Günter Käbelmann in 'Gedenkenstätten für Nordahl Grieg (norwegische Literat) und seiner mit ihm verunglückten Flieger-Kameraden aus Grossbritannien und Australien', 26.11.2003, in Perl files; letter dated 28.6.1949, RAAF HQ London to Air Board Melbourne, Attachment 2 to 11.12.2013 letter, Norwegian Embassy Berlin to British Embassy Berlin, in Perl files.

p. 213 Announcement of Grieg's death: Interview with Antonie Josch (née Sander) on 4.11.2020, in Perl files – the date of the relevant transmission is given in this source as 4.12.1943, but as at that date the German authorities had not advised the ICRC of the identities of the members of Grieg's crew whose bodies had been identified, and therefore the Red Cross had not yet advised the Air Ministry of the deaths of the men in that crew. The OKW did not advise the ICRC of such details until 14.1.1944. As a result, Grieg's death was first announced in Allied media in early February 1944, suggesting that the correct date for the transmission monitored by Sander would be 4.2.1944 not 4.12.1943. The February date is supported by the biographical poster, 'Politischen Positionen Nordahl Griegs', produced by the Kleinmachnow Heimatverein, which states that the Norwegian Government made its official announcement of his death in February 1944, in Perl files.

p. 214 The crash site: 'Erinnerung an einen mutigen Norweger', *Märkische Allgemeine Zeitung*, 1.12.2003, in Perl files; conversation with Heinz Ortleb, reported by Dag Solstad, translated from Norwegian into German by Ingeborg Sperling, 22.11.2004, in Perl files.

10 - Reporting the raid

p. 216 G-George/460's return: '"G for George" Lancaster named after Loxton cat', *Murray Pioneer*, 16.12.1943, in <trove.nla.gov.au>.

p. 218 McIntyre's account: Wilson, *Bomber Boys*, p. 419.

p. 218 McIntyre's fate: Watson, '460 Squadron Pilots and Crews', <www.ozatwar.com/460sqdn/>.

p. 220 Murrow's reporting: Murrow, 'Orchestrated hell'; 'Reported for lost comrades', the *Sun* (Sydney), 6.12.1943, in <trove.nla.gov.au/>; *Daily Mirror* (New York), quoted in 'Reported for Lost Comrades', the *Sun* (Sydney), 6.12.1943, in <trove.nla.gov.au/>.

p. 225 Actual results of raid: Report by 1. Flak Division, 13.12.1943, in Perl files; Middlebrook & Everitt, *Bomber Command War Diaries*, p. 456; Report by Oberbürgermeister Berlin, January 1944, in Perl files.

p. 226 King's reporting: King, 'Terrible Picture of Devastation', in Perl files.

p. 227 RAF raid statistics: Richard Reid, 'Bomber Command', Australians in World War II Series, Australian War Memorial, <anzacportal.dva.gov.au>; Chorley, *RAF Bomber Command Losses, Volume 4*, pp. 408–414.

p. 227 Frank reporting of raids' brutality: 'Berlin blasted', *Army News*, 4.12.1943, in <trove.nla.gov.au>; 'Berlin again', *The Daily News*, 3.12.1943, in <trove.nla.gov.au>; 'The battle for Berlin', *The Dowerin Guardian and Amery Line Advocate*, 4.12.1943, in <trove.nla.gov.au>.

p. 229 Crew bombing reports: Unit diaries for 50, 460, 467 & 619 Squadrons, in Perl files.

p. 231 467 Squadron survival rates: computed from data in 467 Squadron unit diary.

p. 232 *Danville* reporting: *Danville Morning News*, 4.12.1943, <www.newspapers.com>.

p. 234 Bednall's reporting: 'Hell let loose. Eye-witness of Berlin raid', *Daily Telegraph & North Murchison and Pilbara Gazette*, 30.1.1943, <trove.nla.gov.au>; *Canberra Times*, 19.1.1943, <trove.nla.gov.au>.

p. 234 Portal's predictions: Greenhous et al, *The Crucible of War*, p. 657.

p. 234 Harris statements: Neillands, *Bomber War*, p. 283; Greenhous et al, *The Crucible of War*, pp. 725–726.

p. 237 German civilians' attitudes: Jörg Friedrich, *The Fire* (New York: Columbia University Press, 2008), p. 421.
p. 237 Reporting on the lost journalists: 'Three correspondents fail to return from raid on Germany', *Lincoln Evening State Journal*, 3.12.1943, <www.newspapers.com>; '3 Writers lost in Berlin Raid', the *Evening Sun* (Baltimore), 3.12.1943, in Perl files; 'Sydney journalist missing in Berlin raid', *Argus & Sydney Morning Herald*, 6.12.1943, <trove.nla.gov.au>; 'Poet Killed in RAF Raid', *Sydney Morning Herald*, 7.2.1944, <trove.nla.gov.au>.
p. 239 Tributes to Grieg: 'Aufbau', Leo Baeck Institute, New York/Berlin, <old.lbi.org>; 'Joseph Auslander', <poets.org>; 'For Nordahl Grieg 1902–1943', *Aufbau*, 10.3.1944.

11 - Prisoners of war

p. 240 *Dulag Luft: Durchgangslager der Luftwaffe* (Luftwaffe Transit Camp); 'DULAG LUFT – Interrogation Camp', <www.b24.net>.
p. 240 '1200 flyers': *Abteilung Ausland* minute, 1.9.1943, in Perl files.
p. 241 Bennett's experience: Bennett, *Parachute to Berlin*, pp. 57–65.
p. 242 Bönningshaus's identity: *Abteilung Ausland* minute, 24.4.1944, in Perl files.
p. 248 German spies in UK: Christopher Andrew, *The Defence of the Realm: The authorized history of MI5* (Lindon: Allen Lane, 2009), p. 211.
p. 249 Signals intelligence: RV Jones, *Most Secret War: British Scientific Intelligence 1939–1945* (London: Coronet Books, 1978), pp. 491–493.
p. 249 50 Squadron POWs: tallied from data in 'No. 50 Squadron Royal Air Force; in 'World War Two: The Diary of a WWII Bomber Squadron – Part 5, 1942–1943', <www.no-50-and-no-61-squadrons-association.co.uk>.
p. 251 Ginn's interrogation: Norman Ginn interview, in Perl files.

12 - A grand tour

p. 254 Bennett's tour: Bennett, *Parachute to Berlin*, pp. 65–115.
p. 258 Strempel's career background: Miguel H Bronschud, *The Secret Castle: The key to good and evil* (Bytelt Press, 2007), p. 418, in <books.google.com.au>.
p. 258 Foreign Office: the case was handled by Amt VI of the Auswärtiges Amt, *Abteilung Ausland* minute, 9.5.1944, in Perl files.
p. 260 Bennett's handling: *Abteilung Ausland* minutes, 26.4.1944, 27.4.1944 & 9.5.1944; correspondence 26.6.1944 & 13.7.1944, in Perl files.
p. 263 Restrictions on music venues: Guido Fackler, 'Jazz under the Nazis', *Music and the Holocaust*, <holocaustmusic.ort.org>.
p. 265 Railway deportations: 'Railway Lines used for Deportations', *Geschicts Parcours Yorckbrücken*, <yorckbruecken.de>.
p. 271 Actual RAF raids during Bennett's tour: Middlebrook, *The Berlin Raids*, pp. 173, 176–177, 180–183, 189–197, 202–203; Middlebrook & Everitt, *Bomber Command War Diaries*, pp. 412, 460; Boiten, *Nachtjagd War Diaries*, p. 318.

p. 288 Thurnhofer's explanation: Peter Thurnhofer, 'Process from my point of view (Peter, son of Mrs Thurnhofer)', <thurnhofer-istrien.com/3-bennet>.
p. 292 5 March 1943 Essen raid: Middlebrook & Everitt, *Bomber Command War Diaries*, pp. 365–366.

13 - Personal impacts

p. 296 Comparison of 460 Squadron's losses: Greenhous et al, *Crucible of War*, p. 718.
p. 296 460 Squadron's worst nights: Firkins, *Strike and Strike Again*, pp. 41, 50, 53, 57, 66, 85, 94.
p. 296 Corser's crew: John Watson, '460 Squadron Pilots and Crews', <www.460squadronraaf.com>.
p. 297 Crew survival rates: tallied from Chorley, *RAF Bomber Command Losses, Volume 4*, pp. 408–414; the rate this night was better than the 10.9 per cent average survival rate from Lancasters, but including the Halifax crew survival rate of 29 per cent, is broadly indicative overall – see Greenhous et al, *The Crucible of War*, p. 755.
p. 297 460 Squadron overall loss rate: tallied from data in 460 Sqn unit diary.
p. 297 Ginn's ignorance: Norm Ginn interview, in Perl files.
p. 298 Bednall's perspective: personal memoir in NLA: MS 5546, Box 3, Folder 26.
p. 298 Edwards' good luck charm: 'Leipzig Raid', *Kalgoorlie Miner*, 8 December 1943, <trove.nla.gov.au>.
p. 299 Leipzig raid losses: Boiten, *Nachtjagd War Diaries*, vol. 1, p. 312.
p. 299 Abercromby's farewell: 619 Sqn unit diary.
p. 300 Abercromby's final operation: Middlebrook & Everitt, *Bomber Command War Diaries*, p. 462.
p. 300 D-Dog/619's final operation: Middlebrook & Everitt, *Bomber Command War Diaries*, p. 463; Investigation Report, No. 4 MR & E Unit, 11.11.1947, in Perl files.
p. 300 King's tribute to G-George/467: King, 'Over Berlin in a Lancaster', the *Age*, 6.12.1943, in Perl files.
p. 301 G-George/467's crash: '1943 Incident Logs', <www.bcar.org.uk>; 467 Sqn unit diary; NAA: A705, 166/14/135.
p. 302 G-George/467's flying hours: NAA: A705, 166/14/135.
p. 302 467 Squadron losses: Alan Storr, *Second World War fatalities: No. 467 Squadron RAAF* (Canberra, Australian War Memorial, 2005).
p. 302 Forbes's tour with 463 Squadron: Richard Reid, 'Bomber Command', Australians in World War II Series, Australian War Memorial, <anzacportal.dva.gov.au>.
p. 304 50 Squadron losses: 'No. 50 Squadron Royal Air Force: The diary of a WWII bomber squadron', pp. 79, 85, <www.no-50-and-no-61-squadrons-association.co.uk>.
p. 305 460 Squadron survival rate: computed from data in 460 Sqn unit diary & <www.ww2roll.gov.au>.

p. 305   467 Squadron survival rate: computed from data in 467 Sqn unit diary & <www.ww2roll.gov.au>.
p. 305   Night school: Tony Brady, *The Empire Has an Answer* (Sydney: Big Sky Publishing, 2019), pp. 56–62.
p. 306   Ginn's motivations: Norm Ginn interview, in Perl files.
p. 306   Kan casualty correspondence: NAA: A705, 166/22/154.
p. 308   460 Squadron personnel casualties: 'No. 460 Squadron', <www.awm.gov.au>.
p. 308   460 Squadron losses in Battle of Berlin: Firkins, *Strike and Return*, pp. 94, 99, 101.
p. 309   RAAF monthly casualty rate: Herington, *Air Power over Europe*, pp. 508–509.
p. 312   Kan's RAAF career: NAA: A705, 166/22/154; 460 Sqn unit diary; 'Index of all aircrew 460 Squadron (RAAF)', <www.ozatwar.com/460sqdn>.

14 - Aftermaths

p. 314   Bennett's article: Bennett, 'Inside Nazi Europe', the *Despatch* (Moline, Illinois), 24.1.1944, <Newspapers.com>.
p. 314   Acclaim for Bennett: 'Lowell Bennett Escapes!', the *Despatch* (Moline, Illinois), 24.1.144; & 'Lowell Bennett Escapes!', the *Despatch* (Moline, Illinois), 24.1.144, in <Newspapers.com>, in Perl files.
p. 314   Bennett in POW camp: Bennett, *Parachute to Berlin*, pp. 157, 171, 191.
p. 315   Murrow's D-Day reporting: Murrow, 'Eisenhower's "Order of the Day"/ D-Day', 6.6.1944, *History of American Journalism*, <history.journalism.ku.edu/>.
p. 315   Murrow and radio journalism: 'World War II on the air: Edward R Murrow and the broadcasts that riveted a nation', *History of American Journalism*, <history.journalism.ku.edu/>.
p. 315   Murrow at Buchenwald: Murrow, 'Buchenwald', 15.4.1945, *History of American Journalism*, <history.journalism.ku.edu/>.
p. 315   Bennett at Barth concentration camp: Bennett, *Parachute to Berlin*, p. 242.
p. 316   Murrow's post-war career: Craig Chamberlain, 'Rare "Hear it Now" Recordings Lend Insight on Murrow and News History', *News Bureau Illinois*, <news.illinois.edu/>; 'Edward R Murrow: Good Night and Good Luck', 25.4.2014, <www.legacy.com/>.
p. 316   King's post-Berlin reporting: 'Science Aids Air War', *Sydney Morning Herald*, 1.2.1944, <trove.nla.gov.au/>; 'British Morale High', *National Advocate* (Bathurst, NSW), 12.4.1944; 'Personal Vice-Regal', *Sydney Morning Herald*, 3.4.1944, <trove.nla.gov.au/>; 'Three Days to London', *Sydney Morning Herald*, 6.6.1945, <trove.nla.gov.au/>.
p. 317   Elisabeth Bennett: Enid Elisabeth Bennett (née Walker) – Joseph Cress, 'Father inspires son to serve U.S. interests abroad', the *Sentinel*, 17.6.2016, in <cumberlink.com/>.
p. 317   Bennett's next book: Lowell Bennett, *Berlin Bastion: The epic of post-war Berlin* (Frankfurt/Main, F. Rudl, 1951).
p. 318   Stockton's grave: 'Reporter Norman Stockton', <www.cwgc.org/>.

p. 319 Commemoration of Grieg: 'Erinnerung an einen mutigen Norweger', *Märkische Allgemeine Zeitung*, 1.12.2003, in Perl files; Manfred Kluger, recorded by Günter Käbelmann in 'Gedenkenstätten für Nordahl Grieg (norwegische Literat) und seiner mit ihm verunglückten Flieger-Kameraden aus Grossbritannien und Australien', 26.11.2003, in Perl files; Günter Käbelmann, 'Wie kam es zum Denkmal "Nordahl Grieg" in der norwegischen Botschaft in Berlin?', 26.8.2002, in Perl files; Günter Käbelmann, 'Chronik über die (Kleinmachnower) Geschichte der Nordahl Grieg Ehrung', 27.7.2005, in Perl files; Konstanze Wild, 'Absturz bei Machnower See', *Märkische Allgemeine Zeitung*, 11.1.2006, in Perl files.

p. 319 Oslo memorial: Bjørn A Bojesen, 'Norway Says Never Again', *Norwegian Language Blog*, 22.7.2021.

p. 321 Bomber Command's dead: *Bomber Command's losses*, <www.bombercommandmuseum.ca>.

INDEX

Abercromby, W 'Jock' 22, 27, 35, 67–68, 89–90, 92, 121, 140–41, 164, 230, 299–300
Aircrew
    bodies of, recovery, identification and burial of 206–8, 210–12
    briefing, pre-raid 61–68
    crew roles 68, 79–82, 84, 91, 161
    debriefing 216–18, 224–25, 230–31
    escape and evasion kit 69–70, 167
    fatalism of 35, 48, 59–60, 67, 92
    flying kit 69–71, 78, 80, 217
    in-flight rations 76, 91
    morale of 35, 47, 62–65, 80–81, 85, 88, 90, 113, 118–20, 143, 178, 308
    motivations of 77, 305
    reactions to seeing bomb damage 183–85, 191
    'special pre-mission meal' 68
    superstition 72–73, 298
    tours of operations 15, 27, 35, 59, 231–32, 302, 304, 313
Air Ministry 2, 9–12, 50
Air Raids, experience of from the ground 192, 202–9, 266–71, 283–85
Air Raid Precautions, *see* Civil defence
Air Raid Wardens, German 100–2
Alford, John 112
Alford, Tom 35, 62, 158–61, 296, 305
American Jewish Joint Distribution Committee 25
Anderson, 'Jack' 107–10
Anderson, Neville 64, 82, 116–21, 173–74, 309
Anundskås, Tor 48
'American Pool' (US press agencies) 9
Argus 37, 238
Arthur, Frank 33, 306–7
Associated Press 9
Aufbau 239
Auslander, Joseph 239

Baker, Bob 224
Baling out (parachuting) 108–10, 112, 119, 130–31, 145–46, 150, 153–55, 159–61
Barth concentration camp 315
Bartlett, Les 60–61, 69, 76, 78, 81, 85, 114–15
BBC (British Broadcasting Corporation) 50, 52
Bednall, Colin 33, 51, 233–34, 295–99
Bennett, Lowell 1–2, 7, 9–13, 26–33, 57, 65–66, 68–69, 71–72, 74–79, 81, 83, 88–92, 124–30, 134–35, 145–47, 153–55, 162–66, 168–72, 174–78, 184–87, 190–200, 220–21, 237–38, 240–48, 252–94, 314–18
    article published from inside Germany 314
    books published 28, 288, 317, 324
    chronology of visitations within Germany 271–73, 286–88
    cultivation of by captors 248, 252–60, 274–76, 290, 294, 314–16
    observations of bombed cities 261–93
    premonition 11, 68, 72, 86, 127, 153
Bennett, Elizabeth 11, 27, 29, 31, 317
Berlin
    as a target 4–5, 51
    bombing damage to 6–7, 183–90, 196, 225, 236, 256–57, 261–63
    burning of by bombing 125, 138, 142–45, 164, 189–90
    defences against air raids 133–34, 152
Bishop, Marie 36
'Blockbuster' bombs, *see* Bomb loads
Bochum, damage to 291
Bolton, Ian 26–28, 57, 59, 67, 83–84, 86, 90, 126–29, 131, 150–51, 166–67, 176–79, 249–50, 304, 315

Bomb loads, of Lancaster bomber
  74–75, 137, 205
  'Cookie' 4000-pound demolition
    bombs 75, 96, 123, 142, 148,
    187, 234
  incendiaries 75, 143, 148, 187
Bomb shelters 193
Bomber Command, RAF
  aircraft mission tallies 77–78
  Berlin raids 2–7
  firestorm raids 229–31
  Hamburg raids 4
  losses 5–6, 225, 227
  loss rates 17, 35, 50, 60, 73, 247,
    296–97, 299, 304–5, 308–10,
    321
  navigational inexactitude 222–26
  operational briefings 61–68
  public relations campaign 7–8,
    10–12, 33, 36, 50–53
  solicitude for journalists' lives 22,
    27, 35–36, 49
  squadrons
    No 50 26–28, 61, 66–68, 72–74,
      85, 231, 244, 249–50, 304
    No. 83 299–300
    No. 460 33, 62–63, 64–65, 73,
      75, 80, 84, 216–19, 296–97,
      304–5, 308, 312–13
    No. 463 15, 304
    No. 467 15, 17, 65, 70, 76–78,
      83, 302–3
    No. 619 20, 65, 68, 73, 76, 220,
      225, 230, 299–300
  targeting of civilians 234–35
'Bomber stream' tactic 88, 90–91, 111,
  116–17, 132, 156
Bönninghaus, Joseph 242–50,
  252–94, 316
Borner, Joseph, *see* Bönninghaus
Boyd AG 110
Bremen, damage to 282–83
Buchenwald death camp 315
Burials, of airmen 173–74
Burt, RF 231

Canberra Times 234
Capture, experience of 170–78, 181–83

Casualty classification and notification
  system 191, 306–12, 318–19
Catty, Alf 119, 173–74, 309
CBS (Columbia Broadcasting System)
  12, 20–21, 25, 315
Churchill, Winston 5, 233
Civil Defence, German 94–98, 100–2,
  193
Civilians, German
  casualties 97, 225
  experiences of bombing 122–24,
    147–49, 179–180
  unsympathetic attitudes towards
    Berlin bombing 235–36
Cole, George 121, 173–74
Cologne, damage to 294
Commonwealth War Graves 318
Considine, Bob 30
Corser, Edward 296, 313
Cronkite, William 26, 54, 56
Crouch, Henry 230

Daily Mail 295
Daley, Eric 35, 158-161
Danville Morning News 232–33
Dawkins A 107–8, 110
D-Day 5, 31
Daily Express 37
Daily Mail 51
Daily Telegraph 37
Decoy fires, German 156–57
Dolan, Leo V 32
Drakeford, Arthur 306
Dulag Luft, *see* POWs, processing of
Düsseldorf, damage to 294

Edwards, Colin 296
Edwards, Fred 111
Edwards, Hughie 216, 298
Einstein, Albert 25
'Empire Press' (Commonwealth press
  agencies) 19
English, James 35, 82, 115, 117–20, 174,
  296
Essen, damage to 291–94
Evening Standard 238

Fire Brigade, volunteer 149, 204–9
Flak (anti-aircraft guns, German) 89–90, 99–100, 152, 204
Flak-helpers (boy soldiers, German) 98–100, 148
Forbes, William 'Bill' 15, 17, 76, 83, 87, 134–37, 163, 300, 302, 304
Forrester, Robert 74–75, 86
Friedrich, Jörg 237
Frizzell, Cecil 302

Gale, Stewart 51
Garlick, John 107–8
Gelsenkirchen, damage to 291
G-George (Lancaster serial W4783), from 460 Squadron 216–18
Ginn, Norman 35, 62, 85, 159–61, 167–68, 180–85, 251–52, 296–97, 305–6
Godwin, Ken 224–25
Grieg, Nordahl 12, 40–49, 84, 151–53, 201, 203, 210–15, 237–39, 244–45, 295–97, 313, 318–21
Grime, William 135, 137
Guard, Harold 39

H2S, *see* Radar, air to ground
Hamburg, bomb damage 278–82
Harris, Arthur 'Bomber' 4–5, 7, 10, 14, 234–35
Hearst, William Randolph 29–30
Heffernan, JA 300
Hind, Guy 112
Hitler, Adolf 8–9, 77
Hore-Brown, David 159
Hottelet, Dick 23

ICRC (International Committee of the Red Cross) 211, 304, 309
Imperial Airways 37
INS (International News Service) 1–2, 9–10, 29–32, 317
Institute of International Education 24

Japan, hostilities with 37–39
Jews, Nazi atrocities against 265–66
Johnen, Wilhelm 139, 146–47

Journalists
  identification with the allied cause 20, 24–26, 44–49, 222, 233
  losses in war reporting 237–38
  motivations for flying on a raid 11, 20, 23–24, 26, 30–34, 39–40, 48–49, 51, 54–55, 305
  reportage 221–22, 224–26, 227, 232–34, 237–39, 300, 315–16
  selection of 2–3, 9–10, 19, 23, 32, 40, 50–53

Käbelmann, Günter 209, 321
Kan, Alex 118, 121, 173–74, 306–12
Kan, Hartog 306–11
Keith, AS 231
King, Alfred 3, 12, 15–20, 36, 58, 65, 76–78, 83, 87, 91–92, 102–3, 132–38, 140, 145, 163, 219, 226–27, 238, 295, 299–301, 304, 316–17
Kleinmachnow 201–10, 320–21

Langslow, Melville 309
Leask, Laurie 158–61, 168, 180–81
Lincoln Evening State Journal 238
Litherland, HA 231
Luftwaffe
  air defence system 93–94, 104–5, 111, 132, 134–35, 249
  decoy fires 156–57
  night fighters 104–7, 134–35, 139–40
  processing and burial of dead allied airmen 210–13
  searchlights 141, 144

MacArthur, Douglas 38
MacDonald, Jamie 51–53
Marz, Franz 204–9, 321
McCarthy, Senator Joe 316
McFarlane, Robert 66–67
McGilvray, JWE 230
McIntyre, Ron 218–19
Miller, Dusty 119, 173–74
Miller, Frank 83, 103
Mitchell, Alan 49, 84, 150–52, 296, 322
Moody, Ron 178–79

Münster, damage to 288–90
Murrow, Edward 'Ed' 12, 20–26, 28, 65–67, 69, 73–74, 84, 86–87, 89–90, 92, 115, 121–22, 140–45, 163–64, 219–22, 225, 230, 238, 295, 299–300, 315–16

Nazi persecution of and genocide against Jews 24–25
New York Times 51–52, 54
Norway
    government-in-exile 12, 44
    invasion of by Germany 43–44

Oberursel, *see* POWs, processing of
Ölberg, Peter 319
Operation Torch 28
Osnabrück, damage to 292

Parachuting, *see* Baling out
Parker, Laurie 77, 301
Pathfinders 125, 134, 136, 139–40, 156–57, 223, 226, 246
Pidsley, Reg 50
Plowright, Phil 62
Portal, Charles 234
Post, Bob 54–56
Power, Dick 224
POWs (prisoners of war)
    escape attempts 169–70, 197–98
    evasion of capture, attempted 167–69
    interrogation of 240–52
    morale of 178, 195
    psychological torture of 251
    supervised movement within Germany 194–200
    processing of 176, 191–94, 240–41
    solitary confinement of 192–94, 241–42, 251

Radar
    air to air, German 105–6, 111
    air to ground, British 105, 116–17, 156
    ground to air, German 93–94
Reynolds, Colin 230, 301–2
Robertson, James 83

Rodin, Ivan 121, 174
Rooney, Andy 55–56
Rumble, RM 230
Rytter, Olav 47

Sander, Antonie 213–14
'Scarecrow flares' 114–15
Sevareid, Eric 23
Shirer, William 25
Shoot-downs
    experience of 107–11, 112–13, 117–19, 126–31, 150, 158–61
    observation of 113–15, 125–26, 149–50, 154, 204–5
    survival chances from 112–13, 161, 177–78
Smith, Milton 230
Smith, WG 231
South China Daily Telegraph 36
South China Morning Post 36
Spies, erroneous belief in ubiquity of 248–49
Stafford, Merv 224
Stars and Stripes 55
Steiner, Dr, *see* Strempel
Stockton (née Bishop), Marie 36–37
Stockton, Norman 3, 12, 33–34, 36–40, 62, 64, 82, 115–21, 134–35, 173–74, 220–21, 237–39, 244–45, 295–97, 318
Stout, GS 230
Strempel, Councillor von 258–74
Sydney Morning Herald 3, 17–19, 238, 317
Sydney Sun 3, 40, 119

Take-off 83–87
Tannenbaum, Harold J 53
The Memphis Belle (movie) 53
Thornton-Smith, David 50
Thurnhofer, Margarete 172
Thurnhofer, Peter 288
Torp, Oscar 43

United Press 9, 54
US Army Air Forces 38, 52–54

Vaughan-Thomas, Wynford 50, 52

Wade, William 2, 10, 32–33
Watson, Alex 178
'Weichow Incident' 37–38
Wells, Norman 62, 138–39
Wilson, JN 37

Winsnes, Andreas 46
Wyler, William 53

Zorner, Paul 105–7, 111–13

Ingram Content Group UK Ltd.
Milton Keynes UK
UKHW011139230323
419044UK00004B/205

9 781742 237923